Nationalism as a Claim to a State

Historical Materialism Book Series

The Historical Materialism Book Series is a major publishing initiative of the radical left. The capitalist crisis of the twenty-first century has been met by a resurgence of interest in critical Marxist theory. At the same time, the publishing institutions committed to Marxism have contracted markedly since the high point of the 1970s. The Historical Materialism Book Series is dedicated to addressing this situation by making available important works of Marxist theory. The aim of the series is to publish important theoretical contributions as the basis for vigorous intellectual debate and exchange on the left.

The peer-reviewed series publishes original monographs, translated texts, and reprints of classics across the bounds of academic disciplinary agendas and across the divisions of the left. The series is particularly concerned to encourage the internationalization of Marxist debate and aims to translate significant studies from beyond the English-speaking world.

For a full list of titles in the Historical Materialism Book Series available in paperback from Haymarket Books, visit: www.haymarketbooks.org/series_collections/1-historical-materialism.

Nationalism as a Claim to a State

The Greek Revolution of 1821 and the Formation of Modern Greece

John Milios

Haymarket Books
Chicago, IL

First published in 2023 by Brill Academic Publishers, The Netherlands
© 2023 Koninklijke Brill NV, Leiden, The Netherlands

Published in paperback in 2024 by
Haymarket Books
P.O. Box 180165
Chicago, IL 60618
773-583-7884
www.haymarketbooks.org

ISBN: 979-8-88890-208-0

Distributed to the trade in the US through Consortium Book Sales and
Distribution (www.cbsd.com) and internationally through Ingram
Publisher Services International (www.ingramcontent.com).

This book was published with the generous support of Lannan
Foundation, Wallace Action Fund, and the Marguerite Casey Foundation.

Special discounts are available for bulk purchases by organizations and
institutions. Please call 773-583-7884 or email info@haymarketbooks.org
for more information.

Cover design by David Mabb. Cover art is a detail from *Luibov
Popova Untitled Textile Design on William Morris Wallpaper for Historical
Materialism*, edition of 100, screen print on wallpaper, 2010.

Printed in the United States.

10 9 8 7 6 5 4 3 2 1

Library of Congress Cataloging-in-Publication data is available.

Contents

PART 2
The Revolution and Its State

PART 3
The Revolution as the 'Grand Idea' and as the 'Present'

Acknowledgements

A first version of this book was published in Greek on 15 December 2020 under the title *1821: Tracing the Nation, the State and the Grand Idea* (*1821. Ihnilatontas to Ethnos, to Kratos kai ti Megali Idea*, Alexandreia Publications).

I would like to thank Marios Emmanouilidis and Dimitris C. Sotiropoulos for reading the chapters of the book while they were being written, and for helping me to improve their quality with well-founded comments. I also thank Panagiotis Sotiris for his suggestions regarding the adaptation of the text for an English-literate audience.

I owe thanks to the participants of the seminar 'Theory and History of Capitalism and the National Phenomenon: The Greek Case' (October 2018–March 2019), whose questions, comments and interventions helped me to shape the arguments developed in this book.

A special mention is, of course, owed to Barbara Santos for translating the greater part of the book, for her valuable suggestions and for having improved the overall style of the manuscript.

About *Nationalism as a Claim to a State*

Who were the Greeks whom the Revolution of 1821 sought to liberate into a national-constitutional state? In this fascinating book, distinguished political economist John Milios investigates the processes of economic, social, and political-ideological unification through which, from the second half of the eighteenth century, Greek-speaking and other Orthodox capitalists promoted a broad national politicisation of large Orthodox Christian populations in the Ottoman Empire and turned them into Greek freedom fighters. He shows how the revolution of the masses demanding representative institutions led to the formation of a constitutional bourgeois state and a national capitalist social formation (1821–27) before taking a Bonapartist and, later, monarchist turn. This is the first book to consider the role of capitalism, nationalism, republicanism, racism, and imperialism in the formation of modern Greece.

– *Vassilios Lambropoulos, C.P. Cavafy Professor Emeritus, University of Michigan*

Nationalism as a Claim to a State provides a groundbreaking account of the Greek Revolution and its aftermath. Opposing the myth of Hellenic continuity, Milios analyses the Greek nationalist movement in terms of capitalist interests within – and at odds with – the Ottoman Empire. He emphasises that early proclamations of Hellenic independence also included Albanians, Serbs, and Bulgars; later, the Greek state defined itself against those groups and pursued territorial expansion. Part of a broader historical movement, the emergent Greek state reveals how nationalist ideologies get twisted this way and that to avoid confronting the realities of capitalism. Carefully researched and persuasively argued, Milios's study takes us deep into the Greek Revolution and beyond, offering crucial lessons for the contemporary world.

– *Rush Rehm, Professor, Theater and Performance Studies, and Classics, Stanford University Artistic Director, Stanford Repertory Theater (SRT)*

John Milios offers us a timely and important intervention in the discussions on the character and role of the 1821 Greek Revolution, a necessary antidote to the nationalist consensus which seems to have prevailed in the bicentenary celebrations of that event. Through the lens of political economy, he critically analyses the role of the emerging middle classes in the formation of the nation state of Greece. At the same time, he shows that the protagonists of the national struggle had imperial (I would prefer to call them colonial) ambitions from the very start, ambitions that were burnt in the ashes of Smyrna a century later. The book not only helps us understand the emergence and the fates of Greece as a national and political phenomenon, and its continuing role as a buffer state in global geopolitics, but it also constitutes a valuable contribution to the contemporary discussions on (and struggles towards) ideological, economic, and political decolonisation.

– *Yannis Hamilakis, Brown University, co-author of* Archaeology, Nation, and Race: Confronting the Past, Decolonizing the Future

Introduction

My decision to update a book written in Greek on the Greek Revolution of 1821 – the revolution that gave rise to the modern Greek state – for English-literate readers, a book that counters the approaches of various 'national' narratives that overwhelmed the public sphere during the bicentenary of '1821', was based on a twofold line of reasoning. First, the Greek Revolution was a genuine bourgeois revolution; in theorising its causes, preconditions, dynamics and internal conflicts, the analysis herein necessarily tackles the issue of bourgeois revolutions in general. Second, English-language Marxist historiography has practically ignored the Greek Revolution – with the exception of brief, albeit somewhat intrusive, comments in the works of Eric Hobsbawm, and in some sporadic references in works by other authors.

The Greek Revolution was plotted and initiated by the Friendly Society (*Philiki Etaireia*), a secret society founded in Odessa, in the Russian Empire, on 14 September 1814 by three Greek merchants. It was declared on 24 February 1821 in the semi-autonomous from Ottoman rule (the 'Sublime Porte') principality of Moldavia, i.e. in present-day Romania, by the leader of the Friendly Society, Alexandros Ypsilantis. It spread almost immediately into the neighbouring principality of Wallachia (also in present-day Romania).

The official 'national' (Greek) account of the Revolution, which has consistently praised the contribution of the Friendly Society in the preparation and declaration of the Revolution, bypasses, usually with a brief or epigrammatic reference, the events in Moldavia and Wallachia during the period of February–September 1821. In fact, even before the end of the second decade of its existence, the Greek state, by decree signed on 15 March 1838 by King Otto and the Minister for Ecclesiastical Affairs G. Glarakis, 'decided' and declared that the Revolution had been proclaimed at the monastery of Aghia Lavra in Kalavryta on 25 March 1821 (the day of the celebration of the 'Annunciation of the Virgin Mary' by the Orthodox Church).

The legend of Aghia Lavra, which the Greek state maintains with reverence to this day with annual celebrations of the Revolution, and the downplaying of the Revolution in the Principalities, are intended not only to symbolically link 'Hellenism with Orthodoxy'; they function mainly as a mechanism for capturing the Revolution within the Greek state, and they conceal a question that lies before us: Why did the *Greek Revolution* begin *in Romania*?

This question becomes even more pronounced if one considers in some detail the events that took place in the Principalities. A typical example: in one of the three proclamations issued in Iaşi, the capital of Moldavia, by Alexandros Ypsilantis on 24 February 1821, entitled 'Greek Men, those sojourning in Moldavia and Wallachia!', we read: 'Morea, Epirus, Thessaly, *Serbia, Bulgaria,* the Islands of the Archipelago, *in a few words the whole of Hellas* took up arms, with a view to shake off the onerous yoke of the Barbarians'.

Several Greek historians, not only leftists, but also proponents of mainstream 'national' approaches, have challenged the myth of 'Aghia Lavra'. For example, in the early 1960s Professor of Mediaeval and Modern History at the University of Athens Apostolos P. Daskalakis wrote: '[O]n 25 March no one was at Lavra to declare the revolution, which, after all, had been declared'.[1] However, Daskalakis's argumentation had no effect on the 'official history' of the Revolution and certainly did not deter, for example, Ioannis N. Theodorakopoulos, also a Professor (at the Panteion School of Social Sciences) and member of the Academy of Athens, from declaring three years later, on 25 March 1965, at the monastery of Aghia Lavra: 'Two "hails" express the meaning of today's great day, "Hail, hail Mary" and "Hail, O hail Liberty"'.[2] And in 2021, the official celebration of the bicentenary of the Revolution began, as it has every year since 1838, on 25 March.

Nevertheless, while 'Aghia Lavra' and the '25th of March' may be matters of dispute, contemporary Greek historiography almost unanimously abstains from any attempt to penetrate the riddle of why the Greek Revolution started in what is today Romania. It is worth mentioning here a current example characteristic of this. In the first quarter of 2021, amidst the official celebrations for the bicentenary of the Greek Revolution, a collective volume was published by Harvard University Press entitled *The Greek Revolution: A Critical Dictionary*, edited by Professors Paschalis Kitromilides and Constantinos Tsoukalas. A foreword to the volume was written by the former President of the *Hellenic Republic* Prokopios Pavlopoulos and the book is dedicated 'In honor of the generations of scholars who, across two hundred years, have devoted their intellectual labor to the study of the Greek Revolution'. At the end of the book, on pp. 727–37, a chronology of the major events pertaining to the Greek Revolution is included, which covers the period 1814–34. The chronology begins with the founding of the Friendly Society in Odessa (1814), continues with various events up to 26–29 January 1821, when the Peloponnesian primates convened to decide on how to commence the Revolution, and then 'jumps' to 3 March 1821, when hostilities began in the mountainous east-central part of the Peloponnese, in the area of Kalavryta. The proclamation of the revolution in Moldavia is curiously absent.

---

1 Daskalakis 1961–62, p. 28.
2 Theodorakopoulos 1972, p. 43. 'Hail, O hail Liberty' is a verse of the 'Hymn to Liberty', the Greek national anthem.

Only the '[d]efeat of the Sacred Battalion under Alexandros Ypsilantis' in Wallachia on 7 June 1821 is mentioned (p. 729).

This chasm in the national narrative (and in the lapse of memory) is a symptom of an aporia vis-à-vis the vague boundaries of the 'nation' at the time of the Revolution. During the first decades of the nineteenth century, the exponents of Greek Enlightenment, who were concomitantly forefathers of Greek nationalism, believed Greekness to be identified with Orthodoxy, as the nascent Greek nation was, at the time, the first to emerge in the broader Balkan and Asia Minor region.

The belief that all Christians in the Ottoman Empire were Greeks began with the Greek Enlightenment. It can be traced in the revolutionary writings of the early Greek revolutionary Rigas Pheraios (1757–1798) and the revolutionary pamphlet *Hellenic Nomarchy* (1806), and was maintained with minor modifications until the middle of the nineteenth century. It is also the ideological ground for the 'Grand Idea', the expansionist strategy of the Greek state in the first century of its existence. A constituent part of this belief was, of course, the conviction that the 'Greek nation' had existed since antiquity.

The dominant nationalist narrative concerning the continuity of the Greek nation since antiquity in a paradoxical way nullifies itself. In other words, it denigrates and largely conceals the political and institutional rupture with which the 1821 Revolution was connected: the historically unprecedented institutional and state changes related to the spread of nationalism in the regions where the Revolution had established itself, i.e. the national politicisation of the masses and their demand for institutions of representation (and therefore for a national-constitutional bourgeois state of 'citizens'), which formed a historically new way of integrating the populations into the state, subsuming them under the already prevailing capitalist relations of domination and exploitation.

The basis for the broad national politicisation of the masses – the development of nationalism – mainly in the regions of southern Greece and the islands, was the processes of economic, ideological and political unification, from the second half of the eighteenth century, of the Christian populations and regions linked to the rapid development of capitalist relations and their associated commercial networks. These processes economically and politically unified rural areas with urban centres (centres of long-distance trade with the interior of the Ottoman Empire and abroad). I refer here to unprecedented social developments of enormous importance which lie at the very heart of the Revolution. The ideas of republicanism and constitutionalism, as well as the national politicisation of the masses, were developed within these processes as an aspect of them.

A core facet of nationalism is political, affiliated with the demand for and a claim to a state. National consciousness, in other words, is not primarily related to the mother tongue, traditions and place of origin of the nationally mobilised population, but to the demand for 'national freedom' and 'illumination'; and, in the case at hand, it was related to the demand for an independent constitutional-democratic state which was supposedly destined to reconstitute the heritage of ancient Greece in the new era, as all the official texts of the Revolution proclaimed:

> Descendants of the wise and philanthropic nation of the Hellenes, contemporaries of the at-present enlightened and based on the rule of law peoples of Europe, and witnesses of the good, which they enjoy under the unbreakable aegis of the laws, it was no longer possible for us to endure the cruel scourge of the Ottoman state to the point of callousness and gullibility, which for about four centuries has been over our heads, and instead of reason, acclaimed arbitrary will as law, persecuted and ordered everything despotically and autocratically.[3]

The first object of my investigation is therefore the historical emergence and the limits of the Greek nation, an object that calls forth the broader theoretical and historical question of the economic, political, cultural and ideological presuppositions of nation-building.

The 1821 Revolution can be assessed and interpreted in terms of its character and dynamics first and foremost by the institutions it created, by the regime it imposed and, naturally, by the official texts that established the guiding indicators of that regime. From the very first moment of its declaration, the Greek Revolution proclaimed its radical enlightenment-bourgeois character. And, from the very first moment, it comprised corresponding bourgeois-representative institutions, thus establishing a constitutional state.

The first Greek state was *de facto* established in 1821–22, when it formed its first republican apparatuses of administration and power, and the constitutional institutions of representation of the masses recognised within it. In 1824 and 1825, the international financial markets anticipated the viability of the Greek state and concluded with it the first loans to modern Greece. From 1826 on, the 'Great Powers' also anticipated the final formation of a form of a Greek state entity and intervened, according to their geopolitical interests each,

---

3 *Resolution of the first National Assembly of the Hellenes in Epidaurus*, on the first day of January of year 1 of Independence [15 January 1822], in Mamoukas 1839, Vol. II, p. 43.

to resolve the 'Greek question' (in 1826: the 'Protocol of St. Petersburg'; in 1827: the naval Battle of Navarino between the 'Great Powers' – Britain, France and Russia – and the Ottoman forces; in 1830: the 'London Protocol').

Throughout the revolutionary struggle, the social, political and ideological antagonisms between the leading political factions within the Greek state became clear. These rivalries, which resulted in two civil wars, as well as the formation of the first three political parties that shaped the central political scene of the country for more than three decades, arose out of controversies over specific political and state issues: the form of the constitution and the state, its federal or centralised character, the role of politicians and the military, the voting system and the political role of the masses and the armed forces and their representative institutions, the preservation or dissolution of local parliaments, the extent of political and individual rights, etc. The outcome of the internal conflicts, i.e. the predominance of constitutionalism in the international environment of a predominantly authoritarian and absolutist Europe, illustrates the diffusion and hegemony in the population of the revolutionary regions of the radical-enlightenment (bourgeois) ideologies.

In factual terms, it is of course perfectly comprehensible that, on the one hand, the Greek Revolution shared similarities with the corresponding revolutions of the time (the American, the French ...); on the other hand, again speaking factually, the Greek Revolution evolved its own particular characteristics, such as the initial absence of the institution of a head of state. A bourgeois revolution, by its very nature, shares certain basic principles and strategic goals wherever it erupts – principles and goals around which its aleatory dynamics have developed. Attempts by journalists and historians alike to discredit the revolutionary constitutions and institutions of the first Greek state, and to demonise the parties that emerged from the internal conflicts, all the while arguing that all of the above were mainly an expression either of 'anarchy' or of foreign influence and dependency, essentially reveal a fear of and disregard for mass movements: the fear of any potential for revolution.

However, bourgeois parties do not split or divide a nation, despite the fact that party rivalries appear, on the surface, to be the causes of social antagonisms: what is a cause may appear as an effect, and vice versa. Bourgeois parties unite a society divided by opposing class interests: they mediate, mitigate and incorporate class antagonisms between the exploiters and the exploited, the governing and the governed, the rulers and the ruled into the parliamentary apparatus, i.e. within the state in the form of 'national interest'. In Greece, this 'national interest', the 'national strategy' into which all parties ultimately converged, was nothing but the expansion of state borders, the 'Grand Idea' as it was later named, the pre-eminently common imperial political goal and 'desire of the nation' and its representatives.

After the Revolution, the modern Greek state became a point of reference for Greek capitalists and Greek communities that continued to flourish in the main centres of the Ottoman Empire, thus providing an economic 'argument' for the imperial vision of the 'Grand Idea'. These capitalist enterprises owned by Greeks, as well as the Greek communities surrounding them, continued to rapidly 'grow' in the Ottoman Empire, namely outside the Greek state and national territory, alongside those within Greece; yet those abroad were overwhelmed by the 'desire' to become part of the new state which, in turn, conceived them as part of a 'second' (wannabe) 'Greece'.

My analysis substantiates the position that none of the uprisings prior to 1821 in what later became Greek territory had the characteristics of a national revolution. This means that the 1821 Revolution was a turning point in the history of the European geographical area. Nevertheless, according to official nationalist historiography, the Revolution of 1821 was nothing but the final, decisive moment of a continuous resistance and an ongoing rebellion of the 'Greeks' against the 'four-century Turkish national yoke' since the conquest of Constantinople in 1453.

Even more, two hundred years after its outbreak, the Greek Revolution of 1821 continues to be a temporal locus for ideological debates and political interventions related to the present. In most of these discussions, an 'ideological use' of the Revolution has been reproduced as an arbitrary portrait of the event and its protagonists, with at times even non-existent 'facts' being constructed in an effort to defend a particular ideological and political stance in the present. Such glorification of the Revolution, which has accompanied the history of the Greek capitalist state from the first decades of its existence until today, has not left leftist historians and intellectuals untouched.

The book is divided into three parts.

In Part 1: The Nation and the Revolution, the subject of investigation is the Greek nation and its geographical and social boundaries. It includes four chapters.

In Chapter 1, 'The Revolution in Moldavia and Wallachia: Questions on the Borders of the Greek Nation', the failure of the Revolution in the Danubian Principalities is examined, and a series of questions as regards the 'meaning' and boundaries of the Greek nation are posited.

Chapter 2, 'The "Hellas" of 1821: Initial Thoughts on the Dissemination of Greek National Politicisation', examines the perceptions of what constituted 'Greece' in the era of the Greek Enlightenment, from the texts of the early revolutionary Rigas Pheraios at the end of the eighteenth century, to those written during the Greek Revolution.

In Chapter 3, 'Approaches to the Nation: A General Theoretical Assessment', a theoretical framework of understanding the nation is posited through a critical analysis of existing theoretical approaches.

In Chapter 4, 'Romans and Greeks in the Ottoman Empire: From Pre-National Social Cohesion to a Greek Nation', the processes that led a part of the Christian 'Romans' (Orthodox Christians) of the Ottoman Empire to national politicisation are analysed, namely their transformation into Greeks embracing the demand for an independent nation state.

Part 2: The Revolution and its State has as its object of analysis the building of the revolutionary republican-constitutional Greek state during the period 1821–27 and its replacement during the subsequent period (1828–43), initially by the Bonapartist dictatorship of Ioannis Kapodistrias, and subsequently by an absolute monarchy. This part includes three chapters.

Chapter 5, 'The First State of the Revolution: The Victorious Period (1821–1824)', analyses the constitutional-democratic institutions, the social and political confrontations and civil wars, the political uplifting of the popular masses and the class rivalries within the forces of the Revolution during its first, victorious period.

Chapter 6, 'The Ebb of the Revolution, the Intervention of the "Great Powers" and the End of Constitutional Republicanism (1825–1833)', examines the unfavourable development of the war of independence after the landing of Ibrahim Pasha's army in the Peloponnese in 1825, the international conjuncture and the de facto recognition of the Greek state through the foreign loans it concluded in 1824 and 1825 with British banks, as well as the interventions of the Great Powers – developments that led to the end of constitutional republicanism immediately following the approval, in 1827, of the most radically democratic constitution in Europe, and the formation of the first three parties of the Greek state. These parties nevertheless functioned as organisers of different forms of resistance to absolutism, leading, ultimately, in 1843–44, to a constitutional monarchy.

Chapter 7, 'The Formation of a Capitalist State and Social Formation', examines the Revolution and its state as a point of no return in the process of consolidating capitalist social relations. The main capitalist branches of the Greek economy in the wake of the Revolution (manufacture, shipping, trade and financial activities) are presented, as well as the relations of the indirect subsumption of small-scale family agriculture under capital. Finally, reference is made to the remnants and resistance of the 'ancien régime' to the capitalist Greek social formation.

Part 3: The Revolution as the 'Grand Idea' and as the 'Present' refers to the legacies of the Revolution, but also to its ideological uses throughout the two centuries of existence of the Greek state.

Chapter 8, '"Hellenisation of the East": The Vision and the Reality', examines the relevance of the ideological and political framework established by the Revolution with the 'Grand Idea', the expansionist strategy of the Greek state during the first century of its existence, a strategy that drew support from the leading position of Greek capital in the Ottoman Empire and was promulgated as 'national liberation' and the 'civilisation of the East'.

Finally, Chapter 9, '1821 "in the Present": On the Ideological Uses of the Revolution', offers a critique of a series of interpretations regarding the Greek nation and the character of the Revolution that have persistently dominated Greek and international historiography and public discourse.

I consider this book a continuation of my previous book, entitled *The Origins of Capitalism as a Social System: The Prevalence of an Aleatory Encounter* (London and New York: Routledge, 2018 and 2019).

The aforementioned book explores the first historical period of the domination of capitalism in Europe with the formation in Venice, from the end of the fourteenth century, of a capitalist social formation and a capitalist state without national characteristics – a (colonialist) state in which, despite all the processes of an early construction of 'patriotism' (obedience to the state associated with the integration of subjects within state apparatuses, the ideological inculcation of 'Venetian values' and the invention of an 'official history', religious and state ceremonies, forms of education, etc.), was *not a nation state*: the state's subjects were not transformed into citizens, the consciousness of 'belonging' of the population did not entail claims on the future of the state and its borders, as later took place, after the French Revolution, in many parts of Europe when and where nationalism prevailed.

If that book, as I was writing it then, seemed like a 'return to the future', the present book comprises a probe into the past of the present: it examines one of the most characteristic examples of the shaping of a *national* capitalist state and a *national* capitalist social formation on the European continent: the Revolution within a non-national Empire, which established one of the first, *stricto sensu, national* capitalist states in Europe.

PART 1

The Nation and the Revolution

∵

CHAPTER 1

The Revolution in Moldavia and Wallachia: Questions on the Borders of the Greek Nation

1   The Declarations of Alexandros Ypsilantis: Hellas in Serbia and
         Bulgaria

The Greek Revolution of 1821 was plotted and initiated by the Friendly Society (*Philiki Etaireia*), a secret society founded in Odessa on 14 September 1814 by three merchants, Nikolaos Skoufas from Arta, Emmanouil Xanthos from the island of Patmos and Anastasios Tsakalov from Ioannina. The declared aim of the Friendly Society was to overthrow the Ottoman Empire and establish a Greek constitutional republic in the empire's territory (see below).

On 21 February 1821, Alexandros Ypsilantis, member and subsequent leader of the Friendly Society ('General Commissioner of the Authority'), and until then a general in the Russian army and aide-de-camp of the Tsar,[1] crossed the River Pruth and entered into Moldavian territory, which formed a semi-autonomous Principality under the domain of the Ottoman Empire. The Prince of Moldavia, Mikhail Soutsos (also known as Mikhail Vodas), was a member of the Friendly Society. He 'burned the signs of princedom',[2] and left at Ypsilantis's disposal his guard, together with 285,000 piastres. Upon his arrival in Iaşi, the capital of Moldavia, Ypsilantis issued on 24 February 1821 three proclamations, all of which were printed at the local printer's shop of Manouil Vernardos. In the first of these, entitled 'Greek Men, those sojourning in Moldavia and Wallachia!', we read:

> Behold, after so many centuries of woe, the phoenix of Hellas is again spreading its wings in splendour and summons under this shadow her true and obeisant progeny! Behold our friend, Motherland Hellas, raising the flag of our forebears in triumph! Morea, Epirus, Thessaly, *Serbia*, *Bulgaria*, the Islands of the Archipelago, *in a few words the whole of Hellas* took up arms, with a view to shake off the onerous yoke of the Barbarians, and setting her sights on the sole victory-bearing weapon of the Orthodox

---

1   While serving as an officer in the Russian army against Napoleon, Ypsilantis lost his right hand in the Battle of Leipzig in 1813 (Evangelides 1934, p. 566).
2   Evangelides 1934, p. 566.

Christians, the sacred, I say, and life-bearing Cross, cries out resoundingly under the protection of a great and mighty force, In hoc signo vinces! Long live liberty![3]

The second proclamation, entitled 'Fight for faith and motherland', is addressed to all Hellenes,[4] while the third, entitled 'Brothers of the Society of Friends', summons the members of the Society into the struggle.[5]

A day earlier, on 23 February 1821, Ypsilantis had issued a proclamation, 'To the Nation of Moldavia-Wallachia', in which he promulgates that *all of Greece from this day raises the flag from all the places under the yoke of tyranny*, and asserts:

Wherefore I avouch to you and assure you ... that you will have every comfort and certitude and in no way shall you be confused by my actions for the reason that the authority and administration of this Principality shall stay as it already is, and faithful to these same laws, shall conduct its affairs ... divine providence graced you with a Master, he who this day governs, Mikhail Voevodas Soutsos ... a father and benefactor alike to you.[6]

---

3   Ypsilantis 1821a, emphasis added.
4   'Fight for Faith and Motherland! The time has come, o Hellenes ... Let national phalanxes be formed, let patriotic legions appear and you will see those old giants of despotism fall by themselves, before our triumphant banners. All the shores of the Ionian and Aegean seas will resound to the sound of our trumpet ... The nation assembled will elect its elders, and to this highest parliament all our acts will yield ... The Motherland will reward her obedient and genuine children with the prizes of Glory and Honour. Those who disobey and turn a deaf ear to this present appeal will be declared bastards and Asiatic germs, their names, as traitors, anathematised and cursed by later generations ... Let us then once again ... invite Liberty to the classical land of Hellas! Let us do battle between Marathon and Thermopylae! Let us fight on the tombs of our fathers, who, so as to leave us free, fought and died there! The blood of the Tyrants is acceptable to the shades of Epameinondas the Theban and of Thrasyboulos the Athenian, who crushed the thirty tyrants, to the shades of Harmodius and Aristogeiton, who destroyed the yoke of Peisistratus, to that of Timoleon, who restored freedom to Corinth and Syracuse, certainly to those of Miltiades and Themistocles, of Leonidas and the Three Hundred, who cut down the innumerable armies of the barbarous Persians, whose most barbarous and inhuman descendants we today, with very little effort, are about to annihilate completely. To arms then, friends! The Motherland calls us!' (Ypsilantis 1821b, also cited in Clogg 1976, pp. 201–3).
5   '... So onwards, o brothers, each of you contribute this one last time by offering above and beyond what is within your power, be it armed men, weapons, money or national costume' (Ypsilantis 1821a).
6   Cited in Photeinos 1846, p. 33.

On 25 February 1821, Ypsilantis issued a proclamation entitled 'To the so-journing Hellenes', essentially addressing himself to the members of the reigning Ottoman apparatuses in Moldavia, since, as far back as the seventeenth century, but primarily after 1711, the governance of the Ottoman dominion in Moldavia and Wallachia had been assumed by *Phanariotes*[7] and other Greek-speaking officers and representatives of the Sublime Porte, the Ottoman central government:

> Ye my friends, fellow compatriots ... forced from adverse conditions to be reduced to a state so as to be set as well behind the chariots of the local masters; contempt and hubris heretofore unheard of against the dwellers on Hellenic land! Behold then a bright course opening before you, the sacred struggle in favour of motherland and faith. Rally to rinse off this hubris unbid, etched upon the flag of liberty.[8]

The Ecumenical Patriarch of Constantinople Gregorios V and the Patriarch of Jerusalem Polykarpos almost at once (in those first days of March 1821) denounced the Revolution with an Encyclical. According to the Encyclical, the insurrectionists 'Rather than being lovers of liberty they proved to be loathers of liberty, and rather than being lovers of country and religion, they proved to be loathers of country, religion and God'. At the same time, Orthodox Christians are called upon to demonstrate 'all possible submission to and compliance with that all-powerful and invincible Reign destined by Providence'.[9]

In the proclamations of the leader of the Friendly Society a clear attempt is made to kindle emotions of enthusiasm and optimism in the addressees for the course of the Revolution, a thing to be expected in such a revolutionary

---

7 *Phanariotes* (or *Phanariots*) were Greek-speaking laymen, mostly descendants of the old Byzantine aristocracy, who held high political positions in the Ottoman administration; they were called *Phanariotes* after the district of Fener where they lived. See also Chapter 4.

8 Cited in Photeinos 1846, p. 34. As Lidia Cotovanu notes, '[T]he ruling class of Wallachia remained divided between, on the one hand, the Boyars who were supported by neighbouring Christian forces in order to strengthen the autonomy of the land, and on the other hand, those who "were content" with the dependency of the region on the Ottoman capital. In a competitive atmosphere as such, the ideological contention that those Greeks established within the principalities is amplified, as they constituted the organisational bodies of Ottoman domination ... To this ideological, metaphorical representation of the *Greeks* as pipelines of foreign domination, is added social disaffection, which stems from the direct personal interaction of local subjects with the *Greek* landowning class, whether they be officials, merchants, or clerics' (Cotovanu 2018, pp. 435–6).

9 Cited in Kremmydas 2016, pp. 65, 70.

undertaking. Reference to the heroic greatness of the ancient 'forebears' serves, amongst others, the same objective.

What is problematic according to the 'facts and figures' of the official historiography of today (or 'national history', not only Greek) is twofold: one, the view regarding the *borders of Greece* (in other words, of the territory where the Greek nation is considered to have lived, and where the Greek *state*, theretofore non-existent, would be created) as, e.g. Serbia and Bulgaria appear as regions that belong to Greece (where 'national phalanxes shall be formed', and 'patriotic legions' shall appear);[10] and two, the dyad of terms that are used to describe both the nation and the dominion where its people reside, in which the independent *state shall be created: Hellenes-Greeks, Hellas-Greece.*[11]

I shall leave such issues open for the time being, as they constitute an essential question of investigation in the book with which we will concern ourselves in the forthcoming chapters. It is worth noting, as a hint of what is to follow, that the perception that the Bulgarians and Serbs were a part of the Greek nation, and thus that the Greek state shall (and must) expand into the areas that these people inhabited, was preponderant throughout the course of the Greek Revolution, that is, even *after* the failure of the movement in Moldavia and Wallachia, the formation of the first Greek revolutionary government and the conspicuous disappearance of the Friendly Society from the foreground. Indicative of this is the articulation of Theodoros Negris (editor in November of 1821 of the *Provisions of Law* that governed the *Areios Pagos* – the temporary administration of 'Eastern Mainland Hellas') from the *year 1824* that follows:

> While it is just for Christians having been born and residing in this free land to enjoy the Rights of the free Hellene citizen, it is equally just for their brothers to enjoy the same, whose Country is not free, as this part of the Nation, which today is free by divine grace, having been liberated by a shared decision of freedom-loving Hellenes from the various Provinces of Turkey. The Serb, the Bulgarian, the Thracian, the Epirote, the Thessalian, the Aetolian, the Phokian, the Lokrian, the Boeotian, the Athenian, the Euboean, the Peloponnesian, the Rhodian, the Cretan, the Samian, the Psarian, the Lemnian, the Koan, the Tenedian, the Mytilenian, the Chi-

---

10   To the contrary, as we have seen, most notably in the Proclamation of 23 February 1821, the 'Nation of Moldavia-Wallachia' is clearly distinguished from the Hellenes (Greeks).

11   Characteristically, in a letter sent by A. Ypsilantis to Society Friend Demetrios Makris on 21 February 1821, the former mandates the following: 'In the Greek Church the Priests shall pray in the Divine Liturgy: "For the erection of Trophies of Victory of us the Pious against the Tyrants"' (Philemon 1834, p. 305).

ote, the Naxian, the Tinian, the Antiochian, the Syrian, the Ephesian, the Vythinian, the Caesarean, the Smyrniote, and the remainder of Christians under the barbarian yoke of the Sultan for centuries, depressed, groaning, they agreed ... to live with one another in freedom ....[12]

We shall see in what follows that this perspective, with slight variations, will remain predominant within the confines of the Greek national ideology up to the middle of the nineteenth century.

2 The Evolution and Failure of the Campaign in Moldavia and Wallachia

The plans of the Friendly Society were grandiose. As most of the members of the Society were in the Peloponnese,[13] and Mani was under a semi-autonomous system, Ypsilantis initially drew up plans to initiate the revolution himself from Mani,[14] and simultaneously or immediately thereafter for the insurrection to break out in the Danubian Principalities under the leadership of the warlords Georgakis Olympios and Tudor (Theodoros) Vladimirescu, both of whom had taken part in the Russo-Ottoman war of 1806–12 under the command of the Russian general Mikhail Kutuzov, as well as in, according to various sources, the Russian delegation at the Congress of Vienna in 1815.[15] Various circumstances as well as internal clashes amongst the leadership of the Society ultimately drove Ypsilantis to alter his plan and to spearhead the outbreak of the Revolution himself in Moldavia and Wallachia.

It was assumed that the Revolution would sweep throughout the entire Ottoman Empire and lead to its demise, with the creation of the new Greek state in its place.

> ... [T]he insurgents would march towards Constantinople, where initiates were already present, the objective being the assassination of the sultan,

---

12 Negris 1824, cited in Stoikou 2008, pp. 109–10, and in part in Skopetea 1988, p. 25.

13 A. Ypsilantis, in a message to the members of the Friendly Society on the Peloponnese on 8 October 1820, notes, *inter alia*: 'In such critical times as these present ones, no other province of our Motherland has shown such zeal towards the felicitous outcome of the sacred aims of our Genus, as your country-loving spirits, o Peloponnesians!' (Philemon 1834, pp. 281, 293). Genus [Γένος] initially meant all Orthodox Christians of the empire (a non-national or non-ethnic categorisation), and later the Orthodox Greeks.

14 Philemon 1834, pp. 272–3.

15 Olympios had also distinguished himself in the Serbian uprising of 1804.

the setting fire to the naval base of the Golden Horn (Tarsanas), as well as to the fleet, and the torching of Byzantium.[16]

In the Principalities, Alexandros Ypsilantis banked his hopes on the formation of the troops necessary to fulfil the plans of the Society by enlisting the local warlords. This assessment originated in a deficient understanding of the prevailing conditions there, which to a degree was rooted in the incompetence of his collaborators and counsellors.[17]

The majority of the Inhabitants of the two Provinces of Moldavia and of Wallachia ... were unworthy of arms ... The so-called Playashes, Voundori, Voutikashes and Pandours (or the mountaineers)[18] perceived as the most proficient and well-trained at such things; the Lords nevertheless ... nurtured animosity towards the Hellenes, as they had been under the latter's rule for many a year. Of the occasional Hellene sporadically found in this

---

16   Evangelides 1934, p. 566; see also Philemon 1834, p. 310, Philemon 1859, pp. 47 ff. Philemon
      (1859) delineates the plans put forth for approval by Alexandros Ypsilantis. In one of those
      plans, which had been drawn up by Friends member warlord Savvas Kaminaris Phokianos
      (see below), we read: 'First and foremost Serbia shall take action, and take care of, if pos-
      sible, and by no deceitful means, to take over the fort ... When the Serbs rebel, the Vosnaks
      shall want to take up arms and attack them. But the sworn Erjekoval and Staravlatal Chris-
      tians of the system will attack the Voznaks from behind ... It is then that the Turkish
      neighbours shall decide to run against the Christians; but the attacking Montenegrins then
      hit from the side ... The pasha of Skodras, upon learning of this rebellion, will take up arms
      ... Then, the Merititises, who are Latin ... whom we have to buy out with piastres and firmly
      affix them by an oath, set them against the Skodrians ... the Hellenes of the Aegean sea
      with their fleet will then move ... against Constantinople ...' (Philemon 1959, pp. 77–9).
17   'All the same, the people who were forming Ypsilantis's Council did not possess, it seems,
      the requisite political and military minds' (Philemon 1834, p. 296).
18   Thomas Gordon describes as follows the different groups bearing arms in the Principalit-
      ies: 'Formerly, the native force of the principalities was by no means despicable, consisting
      of *Pandours*, or militia, headed by the nobility, and enjoying considerable privileges. Since
      the sway of the Phanariotes began, however, military service was abolished, the Boyards
      (or nobles) sunk into sloth and effeminacy; and the princes, wanting money and not
      swords, trampled underfoot the franchises of the soldiery, and did all they could to depress
      the spirits of their subjects. Yet there was still a semblance of provincial militia arranged
      under the following denominations: – First, the *Pandours* of Little Wallachia, (the district
      between the Danube and the Olta), where that institution, though languishing, had been
      suffered to exist; they were estimated at 10,000. Secondly, the *Playashes*, or mountain-
      eers, guarding the defiles toward the Austrian frontier, and on that account exempt from
      tribute. Thirdly, the *Potokeshes*, who are charged to watch over the security of the roads.
      Fourthly, the *Vounatores*, or huntsmen of the Boyards, whose only occupation is to provide
      their masters with game' (Gordon 1872, Vol. 1, pp. 94–5).

Province most were those called the Arkatashes ... those among them who would be able to bear arms were a few Epirotes, Thessalians, Macedonians, Acharnians, Bulgarians, Serbs, amongst others, all understood to be under the general name Albanians.[19] But just as their numbers reached 4000 ... moving forward, we find that the squalid and phlegmatic Bulgaria, the once illustrious Macedonia, became impoverished of any wisdom, were steeped in tyranny, and worst of all, were in no position to recognise even the true significance of the word Liberty.[20]

The analysis cited above by Philemon[21] apprises us not only of the sketchy and tenuous military strength of Ypsilantis's undertaking, but also of a *national politicisation* of scant proportion of the populations of 'Hellas', in spite of the heady optimism of the Friends.

With the declaration of the Revolution by Alexandros Ypsilantis, the warlords Vasileios Karavias, Georgios Argyropoulos and Georgios Arvanitakis seized Galaţi, the most significant harbour of Moldavia, and 'proceeded with massacres of the Turks and amongst them was the garrison commander Toptzis agha'.[22] When these events became known, the Sublime Porte dispatched numerous troops to the Principalities, which entered Moldavia on 1 May 1821, to quash the Revolution.

By the end of April, Alexandros Ypsilantis, bearing the title of 'Sovereign General Commander', declared that he had managed to assemble troops of 13,345 men, which had been divided into five Army Corps, and into two other corps, the Sacred Battalion (400 fighters) and the Troops of Moldavia (300 men).[23] Each Army Corps was divided into *tagmatarchies* (Commanding Units), *Chiliarchies* (battalions of 1,000 men) and *Lochous* (Companies). The First and Second Corps were commanded by Nikolaos and Georgios Ypsilantis respectively, brothers of Alexandros, the Third by Georgakis Olympios, the Fourth by Savvas Kaminaris Phokianos,[24] and the Fifth Corps, the greatest in number with 6,000 men, by Tudor Vladimirescu. As intelligence of the approaching Ottoman army reached them, however, and due to rivalries a-

---

19 According to Ilias Photeinos, in the Principalities, 'Those Bulgarians, Serbs, Hellenes and/or natives found to be clothed in the garments customary to the Ottomans (the osmanlitika) or in Hellenic costume, are commonly referred to in the native locution as Arnaout, namely, Albanian to this day' (Photeinos 1846, p. 11).

20 Philemon 1834, pp. 296–8; see also Cotovanu 2018, p. 431 and note 6.

21 Philemon 1834.

22 Evangelides 1934, p. 566.

23 Statistics from Todorov 1982, and Gordon 1872, Vol. 1, pp. 141–2.

24 See also note 16.

mongst the commanders of the various military units, the army began to 'shed its leaves' to about one-third of its original size.[25]

Of the warlords who were an integral part of Alexandros Ypsilantis's activity in the Danubian Principalities, most influential was Tudor Vladimirescu, who had initiated his own action even before the arrival of Ypsilantis in Moldavia. On 23 January 1821, he addressed a proclamation 'To all the people of the city of Bucharest and the rest of the states and villages of the Romanian Genus', calling upon them to take up arms against the local lords:

> ... Our rulers ... how long shall we suffer being bled dry? How long shall we continue to desire to be enslaved? ... Well therefore make haste, brothers! Let us eradicate evil with evil ... [M]ake haste, then, everyone, to come most swiftly, may those possessing arms come with arms, may those lacking such come with staffs and clubs ... the land that has wrongly and unjustly been possessed by those thieving Masters, that is, those who desired not to be in accord with our spirit, and who desired not to follow our course of action, I hereby promise that the land shall be reclaimed for the benefit of all.[26]

In contrast to Ypsilantis, who had given assurance 'to the Nation of Moldavia-Wallachia' that 'the authority and administration of this Principality shall stay as it already is, and faithful to these same laws' (see above), Vladimirescu had declared an insurgency against the 'malevolent Masters', into which he most likely classified 'the *Greek* landowning class as well, whether they be officials, merchants, or clerics'.[27]

Vladimirescu, assessing that the Ottoman army advancing into the Principalities would not be able to be confronted, asked Ypsilantis to abandon Wallachia so as to avert bloodshed and slaughter, and pulled out of Bucharest without a fight. At the same time, he appealed to the Sublime Porte, declaring his fidelity and, contending that his actions did not challenge Ottoman sovereignty but had to do with the local lords, he petitioned for certain reforms pertaining to the Ottoman system of dominance, in which he himself would

---

25 According to a decree issued by Alexandros Ypsilantis on 26 April 1821, 'The Prince is obliged to alter his plan of organizing the army in divisions, and to cease making promotions, on account of the jealousy and emulation of his officers' (Gordon 1872, Vol. 1, p. 142).

26 Cited in Photeinos 1846, pp. 7–9, 'translated from the Vlach language'.

27 Cotovanu 2018.

maintain and amplify his role as a military lord.[28] Nevertheless, taking advantage of a degree of upheaval within his troops, the warlords Georgakis Olympios, Hadži-Prodan and Dimitri Makedonski apprehended Vladimirescu and handed him over to Alexandros Ypsilantis, who summarily ordered his execution, which took place on 28 May 1821.

On 7 June, what remained of Ypsilantis's army, considering that the greater part of his soldiery had deserted him, were defeated by the Ottoman army near Drăgăşani, in Wallachia, where the Sacred Battalion was also decimated. Prior to that battle, warlord Savvas Kaminaris Phokianos had surrendered to the Ottomans, and his troops, under his command, fought alongside the Ottoman army against Ypsilantis at Drăgăşani.[29] Those remaining under the command of Ypsilantis following the Battle of Drăgăşani decided to abandon the campaign and sought refuge in the Austrian Empire. Ypsilantis followed suit, though he disagreed with the decision. There, he addressed them for the last time:

> Soldiers! What shall I say? Begone with blasphemy! I desire not to sully that comely and glorious name, as I address you, a herd of unmanly and unworthy rabble, and I shall address you accordingly. Cowardly and slavish manikins! Your treachery and conspiracies which you underhandedly effected force me to take leave of you. From this moment on, any affiliation of mine with you is henceforth dissolved.[30]

Following the insurrectionists' defeat at Drăgăşani, the company under Georgakis Olympios and a second armed band led by Ioannis Pharmakis were still intact. These armed divisions fled to the mountainous regions of Moldavia, pursued by the Ottoman army and the collaborating forces of Savvas Kaminaris Phokianos. Eventually, in July of 1821, the majority of them resolved, under the command of the former colonel of the Russian army Wallachian Prince Kantakouzinos and 'Chiliarchos' Vassili Todor, that it would be pointless to press on with the campaign, and they crossed the border into the Rus-

---

28   In the memorandum he sent to the Sublime Porte, Vladimirescu petitions: '[T]hat the prevailing custom of appointing exclusively Greek Phanariotes as Principals of Wallachia be abolished ... [T]hat the taxes of the villagers be determined as a result of common agreement for seven years, and within that time period taxes shall not increase, nor shall they decrease ... An amount of five hundred thousand piastres shall be made at last in advance to cover the necessary expenses of [Vladimirescu's] troops ...' (Photeinos 1846, p. 27).

29   In the wake of the hostilities, the Ottomans set a trap to capture Kaminaris and slayed him (Evangelides 1933, p. 405).

30   Cited in Photeinos 1846, p. 160.

sian Empire in the region of Bessarabia, where they surrendered to Russian authorities. Georgakis Olympios and Ioannis Pharmakis carried on the struggle until the beginning of September 1821, whereupon Olympios, in order to evade arrest, blew himself and his small band of comrades up at the Sekkos monastery, while Pharmakis surrendered to the Ottoman army and was executed.

In 1982, Nikolai Todorov published the 'State Files of the County of Odessa, Secretary to the Governorate of Novorissiksy and Bessarabia' in Greek, in which the names and personal information of 1,002 combatants who had crossed the border at Bessarabia and surrendered to the Russian authorities in the township of *Orgiev* in July of 1821 are recorded.[31] In this file, 'the nationality and citizenship of every man are documented'.[32]

According to 'nationality', 503 of the 1002 registered declared themselves to be Greek, 199 as Moldavians, 132 as Bulgarians, 72 as Serbs, 15 as Ukrainians (Little Russians), 14 as Russians, nine as Wallachians, seven as Albanians, six as Roma, as well as four as Hungarians, Poles and Dalmations respectively, three as Lipovans (Russian 'heretics'), French, Christianised Ottomans, Arnaouts and christened Jews respectively, two as Montenegrins, Italians of Austrian citizenship, Prussians and Bosnians respectively, and one respectively as being Saxon, Neapolitan, German of Austrian citizenship, and a Spaniard, while the remaining six had no clear 'nationality'. As the registry also contains a record of the place of birth and residency of each combatant, it becomes apparent that approximately one-third of those registered had declared permanent residency in the Principalities, while the remainder had gone there from Russia and elsewhere in the early months of 1821.

3   Questions for Consideration: Nation, State and Borders of Claimed Territory

From the files presented that detail the statistics of the 1,002 revolutionary fighters in the Principalities who sought refuge in the Russian Empire (a number of some consequence, given that the total number of those who ended up fighting against the Ottomans in the Principalities did not exceed 5,000), but also from the course of events in Moldavia and Wallachia that we outlined earlier, a number of questions of significant theoretical and historical value arise:

---

31   Todorov 1982, pp. 191–294.
32   Todorov 1982, p. 191.

- Was the Revolution of Alexandros Ypsilantis in Moldavia and Wallachia *transnational* (considering that just barely over half – 50.20 percent to be precise! – of the fighters declared themselves to be Greeks)?
- If we consider that it was presumed to be the *Greek Revolution of 1821* – since in any event Alexandros Ypsilantis declared the campaign in the name of Greek independence – were *such an exceedingly high number* of participants in the hostilities in the Principalities (49.80 percent calls of the those fighting) in fact *'Philhellenes'*?
- Were the 'Philhellenes' perhaps, in fact, much fewer, if we heed Alexandros Ypsilantis's proclamation in Iași on 24 February 1821, according to which *Serbia and Bulgaria (together with the Morea, etc.) constitute 'all of Hellas'*?
- Perhaps the designations 'Hellene-Greek', Bulgarian, Moldavian, etc. (also) referred to *other components* beyond what the present-day national(ist) take on things conceives.
- Perhaps amidst the Revolution of 1821 (i.e. the national politicisation and the armed struggle that pursued the foundation of a Greek *state*) there coexisted actions of *military leaders of the 'ancien régime'* who jumped on the bandwagon of the Revolution, provided that it could promote *their social-power positions*. And I do not refer here to the more obvious cases of Tudor Vladimirescu and Savvas Kaminaris Phokianos, but put forth the question for consideration and investigation into all that took place during the Revolution that lay the foundation for the first Greek state in the southern part of present-day Greece.
- Perhaps all of the pre-1821 'revolutions' were not, in fact, 'struggles for national liberation' as is usually claimed, but insurrections that aimed at the intensification of the power, autonomy and ascendancy of religious groups, certain regions, local lords (primates or *kotsambasides*) or warlords (of the local war aristocracy), either within the confines of the Ottoman regime, and/or under the aegis of a certain Christian power.
- Additionally, were there age-old *'nationalities'* that had been roused, or does national politicisation (the nationalism that forms and holds the nation together) constitute *an innovative and therefore as such 'subversive' social stance* in the context of late 'modernity' (of the nineteenth century) that makes a claim for and/or demands (and forms) 'a state with civil rights', establishing thus a new form of sovereignty holding together the power of the dominant class over the dominated? In this case, how can the structural elements of social cohesion of social groups and regions *prior to* the national politicisation-homogenisation of the populations be traced?
- To what extent were the ideas of the revolutionaries regarding the borders of 'Hellas' determined by the pre-revolutionary 'calls to rise' of the national

enlightenment-revolutionaries (such as Rigas Pheraios, or the author of *Hellenic Nomarchy*, or Adamantios Korais, etc. [see below])?
- Finally, to what extent did these ideas determine the subsequent *Megali Idea* (the Grand Idea) and the permanent expansionist politics of the Greek state?

These questions constitute the objective of our research in the chapters that follow.

The 'Hellas' of 1821: Initial Thoughts on the Dissemination of Greek National Politicisation

1   The Boundaries of 'Hellas', Beginning with Rigas Pheraios (1797) to 1821

While the Revolution in Moldavia and Wallachia was progressing, and in fact before the pivotal battle of Drăgășani in June of 1821, the insurrection broke out in the Peloponnese, Mainland Greece as well as on the islands. On 17 March, the Towers of Kalavryta were besieged, and subsequently occupied on 21 March, while Kalamata was seized on 23 March. On 26 March the Revolution was declared on the island of Spetses, on the 28th on the island of Hydra and the very next day in Livadeia. On 1 April 1821 Thebes was taken.[1]

We have seen that throughout the duration of the struggle, there reigned the widespread belief amongst the insurrectionists that the boundaries of 'Hellas' (of the Greek nation) would expand all throughout the Balkans and beyond (for numbered amongst Hellenes were 'the Serb, the Bulgarian, the Thracian, ... the Peloponnesian, ... the Antiochian, the Syrian, the Ephesian, the Vythinian, the Caesarean, the Smyrniote ...').[2]

This belief was preserved for a number of decades following the found-ation of the Greek state, even after the presence of Bulgarian nationalism had become apparent. In the middle of the nineteenth century, the views introduced by the Greek Enlightenment were still influential, according to

---

1   On 27 March 1821 Alexandros Ypsilantis seized Bucharest. There are thus discrepancies in the perspective of Vassilis Kremmydas that 'while the troops from Mani ... were seizing ... Kala-mata on 23 March 1821, the Friendly Society found itself in the difficult position of having to deal with two problems, the Encyclical, to be precise, of the Patriarchate, and the failure of Alexandros Ypsilantis in the Para-Danubian Principalities' (Kremmydas 2016a, p. 73). Prior to September of 1821 (or at least before June: the battle of Drăgășani), no one could speak of any failure on the part of A. Ypsilantis; the Greek Revolution in what is today Romania was still going on, and, with the limited means of conveying information in those days, word of defeat reached the southern Greek territory considerably after March of 1821. More specific-ally, Demetrios Ypsilantis, brother of Alexandros, bearing credentials of the 'Plenipotentiary of the General Committee of the Authority', arrived on Hydra by way of Trieste on 8 June 1821, without conveying news of any 'failure in the Para-Danubian Principalities'. The Greek Revolution in the territory of what is today Romania cannot be easily dismissed as incidental.

2   See Negris 1824, op. cit.

which the Orthodox populations of the Byzantine, and subsequently Ottoman, Empire were Greeks, subject to various obscurantist despots (Romans
or Turks),[3] and thus there was still considerable resistance to the dynamic-
ally emerging 'Zambelio-Paparrigopoulian school' (of historians S. Zambelios
and C. Paparrigopoulos)[4] concerning the Greekness of the Byzantine state. As
such, the inclusion of Bulgarians as Greeks could be traced back to the earlier
clashes between the mediaeval tsars of Bulgaria and the Roman emperors of
Byzantium. Ikesios Latris (1799–1881), counsellor to Admiral Miaoulis during
the Revolution of 1821, and subsequently Governor of the islands of Milos and
Siphnos and publisher of the newspaper *Panarmonion*, wrote in 1860:

> Those who were then called Bulgarians were in fact by no means the first
> marauding foreigners, but Hellenic Thracians, who were justifiably hos-
> tile to the reigning aristocracy of Byzantium, the majority of whom were
> from old Rome and were tyrannical by nature and used to violent ways
> as was customary in ancient Rome, something which irritated and roused
> the Hellenic peoples, who were by nature social, embracers of liberty, and
> fearless. The then erroneously named Bulgarians that were fighting the
> Empire of Byzantium, whilst the majority were speakers of our tongue,
> were in fact fighting the Roman system and not that of the Hellenes, and
> as the same genus, not as foreigners, nor as foes to Hellenism.[5]

---

3   Adamantios Korais (1748–1833), a major figure of the Greek Enlightenment, wrote in 1819:
    'Behold our painting, since Philip trod upon us until the year 1453. We went through various
    despots, mute and foolish as herds of animals, though we did not change the wretchedness
    of the situation' (Korais 1819, pp. 4–5). Regarding the battle of representatives of the Enlight-
    enment with their 'confederated rivals' during the period 1819–21, see Iliou 1974. As Ioannis
    Zelepos observed, 'between the French Revolution and the inception of the Greek campaign
    for liberation in 1821 ... the religious attack against the enlightenment is expressed *inter alia* by
    means of the disparagement of ancient Greek culture and civilization, but in general of the
    ancient Greeks as well' (Zelepos 2018, pp. 345–6). Regarding the 'transition from the Kora-
    ist interpretative framework to the *Zambeliopaparrigopoulian* one', that is, in the framework
    of the historical continuity of Hellenism according to the conservative historians Spyridon
    Zambelios and Constantinos Paparrigopoulos, see Koumbourlis 2018. See also Chapter 9.
4   See Xifaras 1993a, 1993b. For a systematic presentation of the views formulated by representat-
    ives of official institutions of the Greek state in the first decades of independence that pertain
    to the 'non-Greekness' of Byzantium, see Platis 2008.
5   Cited in Lyberatos 2018, p. 422. This 'historical' documentation of the 'Greekness' of the Bul-
    garians, as baffling as it may seem today, is not necessarily any more arbitrary than other
    narratives, as, for example, that pertaining to the 'Greekness' of Byzantium. Former prime
    minister (in 1945 and 1967) and professor Panagiotis Kanellopoulos (1982, see also in what fol-
    lows) writes the following: 'Simeon was the more glorified sovereign of the first Bulgarian state
    ... (893–927) ... he aimed to transfer the base of the Bulgarian state to Constantinople and be

Perspectives on the Greekness of the Christian Balkan peoples did not, naturally, originate in the Revolution; it was the common creed of those who espoused the 'national-revolutionary' vision of the formation of a new Greek constitutional *state*, and of course of the nationalist intellectual groups and insurgent nationalist movements in countries in Europe beyond Ottoman borders.

The Vienna-based early Greek revolutionary Rigas Pheraios (1757–98) begins the final text of his 'Constitution'[6] by summoning the people[s] of the future 'Hellenic Republic' as follows:

> The people, descendants of the Hellenes,[7] wherever they may reside, Roumeli, Asia Minor, the islands of the Mediterranean, Wallachobogdania, and all those who despair under the most insufferable tyranny of the most abominable Ottoman despotism ... Christians and Turks alike.[8]

And further down, he elucidates:

> There is only one Hellenic Republic, with all the various genera and religions included in her bosom ... The Hellenic people, namely those dwelling within this realm, no religion and language excepting, are divided

---

crowned there as successor to the Roman emperors ... Simeon, who was educated in Constantinople, felt himself to be "about half Greek" (semi graecum), as the Italian – Lombard – historiographer Liudbrand or Luitbrand, [B]ishop of Cremona, wrote some decades after his [Simeon's] death' (Kanellopoulos 1982, pp. 12–13). Regarding the subsequent Tsar of the Bulgarians, Samuel (997–1014), and his clash with the Byzantine emperor Vasileios (Basil) II (the 'Bulgar-slayer'), Dionysios Zakythinos (1903–93) writes: 'Without any regard for nation, the people cross over from one faction to another. In a word, the longstanding and ravaging duel between Vasileios II and Samuel create an atmosphere, in part, of an internal *crisis*, revolution and sedition on the one side, and cruel suppression of the revolt on the other' (cited in Kanellopoulos 1982, p. 22, emphasis added). For the meaning of the terms Graecum, Roman (Romaios), the Romaic language, etc., see below and Chapter 4.

6 'New Political Administration of the Inhabitants of Rumele, Asia Minor, the Mediterranean Islands and Moldobogdania' (Text in Stathis 1996, pp. 183 ff., and its translation in Rhigas 2008, pp. 65 ff.). Roderick Beaton translates the title of Rigas's 'Constitution' as the *New Civil Government of the Inhabitants of European Turkey, Asia Minor and the Mediterranean Islands and Wallachia and Moldavia* (Beaton 2019, p. 54).

7 As Roderick Beaton notes, 'It was a conscious and, it would seem, a little-contested policy choice, beginning around 1800, to *reassert* kinship with the lost civilization of classical antiquity. It has also been a highly selective one. Think of all those ancient practices that have been entirely airbrushed out: nudity, pederasty, slavery, submission of women, infanticide, paganism, animal sacrifice' (Beaton 2019, p. 7).

8 Cited in Stathis 1996, p. 183.

into primary assemblies in the local provinces ... through exercising their imperial power ... He who speaks the colloquial or the Hellenic language, though he may live in the Antipodes (as the Hellenic leaven has expanded into the two hemispheres), is both Hellene and a citizen. He who is a Christian, and does not speak the colloquial or Hellenic language, but only supports Hellas, is a citizen ... The sovereign people are all those who dwell in this realm irrespective of religion and dialect, Hellenes, Bulgarians, Albanians, Wallachians, Armenians, Turks, and any other kind of genus.[9]

In Rigas Pheraios's 'Constitution' (as in his *Thourios*, the Greek battle hymn composed by Rigas), the term 'Hellene' signifies as much the inhabitant-citizen of the Republic as that of the Hellenophone who resides beyond her borders, but also that of he/she who resides in the southern Balkans and on the islands (when he/she is distinguished from the Serb or Bulgarian future citizen of Hellas), whereas the term 'Turk' and its derivatives are primarily used synonymously with being a Muslim, the Islamic religion, etc.[10] Despite the persistent promulgation of religious tolerance, Christians enjoy the privilege of citizenship – Greekness – (provided it is what they seek – 'they support Hellas'), while the 'any other kind of genus' ('Hellenes, Bulgarians, Albanians ...') is likely determined by linguistic criteria. Nevertheless, priority is given to those who speak the 'colloquial' and 'Hellenic' languages (the latter clearly being the archaic *Katharevousa* Greek language of the Christian apparatuses of the Ottoman Empire, commerce and the lettered class).[11] Moreover, the two languages are not of equal stature, as:

---

9   Cited in Stathis 1996, pp. 197–8.

10   '... [T]he freedom of all religions, Christianity, Turkism, Judaism etc., is not restricted under the present administration' (Rigas, op. cit., p. 79).

11   Rigas's vision drew from several sources and was one of the most advanced in the context of the Enlightenment movement (Psarras 2020). A characteristic example: 'Women are even expected to serve in the army, "carrying spears, in case they cannot handle a musket". There is a certain magnificence about all this. In some ways Rigas is far ahead of his time (it was not until 2016 that full combat roles were opened to women in the UK or the US military). The multiculturalism that since the late twentieth century has often been nostalgically attributed to the Ottoman Empire, in the pages of Rigas's *New Civil Government*, becomes harnessed to a modernizing programme that might have turned the cities of the eastern Mediterranean into pluralist, democratic, law-governed communities long before London, Paris or New York. Rigas's "Hellenic Republic" is "Greek" in the way that the English poet Shelley would soon declare that the whole of Europe was: as the *cultural* inheritor of the ancient legacy' (Beaton 2019, p. 56).

All without exception are obliged to be acquainted with letters; the motherland has to make schools in all the villages for male and female children ... The ancient authors of history should be explained, and in the greater cities the French and Italian languages instructed, and *the Hellenic language required.*[12]

In the revolutionary pamphlet *Hellenic Nomarchy, Namely a Discourse on Liberty*, by the Anonymous Hellene, which was published in Italy in 1806,[13] and which the author inscribes to Rigas Pheraios,[14] we encounter a description similar to that of Rigas, and to Ypsilantis's proclamations, etc., as regards the boundaries of 'Hellas':

The Ottoman realm in Europe is divided into the following thirteen provinces, that is, Wallachia, Moldavia, Bulgaria, Serbia, Bosnia, Dalmatia, Albania, Epirus, Thessaly, Livadeia, the Peloponnese, Macedonia and Roumeli. The inhabitants are nearly eighteen million, together with the Islanders of the Archipelagos. The *Christians* to Ottomans, are 115 to 29 ... *Such a great number of Hellenes*, O dear ones, how then are they to live?[15]

The passage above clearly indicates that Greeks were defined by their religious proclivities, while the Ottomans were by definition precluded, something which distinguishes the *Nomarchy* from Rigas's 'Constitution'.

The problem of the 'borders' of Greece shall be addressed in the forthcoming chapters, as it is from there that the 'borders' of the territory claimed by the new Greek state, of the *Megali Idea*, or Grand Idea, largely originate. It is worth noting here that from the end of the nineteenth century onwards, any notion of Greekness in Bulgaria or Serbia rings of paradox. Those belonging to the new Balkan nations claimed their continuous existence as nations since antiquity. Accordingly, the question arises as to how the seemingly 'transnational' character of the Greek Revolution, as well as the launching of the Revolution by the leader of the Friendly Society in Moldavia and Wallachia, may thenceforth be interpreted.

---

12   Cited in Stathis 1996, p. 192, emphasis added.
13   'Written and printed at my own expense for the benefit of the Hellenes, BY AN ANONYMOUS HELLENE. In Italy, 1806' (Anonymous Hellene 1977, p. 7). For the philosophical sources of *Nomarchy*, see Noutsos 1982.
14   'TO THE TOMB of the great and dearly departed Hellene RIGAS, slain for the benefit of the salvation of Hellas, for the sake of gratitude the author thus undertook this opus as a gift. Exoriare aliquis nostris ex ossibus ultor' (Anonymous Hellene 1977, p. 85).
15   Anonymous Hellene 1977, p. 99, emphasis added.

2   Various Assessments of the 'Transnational' Element of the
         Revolution in the National Historiography

Excepting the historical essays that were published the first decades following
the Revolution,[16] which consider the inclusion of Serbia, Bulgaria, etc. within
the boundaries of 'Hellas' (and, correspondingly, the integration of Serbs and
Bulgarians, etc. into the Greek populace) as natural, historians subsequent to
that early period generally skirt the question of the marked and substantive
participation of Bulgarians, Serbs, Moldavians, etc. in the Revolution in the
Principalities, making only cursory and unexamined references. They almost
exclusively cite the proclamation by Alexandros Ypsilantis entitled 'Fight for
faith and motherland', and not the one bearing the title 'Greek Men ...'.[17]

   As, for example, the most recognised national historian to this day, Constantinos Paparrigopoulos (1815–91), plainly states: 'Many other Hellenes, Bulgarians, Serbs supported the activity of the [Friendly] Society in the Principalities',[18] while another established historian of the Revolution, Dionysios Kokkinos, merely alludes to 'Hellenes and Arnaouts'.[19]

   That notwithstanding, three interpretations of the participation of Bulgarians, Serbs, etc. took shape, all of which confirm the 'transnational' nature of the
Revolution in Moldavia and Wallachia, despite their varying points of origin.

   The first 'reading' considers the Revolution in the Principalities to have been
a mistake on the part of Alexandros Ypsilantis, as the population there was not
Greek. The main proponent of this stance was Spyridon Trikoupis (1788–1873),
himself an active participant in the Revolution. In the *History of the Hellenic
Revolution*, published in 1860, he writes:

> Ypsilantis went to initiate the struggle of Hellas in foreign lands without
> having thought what he would do with the inhabitants of those very
> lands.[20]

However, even if this assessment is correct, the question remains: why did the
Society of Friends initiate the Revolution in Romania?

---

16   Philemon 1834, 1859; Photeinos 1846.
17   See Chapter 1 of the present book.
18   Paparrigopoulos 1971, Vol. 15, p. 20.
19   Kokkinos 1956, p. 111. Kokkinos refers to the proclamation 'Greek Men ...', but he 'translates'
      it as 'Those Men of Hellas who are sojourning in Moldavia and Wallachia' (Kokkinos 1956,
      p. 109).
20   Trikoupis 1993, p. 61. George Finlay shares the same opinion: 'Thus terminated this ill-
      judged attempt to make a Greek revolution in foreign provinces, without offering to the

The second perspective, expressed characteristically by the Marxist historian Yanis Kordatos (see also Chapter 9), conceives Rigas Pheraios's political programme as a declaration of a campaign for the creation of a 'Balkan Federation' (and not of a Greek state),[21] as well as for a revolution itself in the Principalities, a 'pan-Balkan insurrection', from whose objectives Ypsilantis deviated, the result being a loss of support from the other Balkan peoples, in spite of their initial involvement in the Revolution:

> What Ypsilantis aimed for was to capitalise on the pan-Balkan insurrection to the benefit of Greek feudal lords, who would replace Turkish authority in Constantinople ... rather than invade Bulgaria, where such an action would likely instigate an uprising of considerable significance, he changed direction and headed towards the Austrian border, evidently determined to abandon the Campaign ... The result ... was the disillusionment of Moldavian and Wallachian farmers, who deserted Ypsilantis's camp. Aside from the Moldavian and Wallachians, equally disillusioned were the Bulgarian *volunteers* ... and all of those genuine leaders of the popular masses.[22]

The third interpretation, characteristically represented by the Bulgarian historian Nikolai Todorov[23] and Panagiotis Kanellopoulos, maintains that the

---

native population any guarantee for a better administration of justice, or any prospect of increasing the liberties of the nation' (Finlay 1859, pp. 169–70).

21 Kordatos writes, characteristically, in 1945: 'Within the next few days, the peoples of the Balkans, emancipated from the influence of the plutocracy, shall seal an agreement and organise into a pan-Balkan federation. The time has come for Rigas's plans to be realised, adapted to the novel political-social conditions created by the Second World War and the victories of the Red Army' (Kordatos 1983, pp. 5–6).

22 Kordatos 1972, pp. 149–50, emphasis added. In the first edition of Kordatos's book (1924), these very same positions are in fact argued regarding the 'pan-Balkan insurrection', which A. Ypsilantis strove to steer 'to the benefit of Hellene feudal lords. The result ... was the disillusionment of Moldavian and Wallachian farmers, who deserted Ypsilantis's camp' (Kordatos 1927, pp. 78–9). At the same time, however, the claim that the Friendly Society were of a 'pure bourgeois spirit' is also articulated! As regards the proclamation 'Fight for faith and motherland' that Ypsilantis 'pushed' in the Principalities, Kordatos writes in 1924: 'That proclamation, by the very nature of its content, is of paramount importance, as its wording attests to the fact that the Directors of the Friendly Society possessed a pure bourgeois spirit and had been influenced by French revolutionary ideas' (Kordatos 1927, p. 76). Regarding the radical transformation of Kordatos's views from 1927 onwards, which resulted in a fourth edition of his *The Social Significance of the 1821 Revolution*, published in 1946 as an entirely different book than the one bearing the same title published in 1924, see Chapter 9 of the present book.

23 Nikolai Todorov (1921–2003) was a professor of history at Sofia University, member of the

Revolution was a struggle for the national liberation of the Greeks in which other Balkan peoples participated as *volunteers*, since many of them expected, amongst other things, the emancipation of their own nations as well, were the Greek Revolution to be victorious.

> Many a Bulgarian, Serb, Montenegrin, Albanian, Romanian took part in the Greek revolution ... The Bulgarians, those immediate neighbours to the Greeks who had for centuries shared the harsh and onerous fate of Ottoman suzerainty, played an active role in the revolution, which they considered to be a shared affair.[24]

Despite their shared action in the Greek Revolution, it was, states Todorov, a case of different national groups, national groups roughly as we know them today. The 'Bulgarians, Serbs, Montenegrins, Albanians, Romanians' thus constituted 'volunteers from the Balkans', according to Todorov.[25] Therefore, in accordance with the prevalent description of the foreign volunteers who fought in the Greek Revolution, they could be referred to as 'Philhellenes'!

Panagiotis Kanellopoulos, who authored the lengthy introduction to the book by Todorov entitled 'Hellenes and Bulgarians',[26] offers the following as an explanation of the aforementioned schema:

> They had, as all the Christian populaces had – not only the Hellenes – their own distinct *popular consciousness*. Each ethnic group had their traditions and legends, their language, their mores and customs, their folk songs ... The mores and customs exhibit a great many similarities, of course, as do the songs of the Hellenes with those of the other Balkan peoples ... Nevertheless, not one of the Christian peoples of the Balkan peninsula forgot, throughout the centuries of thraldom, their *origins* ... *The concept of 'Nation', needless to say, crystallised much later.*[27]

So according to Kanellopoulos, there were *distinct Balkan peoples*, each with its own distinct '*origins*' and '*popular consciousness*', which until the nineteenth century could not be considered as nations. A significant mark of the nine-

---

Bulgarian Academy of Sciences, Ambassador of Bulgaria to Greece (1978–83) and Acting Prime Minister of Bulgaria from 17 July to 1 August 1990.

24   Todorov 1982, p. 67.
25   Todorov 1982.
26   See Todorov 1982, pp. 11–62.
27   In Todorov 1982, p. 48, emphasis added.

teenth century is that only then, during that specific time period, does a consciousness arise in the people, amidst the effects begot by the American and
French Revolutions, that their self-governance is a possibility – and a prospect:

> ... The people, until the hour when the North American colonies rose up
> against the British Crown, and most notably until that great moment of
> the French Revolution, did not know that they could blaze their own his-
> torical trail with leaders that would arise from within their own ranks.
> The fate of the people, until the second half of the eighteenth century,
> had been inextricably wedded to the fate of their rulers – whether their
> powers were inherited or usurped – and to the caste of those who, endow-
> ed with social privilege, stood out from their people.[28]

So did the participation of volunteers from the other Balkan populations in the
Greek Revolution thus constitute an attempt of those populaces to 'blaze their
own historical trail'? Kanellopoulos seems at this point to abandon his case and
goes on to argue that the Bulgarian volunteers were not pursuing 'their own
national objective':

> However, *before* the nineteenth century would *divide the populaces* – that,
> too, being an historical necessity – so that *each* may lay claim to *their own
> national objective*, the Bulgarians tangibly demonstrated their *solidarity
> with the Hellenes*.[29]

It is here that Kanellopoulos's entire analysis seems to flounder. First, for the
reason that the Revolution of 1821 obviously takes place in the nineteenth
century. Second, because the distinct 'origins' and 'popular consciousness' of
distinct 'nations' suddenly appears to be of little consequence. Perhaps, then,
although in the year 1821 the 'nineteenth century' was already in its third decade, the Bulgarians had yet to forge their own appreciable, distinct 'national
objective'? Kanellopoulos does not want to draw his reader down such a path,
in spite of the fact that, as evidenced, his contentions lack consistency and are
contradictory, and lead to such. So as to avoid such an impasse, he hastens to
distance himself from the 'Hellenic Republic' envisaged by Rigas:

> In the 'Hellenic Republic' ... language and education should be, according
> to Rigas, Greek ... [W]ith his great proclamation he imbued a tone that

---

28   In Todorov 1982, p. 41.
29   In Todorov 1982, pp. 60–1, emphasis added.

signalled, without his intending to, for he himself was not a 'nationalist', a drastic diminishment of the historical initiative of the other peoples of the Balkans.[30]

Yet what would constitute the 'Hellenic Republic' if the language and education were not compulsorily Greek? And, as such, if Rigas were not, in fact, the bearer of the new, radical ideology of nationalism, which had begun to ripple throughout Europe in the wake of the French Revolution? The so-called transnational 'Balkan Federation' of Kordatos, perhaps?

3   Language, Origins and the 'Plans of the Friends'

Allow me to posit a separate question that arises from what has already been developed: Would the nascent Greek state have been able to incorporate and gradually assimilate populations speaking other languages to such an extent so as to include the inhabitants of the provinces of Serbia, Bulgaria, etc.? I shall subject this question to further analysis in the upcoming chapters, whose principal objects of study shall be the nation and (Greek) nationalism. Suffice it to be pointed out that the nation, that is, the *national politicisation of a population*, nearly never has language as a primary criterion *in the prospect of the formation/strengthening/expansion of a national state*, though certainly a national tongue tends, in hindsight, to mould and to universalise.

There is a singular aspect to the fact that the language of those inhabitants of the first Greek state was not only Greek (*Demotic* [colloquial] or *Katharevousa* [archaic]), but also Albanian ('*Arvanitika*'), which not only prevailed in certain regions,[31] but in essence comprised the language of the Greek naval fleet up to

---

30   In Todorov 1982, p. 57.
31   See Giohalas 2006, 2011. Thomas Gordon describes as follows the Albanian-speaking regions of Greece: 'Attica, Argolis, Boeotia, Phocis, and the isles of Hydra, Spezzia, Salamis, and Andros, are inhabited by Albanians. They likewise possess several villages in Arcadia, Achaia, and Messenia ... Among themselves those people always converse in their own language; many of them do not understand Greek, and they pronounce it with a strong accent' (Gordon 1872, Vol. 1, p. 34). Roderick Beaton writes in this context: 'Speakers of Greek as a first language seem to have been in the majority throughout most of the islands of the Aegean and the Ionian seas, in Crete and in Cyprus, in the Peloponnese (at this time still more commonly known as the Morea) and the southern mainland of what is now Greece, an area loosely known at the time as Roumeli. Even within that area, significant regions were primarily Albanian-speaking ... Further north in the Balkans, around the Sea of Marmara and down the Aegean coast of Anatolia, there were many Greek speakers

the beginning of the twentieth century, as a high percentage of sailors came from Albanian-speaking areas of the state (the islands of Hydra, Spetses, Poros, Andros, etc.).

Even prior to the Revolution there were dictionaries of the Balkan languages in circulation, such as *Protopeiria*, by Theodoros Anastasios Kavalliotis (1718–89), which was published in Venice in 1770 and which contained a trilingual lexicon (the Romaic [Greek], Wallachian and Alvanitiki languages), the *Introductory Teaching* (*Eisagogiki Didaskalia*) by Daniel Moschopolites (1754–1825), 'consisting of a quadrilingual Lexicon of the four common Dialects, namely, of colloquial Romaic, Moesian Wallachian, the Bulgarian and Arvanitiki languages',[32] which was published in 1802, and the *Lexicon of the Roman and Colloquial Arvanitiki Languages* by Markos Botsaris (1790–1823), a manuscript from 1809 which contains Greek-Albanian dialogues as a kind of 'tutorless method' of learning. Further, a bilingual Holy Scripture (Greek-Albanian) was released in 1827 'by the printing establishment of the Administration'.[33]

Following the Revolution, Dr Karl Reinhold (1834–80), a physician from the Kingdom of Hanover who served as Chief Physician in the Hellenic navy, published a book in 1855 that included a Greek-Albanian dictionary and folkloric material entitled *The Pelasgika: The Naval Dialect* (meaning the Albanian language).[34] As Aristeides Kollias notes:

> Reinhold served in the Greek navy ... It was there that he learned Arvanitika. The language of our navy until the era of the great Admiral of the Balkan wars [1912–13], Pavlos Kountouriotis, was Arvanitika.[35]

---

too, but here they were more evenly interspersed with speakers of other languages. There were Greek-speaking enclaves as far east as the district around Trebizond on the Black Sea, known in Greek by its ancient name of Pontos, and in Cappadocia, the Greek name for the area around Kayseri (Caesarea) in central Anatolia' (Beaton 2019, p. 33).

32   In the introductory texts of the dictionary, the author writes: 'Albanians, Wallachians, Bulgarians, Speakers of other languages, rejoice / And prepare yourselves, all of you to become Romans / Relinquishing the language, voice and mores of barbarians / Where to your Descendants may seem like myths'. http://editions.academyofathens.gr/epetirides/xmlui/handle/20.500.11855/419.

33   *The New Testament of our Lord Jesus Christ, bi-lingual, that is, in Greek and Albanian = Dyiata e re e Zotit sone ke na Spetoi Iesou Christoit be dhi yioche dho me thene Gerkiste, e dhe Skipetartze.*

34   Caroli H.Th. Reinhold (1855), *Noctes Pelasgicae: Dialectos Graeciae Pelasgicas*, Typis Sophoclis Garbola, Athens. https://books.google.gr/books?id=ugJvYWos14UC&pg=PP8&lpg=PP8&dq=Noctes+Pelasgicae:+Dialectos+Graeciae+Pelasgica (retrieved Nov. 19, 2022).

35   Kollias 1997, p. 9.

The monthly periodical *Apollon*, which was published in Piraeus between 1883 and 1892, published a poem in the May 1889 issue (Issue 56) in honour of the Princess Alexandra, daughter of King George and Queen Olga of Greece, occasioned by her engagement to the son of the emperor of Russia, Alexander II. The poem occupies 13 pages and is written in Albanian, with the Greek translation apposed in the adjacent column and with the following frontispiece: 'I extol you in Albanian, in a heroic language, which was spoken by the admiral Miaoulis, Botsaris and all of Souli'.[36]

So if language did not constitute a factor in the demarcation of the nation amongst the Greeks of 1821, there did exist a unifying element in the conviction of the *shared origins from ancient Greece*, which was the birthplace of 'illumination' (the Enlightenment), reason and the sciences.[37] We even saw Rigas's 'Constitution', which is permeated by the revolutionary spirit of the French Revolution, and which does not define the attribute of a citizen based on language or religion, commence with the phrase: 'The people, descendants of the Hellenes'.[38] A discussion of the question in *Hellenic Nomarchy* points to the following:

> Hellas, O my beloved, eight hundred years before Christ, flourished and was at her height of bliss. However, since Philip, father of Alexander the Great, first took hold of the Macedonian sceptre in 375 before Christ, he commenced, alas! to desecrate the free soil of Hellas ... Well, since that time, until 364 Anno Domini, when the kingdom of Rome was divided into East and West, the Hellenes were subjected to frightful tyranny, and endured unprecedented suffering and hardship from the various, cruellest of imperatores, wherever Rome would dispatch them ... Well,

---

36   'DE EPARA VASILOPOULA YIONE LEXANDRA – TO OUR FIRST PRINCESS ALEXANDRA'. The photomechanical reproduction of the original poem appeared in print in the periodical *Besa* (*Μπέσα*), Period II, Issue 1 (November 1995), pp. 10–22. Andreas Miaoulis (1765–1835) was admiral of the Greek navy during the Revolution. Souli is a region in Epirus which actively participated in the Revolution; Markos Botsaris (1788–1823) was a captain of the irregular army of the Souliotes, and was posthumously awarded the title of General.

37   Regarding the Greek Enlightenment during the first two decades of the nineteenth century, see Beaton 2019, pp. 22–5. 'It was, in a way, only a mirror of what was going on throughout the rest of Europe between 1789 and 1815. In the midst of all this turmoil, ideas of national self-determination, of the rights of citizens, of *liberté, égalité, fraternité*, were beginning to circulate, and nowhere more so than in the borderlands where Greek-educated Orthodox Christians made up the elite. For the time being, though, these ideas were for the few' (Beaton 2019, p. 53).

38   Rigas 1797, cited in Stathis 1996, p. 183.

since then, wherever Christianity has been anchored, until 1453, rather than advancing the means for their liberation, alas! the means were being diminished. The superstition and the spurious and pointless fervour of the priests and patriarchs, subjugated the souls of kings ... It was in a situation such as this, my brothers, that Hellas had found herself, when ... the depraved and brutish Ottoman throne was erected in Constantinople.[39]

The reference to the 'ancient ancestors' and the 'illumination' of the East by obliterating the tyranny of the savage and brutish Ottomans (for a more extensive analysis, see Chapter 8) was the rule of thumb in the proclamations at the outset of the Revolution at the various locations when the armed struggle began, for example on the island of Hydra on 16 April 1821:

> The *descendants* of those illustrious men, those who exalted the human race, and with their high virtue *illuminated the world*, now fight for freedom against their oppressors, barbarous offspring of the barbarous Osman, *annihilators of the sciences and arts*, and foes of the hallowed religion of Jesus Christ.[40]

This perspective of the Greek rebels regarding the 'ancient ancestors' (who were, actually, the first to 'illuminate' or 'enlighten' the world, prior to the western Enlightenment) was a common conviction of the 'civilised' world in the period around 1821, following the activity of the Enlightenment and the ideological impact caused by the French Revolution and Napoleon's campaigns in Europe and in Egypt. In fact, this very perspective in part preceded the eighteenth century, at least in the states of the Italian peninsula, whose hallmark feature was the 'invention' of a continuity of the glorification of the ancient (Roman, but Greek as well) past. As Anastasia Papadia-Lala notes regarding Venice and her possessions:

---

39   Anonymous Hellene 1977, pp. 72–3, 75.
40   Cited in Kokkinos 1956, p. 219, emphasis added. In a similar spirit, in Makriyannis's *Memoirs*, when 'Alexander, the king of Russia' encounters Napoleon in Hades, he says to him: 'Napoleon, let us go to see the ancient Hellenes in their place of residence, to find the elder Socrates, Plato, Themistocles, the fine, brave Leonidas and to tell them the gladsome news, that their descendants rose up, where they were lost and expunged from the catalogue of humanity' (Makriyannis 2011, p. 141). Yannis Makriyannis (1797–1864), a merchant, joined the Greek Revolution from its very beginning, and in 1826 was named provisional commander of the garrison at the Acropolis. He was later promoted to a general.

All in all, it can be contended that Greek antiquity – the world of ancient Greece and the ancient Greeks – was considered to be the historical past of the *Greci* of the Venetian period; at the same time, however, Venice incorporated [this antiquity] into her own myth, her contribution promoting the revival of ancient glory ....[41]

As Walter Benjamin notes, the 'glorious ancient past' had also been a motif of the French Revolution:

History is the object of a construction whose place is formed not in homogenous and empty time, but in that which is fulfilled by the here-and-now [*Jetztzeit*]. For Robespierre, Roman antiquity was a past charged with the here-and-now, which he exploded out of the continuum of history. The French revolution thought of itself as a latter day Rome.[42]

In this cultural-ideological context at the beginning of the nineteenth century, with the opposition to the system of *absolute* monarchy being preserved even in the wake of the defeat of Napoleon in 1815, and with the dissident, anti-establishment secret 'societies' proliferating in various countries, the Greek Revolution could expect support from radical circles as much from within Europe as from without. As for the 'Philhellene' movement, as those radicals who were integrated into or aided the Greek Revolution were called, I shall discuss it in subsequent chapters. I shall confine myself here to but a few questions that pertain to the campaign in the Danubian Principalities, and to the Friendly Society's interaction with the Russian 'Decembrists'.

According to Eric Martone,[43] the great Russian poet and man of letters Alexander Pushkin (1799–1837) was a member of the Friendly Society. This bit of information, which is reproduced in the entry 'Alexander Pushkin' in the English version of Wikipedia, is not verified by other sources. What is certain, nevertheless, is that Pushkin was acquainted and in contact with the ruler (Prince) of Wallachia, Mikhail Soutsos, also a member of the Friendly Society, as well as with Pavel Pestel (1793–1826), one of the leaders and the principal theorist of

---

41   Papadia-Lala 2018, p. 176. 'The term *Greco* ... possesses a concrete religious dimension. That being said, in different contexts it acquires a more complex significance, as bespeak its inner conceptual progression, its counterpoints with other population groups, but also its affiliation with topical or other specific attributes' (Papadia-Lala 2018, p. 170).

42   Benjamin 1940. Paraphrasing Benjamin, 'the Greek Revolution thought of itself as a latter day Athens'.

43   Martone 2009.

the *Decembrist* movement in Russia, the aim of which was the assassination of the tsarist family, the overthrow of Tsarism and the transformation of Russia into an egalitarian constitutional republic.[44]

During the period between 1821–23, while in exile in Odessa due to his radical views, Pushkin came into contact with Greek revolutionaries who had settled there following the failed attempt of the Revolution in the Principalities.[45] Ten years later, he encountered Soutsos again and noted in his diary on 24 November 1833: 'Soutsos reminded me that in 1821 I had been to his house in Chișinău [Kishinev] together with Pestel'.[46]

The meeting of Pavel Pestel and Mikhail Soutsos took place the first days of April of 1821. A few days later, in a report to the Commander-in-Chief of the Russian army, Piotr Christianovich Wittgenstein, Pestel wrote the following:

> The desire of the Greeks, should success be achieved, is commended to the formation of a federal republic similar to that of the United States of America. This similitude is not recommended for the highest levels of administration, but on the occasion of, that each specific region shall have its own distinct governance with its own laws and in its general, state-related affairs it shall act in concert with the others [regions]. This foresight of the Greeks had been based upon the exceptional difference between the mores and customs, the perceptions and various ways of thinking *of the various peoples, who reside in Greece.*[47]

---

44   O'Meara 2003; Schwarz-Sochol 1958.

45   According to Grigori L. Arsh, the Russian government had not managed to collect reliable intelligence on the activities of the Friendly Society in Russia. Characteristically, in 1825, while referring to a special governmental committee assigned to investigate the activity of the Society in Russia, it is recorded that 'the upheaval of Greece began in Vienna ... Ypsilantis was not the principal but the instrument of the conspirators' (Arsh 2011, p. 478). Pushkin, on the contrary, compiled extensive 'Notes on the Revolution of Ypsilantis' (Arsh 2011, pp. 504–5). On 2 April 1821, Pushkin wrote in his diary: 'In the evening I called on H. G., who is an excellent Greek woman. We spoke of Al. Ypsilantis. Amongst the five Greeks present only I spoke as a Greek. Everyone displayed a hopelessness regarding the course of the Society's campaign. I am confident that Greece shall triumph and that the 25,000,000 Turks shall relinquish the budding country of Hellas to the rightful heirs of Homer and Themistokles' (Arsh 2011, p. 422).

46   Cited in Iovva 1986, p. 74.

47   Cited in Iovva 1986, p. 71, emphasis added. Nikolai Todorov cites an account by Pestel to Wittgenstein as follows: 'The intent of the Greeks in the event of success is the formation of a federal republic similar to that of the United States of America. The similarity shall not only constitute the basis for the highest of powers but in that each distinct region shall have its own administration, with its own laws and shall act in concert with the others only in the general state affairs' (Todorov 1982, p. 99). While the translation contained

The concept of a new Greek state modelled on the prototype of the United States of America does not emerge only in reports by Pavel Pestel based on information taken from the Greek 'Friends'. As Gunnar Hering (1934–94) notes, when the question of the unification-consolidation of executive power came up during the Revolution,

> the adherents for a change in the form of executive power did not regard monarchy as the sole option, but, during the first civil war [in 1823, J.M.], were already also considering the establishment of a presidential system akin to that of the USA.[48]

As regards the organisation of power on a *federal* level, this had a rather transient quality during the first months of the Revolution in southern Greece, with the formation of three representative-administrative bodies, the 'Peloponnesian Senate', the 'Areios Pagos of Eastern Mainland Greece' and the 'Organisation of Western Mainland Greece'. I shall address this further in Chapter 5 of the present book.

Prior to this, it will be necessary to delve more deeply into the concept of nation on a theoretical level so as to effectively explore the emergence of the Greek nation.

---

in Todorov's book seems to be most precise, nonetheless in the text from which Pestel's account is taken the last sentence has been omitted, where reference is made to the *various peoples who reside in Greece*!

48   Hering 2004, p. 151.

CHAPTER 3

Approaches to the Nation: A General Theoretical Assessment

What has been developed in the previous chapters raises compelling questions regarding the boundaries of the Greek nation in 1821, as well as more general theoretical questions about what constitutes a nation, namely, questions relative to the character of (each) nation and its relation to the historical development of societies. As an initial approach to this question, we shall concern ourselves with those analyses that I think may be useful as regards the issues of the delimitation of the Greek nation as developed in the previous two chapters.

1   The Traditional Ethnocentric Approach

The *traditional national response* to the question posed in this chapter is to detail various criteria or elements that are considered to be characteristic of a human community that constitutes a nation (common ancestry, common historical experiences, language, religion, common folk traditions and culture, the feeling of 'belonging', common destiny, etc.). It claims that these elements represent an unbroken continuity over centuries; or, to put it differently, that the nation has characterised human societies since nearly the dawn of history. This approach therefore conceives of the nation as a community whose existence is not reducible to any social and/or political system in question, and is maintained despite changing circumstances and the succession of social systems; therefore, the nation consistently comprises a 'given' that precedes the forms of organisation of society generally examined by historical research and the social sciences. Besides, we have already seen that in all the texts related in one way or another to the 1821 Revolution (from the 'national' songs of Rigas Pheraios and the texts of Adamantios Korais, to the topical proclamations of the revolutionary struggle), the continuity of the Greek nation from antiquity is a permanent motif. Although the pattern changes in the second half of the nineteenth century with the incorporation of the Macedonian, Hellenistic and Byzantine periods into Greek national history as eras of *Greek domination* (rather than subjugation to barbarian rulers), the idea of *transhistorical continuity* remains unchanged.

The problematique concerning the existence of a nation for many centuries (or even millennia) is not peculiar to Greece, but is reproduced in the official discourse of every modern state, first and foremost in Europe.[1] Let us see how Arnold Toynbee (1889–1975), Professor of History at King's College, University of London, and later at the London School of Economics, formulates this particular view of the Greek nation (see also Chapter 9):

> Four thousand years of Greek history have produced four Greek heritages, each of which has had an effect on the life of the Greeks on later stages of their history. The Hellenic Greeks received a heritage from the Mycenaean Greeks, the Byzantine Greeks received one from the Hellenic Greeks, the Modern Greeks have received one heritage from the Byzantines and a second from the Hellenes. If we compare the respective effects of these heritages with each other, we are likely to conclude that the influence of the past is most beneficial when the memory of the past is faint and when the veneration for it is temperate.[2]

This viewpoint, as with corresponding ones in other European nations,[3] necessarily embodies a racial element, as the nation in question maintains a self-referential continuity through the centuries, in spite of dramatic changes in the historical timeline and in conditions that evolve over centuries that affect societies.

2   The 'Objective' Approach

The traditional ethnocentric approach was initially criticised by Marxism as it had developed in the late nineteenth and early twentieth centuries. In an essay written in 1911, Joseph Stalin noted:

---

1   As stressed by Eric Hobsbawm in 1983, '[M]odern nations ... generally claim to be the opposite of novel, namely rooted in the remotest antiquity, and the opposite of constructed, namely human communities so "natural" as to require no definition other than self-assertion' (Hobsbawm 2013, p. 44).

2   Toynbee 1981, pp. 268–9.

3   If 'Hellenism' accounts for (according to Toynbee) four millennia of history, 'Gallicism' is satisfied with only two thousand years of historical continuity. Its origins are considered to go back to 52 A.D., when the Gauls, under Vercingetorix, fought against Julius Caesar in the region of Mont Beuvray, where, a few months before his death, former President François Mitterrand asked to be buried ('Letzte Ruhe bei Vercingetorix', *Die Welt*, 18 August 1995).

What is a nation? A nation is primarily a community, a definite community of people. This community is not racial, nor is it tribal. The modern Italian nation was formed from Romans, Teutons, Etruscans, Greeks,
Arabs, and so forth. The French nation was formed from Gauls, Romans,
Britons, Teutons, and so on. The same must be said of the British, the
Germans and others ... Thus, a nation is not a racial or tribal, but a historically constituted community of people ... A nation is not merely a
historical category but a historical category belonging to a definite epoch,
the epoch of rising capitalism. The process of elimination of feudalism
and development of capitalism is at the same time a process of the constitution of people into nations ... *A nation is a historically constituted,
stable community of people, formed on the basis of a common language,
territory, economic life, and psychological make-up manifested in a common culture.*[4]

The view that the nation is formed during an era of 'rising capitalism' (in a community of economic life under capitalist conditions, with an internal market,
etc.) is rather common among Marxist writers of the period. What is also common is the notion, accepted by non-Marxists as well, of the (pre-)existence of
'genera' or 'tribes' that united as a nation in a particular territory, resulting in
the formation of a common culture.

These approaches certainly give rise to other questions, such as where on
the timeline the 'era of rising capitalism' actually took place, and why or how
an amalgam of pre-national communities ('tribes', 'clans', etc.) resulted in the
formation of a particular nation. One could ask, for example, through what specific process was an amalgam of 'Romans, Germans, Etruscans, Greeks, Arabs'
transformed specifically into the Italian nation, while a similar amalgam of
'tribes' or other pre-national communities was transformed into the Belgian
nation, etc. To this are added additional criteria (preconditions for ethnogenesis) such as the community of territory, community of culture and a common
language.[5]

The approaches to which we refer in this section attempt to formulate a
framework of non-racial, 'objective' criteria and processes underlying the formation of nations, as opposed to 'subjective' approaches, which lay emphasis on
the self-consciousness of each nation, that is, that *a nation is constituted by
those who believe that they belong to the same nation* (and of course adopt a *com-*

---

4 Stalin 1913, https://www.marxists.org/reference/archive/stalin/works/1913/03a.htm.
5 Ibid.

mon understanding of their origin, history, culture, destiny, etc.) *and act accordingly*. In fact, Stalin, in the text from 1911 under consideration here, attempts to place particular emphasis on the criterion of a common language, probably to underscore the 'objective' character of ethnogenesis: 'a national community is incomprehensible without a common language'.

> But not every stable community constitutes a nation ... What distinguishes a national community from a state community? The fact, among others, that a national community is inconceivable without a common language, while a state need not have a common language ... We are referring, of course, to the spoken languages of the people and not to the official governmental languages. Thus, *a common language* is one of the characteristic features of a nation ... A *common* language for every nation, but not necessarily different languages for different nations! There is no nation which at one and the same time speaks several languages, but this does not mean that there cannot be two nations speaking the same language![6]

However, contrary to the claim that the nation is *'incomprehensible' without a common spoken language*, in the previous two chapters of this book we saw that, although archaic-'purist' Greek (*Katharevousa*) was the official language of declarations, texts, etc. of the 1821 Revolution, as well as the language of the state-ecclesiastical administrative apparatuses of the Ottoman Empire directed towards the Orthodox populations of the state (see more in Chapter 4), the fighters recruited via nationalism and populations who were involved in the formation of the first Greek state in the southern part of the Greek penin-

---

6   Ibid. Stalin's position is rooted in the polemic of Karl Kautsky, the most recognised theorist of the Marxist social democratic movement at the time ('Nationality and Internationality', 1908), in contrast to Otto Bauer's work, *The Question of Nationalities and Social Democracy* (Die Nationalitätenfrage und die Sozialdemokratie, 1907). Bauer defines the nation as 'a community of character', and explains: 'But here it is not the community of fate, but the sameness of fate that has produced the community of character (Aber hier ist es nicht die Schicksalsgemeinschaft, sondern die Gleichartigkeit des Schicksals, die die Charaktergemeinschaft erzeugt hat) ... That which constitutes the nation is no longer the consanguinity and the cultural unity of the masses, but the cultural unity of the dominant classes perched above these masses and living off their labor' (Bauer 1907, Bauer 2000, pp. 100, 106–7). Kautsky, criticising Bauer, writes: 'Yet Bauer's specific definition of the nation is either so vague that it does not show how and why the nation is different to any other social formation ... the commonality of destiny and culture does not form anything that strictly distinguishes one nation from another ... Bauer refuses to recognise ... that in fact, the most powerful of the threads uniting the nation, is language' (Kautsky 2009, pp. 374, 377).

sula were not all Greek-speaking. In fact, certain regions and national (Greek) populations and fighters who played a decisive role in the rescue, and final, favourable outcome, of the Revolution (on Hydra, Poros, Spetses, etc. ...) were in their vast majority Albanian-speaking.[7]

Apart from this, all of the texts of the Revolution (proclamations from the beginning of the struggle, decisions on the part of the revolutionary adminis-trations and national assemblies, newspapers from revolutionary Greece, etc.) do not seem to attach any importance to the other 'objective criterion' of the nation under consideration, to a particular 'cultural community' (or 'dis-tinct popular consciousness',[8] as Kanellopoulos puts it). Ultimately, the entire Balkans and Asia Minor were regarded by the revolutionaries as a 'community of territory'.

In conclusion, in spite of the abandonment of the racial criterion, the 'object-ive approach' does not succeed in eliminating the questions and ambiguities regarding the nature of the processes that have led to the actual formation of *specific* nations. This finding pertains even more to non-Marxist conceptions of the nation, not only to the traditional ones that claim an 'uninterrupted national continuity' over the centuries, but also those which, having aban-doned racial criteria, either simply describe the characteristics of the nation (language, territory, religion, culture, and so on), or present as a basic criterion and characteristic the 'subjective' element of the nation, the consciousness of 'belonging' of those who make up a nation.

3   The 'Subjective' Approach

A typical case of an analysis that propounds the 'subjective' or 'internal' cri-terion in the interpretation of the nation is a study of nationalism by Alex-andros Papanastasiou (1876–1936), a socialist lawyer and politician who also served as prime minister of Greece, published in the *Review of Social and Polit-ical Sciences* in 1916:

> The facts prove that the penetration of a language into a people ... does not necessarily alter its national feeling, nor does the commonality of language prevent the division of a nation into separate ones ... It is there-

---

7   Hobsbawm notes about the French language: 'in 1789 50% of Frenchmen did not speak it at all, only 12–13% spoke it "correctly" ... In northern and southern France virtually nobody talked French' (1990, p. 60).

8   Kanellopoulos 1982, p. 48; see Chapter 2.

fore now admitted that *the commonality of language is not a sure sign of a nation ... Customs and manners* do not have absolute uniformity in nations and, moreover, there are many similarities between the various nations with regard to them ... From the foregoing it is evident that *external* traits ... cannot define a multitude and that *the surest trait is internal, is the consciousness, the recognition of those* who constitute a nation, that they constitute a separate whole, different from others of the same kind ... From this consciousness, which certainly characterises the existence of the nation, there flow common feelings that connect the members of this nation and *a will* to *unified action.*[9]

Nevertheless, as has already been suggested, the 'subjective' approach in essence reproduces a circular argument, since there exists no adequate objective characteristic or criterion (e.g. a common language or culture): a *nation* (a community of people with a belief of 'belonging') *is the nation* ('the recognition of those who constitute a nation that they constitute a distinct entity'). Alternatively stated, the definition according to which the nation expresses the common conviction (and will) of a group of people that they themselves constitute the nation brings further issues to the fore, such as that of territory (of state and soil alike), while simultaneously defining the nation through itself (*circulus in probando*).[10]

---

9   Papanastasiou 1992, p. 29. Papanastasiou's analysis is not, of course, devoid of contradictions. For example, he claims that the nation *pre-exists* the 'will for unified action'. Further, he declares: 'However, *the nation is not born at once, the day that it expresses a will for unified action* ... A people can constitute a nation to a greater or lesser degree' (Papanastasiou 1992, pp. 30–1). Therefore, the traditional, 'uninterrupted existence of the nation through the ages', which at some point results in its 'awakening', is far from being excluded, even in times when no evidence of a 'national consciousness' can be traced. Here Papanastasiou's argumentation contradicts itself.

10   Otto Bauer aptly pointed out the circularity of the argument of the 'subjective' (or 'psychological', as he calls it) approach: 'This psychological theory of the nation seemed all the more acceptable when one was not able to locate an objective feature of the nation, when all attempts to discover the bond that unified the nation as a community either in language, in common descent, or in the fact of belonging to a state appeared to fail due to the diversity of national phenomena. However, this psychological theory is not only unsatisfactory, but actually incorrect. It is unsatisfactory because, even supposing it were correct that the nation is formed by those conscious of their affinity with one another, the question would remain: why is it that I feel myself to be connected with these rather than with those people? What are the "indissoluble ties" by which I know myself to be linked to the other members of my nation? If I am conscious of my nationality, of what am I actually conscious? What is it that compels me to feel myself one with all Germans and not with the English or the French? Moreover, is it actually true

To dispel (or obscure) the circularity of the argument, the proponents of the 'subjective' approach to the nation have in recent decades resorted to a tactic of dual nature: on the one hand, they assign a new definition to the concept of national 'belonging', and on the other, they attempt to describe the mechanisms that have forged this 'belonging'.

The two most well-known of such efforts, both published for the first time in 1983, are the *'invention of tradition' approach* formulated by a group of British historians, with Eric Hobsbawm and Terence Ranger as 'moderators',[11] and Benedict Anderson's approach to the nation as an 'imagined community'.[12]

Regarding the first approach, Hobsbawm clarifies:

> 'Invented tradition' is taken to mean a set of practices, normally governed by overtly or tacitly accepted rules and of a ritual or symbolic nature, which seek to inculcate certain values and norms of behaviour by repetition, which automatically implies continuity with the past. In fact, where possible, they normally attempt to establish continuity with a suitable historic past.[13]

The aim of the research was to identify and describe both the function of primarily state apparatuses and (national) intellectuals in 'inventing' a history as a national history, as well as to identify and describe the invention of a series of corresponding national symbols and rituals that served to educate the population as to how to be (a part of) the nation, as a national community, based on the insight that 'much of what *subjectively* makes up the modern "nation" consists of such constructs'.[14]

The 'invention of tradition' is not, however, a practice of nation states or nationalist intellectuals alone. In pre-national states, such as those of the Italian peninsula prior to the nineteenth century, a similar process of 'constructing' tradition and 'historical continuity' from a 'glorious ancient past' (from Roman antiquity, but also from the ancient Greek civilisation; see the citation of Papadia-Lala in Chapter 2, section 3) is also recorded. Venice, in the more than eight centuries of her existence as an independent state and

---

that all members of a nation are always conscious of their affinity with one another?' (Bauer 1907, Bauer 2000, pp. 120–1).

11   Hobsbawm and Ranger 2013.
12   Anderson 2006.
13   Hobsbawm 2013, p. 1.
14   Hobsbawm 2013, p. 14, emphasis added. 'Standard national languages, to be learned in schools and written, let alone spoken, by more than a smallish elite, are largely constructs of varying, but often brief, age' (Hobsbawm 2013, p. 14).

empire,[15] until her collapse in 1797 brought about by Napoleon's army, was never a national state: the destructive, recurrent wars between the state of Venice and that of Genoa in early modern times were never considered 'civil wars', not even by nationalist Italian historians seeking the continuity of 'Italianism' over the centuries. Nevertheless, the state apparatuses systematically nurtured the populations of the empire with 'Venetian values', while at the same time systematically 'inventing' a Venetian history, without the populations of the city or the empire forming any *national* (Venetian, Italian or other) consciousness.[16]

The 'invented tradition' is therefore not necessarily a 'national' one. How (under what conditions) does it become 'national', and at the same time 'active' (accepted by the population)? The questions remain.

In the other aforementioned 'subjective' approach, that of the nation as an 'imagined community', Benedict Anderson elucidates in his introduction that all communities that are not based on the direct acquaintance and relationship of the individuals participating in them (as opposed, for example, to the 'community' of members of a family or a small village) should be considered 'imagined'. These are therefore not 'fictitious' communities, but communities that are perceived mentally: imagined. Hence the following definition of a nation:

> It is an imagined political community – and imagined as both inherently limited and sovereign. It is imagined because the members of even the smallest nation will never know most of their fellow-members, meet them, or even hear of them, yet in the minds of each lives the image of their communion ... [The nation] is imagined as a community, because, regardless of the actual inequality and exploitation that may prevail in each, the nation is always conceived as a deep, horizontal comradeship.[17]

Nevertheless, the question is not to assign new terms to the various attributes of national 'belonging',[18] but to interpret *how* and *why* they came about. In

---

15   Cf. Milios 2018.

16   'From the fifteenth century on, the Venetian state systematically directed the production of an official "Venetian history" as a means of imprinting forms of "patriotism" into the minds of the city's and the empire's inhabitants: that is, loyalty to the state and consensus on its policies ... In 1486 the Senate rejected the versions of Venetian history written by some prominent scholars and approved the *Rerum Venetarum* (*Of Venetian Matters*) composed "by a second-rate professional humanist called Sabellico" (Lane 1973, p. 220)' (Milios 2018, pp. 208–9). Within a year, 32 of the 33 volumes of the work had been printed!

17   Anderson 2006, pp. 6, 7.

18   Typically, Anderson quotes Seton-Watson's (cyclical-tautological) definition of the nation,

this direction, Anderson principally advances the element of the formation of a common language: 'the revolutionary vernacularising thrust of capitalism', 'the birth of administrative vernaculars', the formation of a 'language-of-state', or 'language of the court', of 'self-conscious language policies pursued by nineteenth-century dynasts confronted with the rise of hostile popular linguistic-nationalisms',[19] to reach the following conclusion:

> What, in a positive sense, made the new communities imaginable was a half-fortuitous, but explosive, interaction between a system of production and productive relations (capitalism), a technology of communications (print), and the fatality of human linguistic diversity ... print-languages laid the bases for national consciousnesses.[20]

At this point it is worth iterating that the existence of a second spoken language in the Greek Revolution that created the Greek state in the southern part of the Balkan peninsula ('a heroic language, spoken by the Admiral Miaoulis, Botsaris and all of Souli', see Chapter 2) far from hampered the national unification and armed political action of the populations of the region.

Beyond this, it is worth noting that both the approach of the 'invented tradition' and that of the 'imagined communities' are based on an 'enlightenment-type' interpretation of the formation of consciousness: that certain pioneers invented and 'taught' the populations traditions, symbols, myths and a (printed) national language which eventually facilitated 'the decline of the imagined community of Christendom'[21] and the formation of a national consciousness (or *national* 'imagined community').

For a 'teaching' to be effective, however, it must be accepted by those to whom it is addressed. How was it that the populations were convinced of the national 'enlightenment teaching', given the pre-existing power of 'the imagined community of Christendom' and its own uninterrupted 'paternal teaching'?[22] Even more so considering that the monarchies of Europe at the begin-

---

according to which 'a nation exists when a significant number of people in a community consider themselves to form a nation, or behave as if they formed one', and he simply adds: 'We may translate "consider themselves" as "imagine themselves"' (Anderson 2006, p. 6).

19   Anderson 2006, pp. 39, 41, 42.

20   Anderson 2006, pp. 42–3, 44.

21   Anderson 2006, p. 42.

22   In the *Paternal Teaching of His Beatitude the Patriarch of the Holy City of Jerusalem Anthimos*, published in 1798 in Constantinople by the patriarchal printing house as a polemic against Rigas Pheraios and the Enlightenment movement in general, we read: 'Deceptive are, Christian brothers, the teachings of these new liberals; and beware, guard your

ning of the nineteenth century were not yet self-defined as national, but as *Christian* states and therefore nor was the 'fatherly state teaching' national – the result being that early *national* movements and corresponding 'fraternities' or conspiratorial societies were actually under persecution![23]

---

patriarchal faith and, as followers of Jesus Christ, your inviolable submission to the political administration, which gives you all that is necessary only for your present life, and most honourable of all, which causes no hindrance or harm to your spiritual salvation' (Anthimos 1798). In the same year (1798), Adamantios Korais replied to this text with the *Fraternal teaching to the Greeks throughout the Ottoman territory* (Korais 1798). 'Obedience to God, Korais thundered: "means nothing other than that we must obey the laws because the laws are nothing other than the unanimous and common opinion of a people, and the voice of a people is the voice of God". Therefore, he concluded, far from owing obedience to the Ottomans, "Those ruled by tyrants have the inalienable right to seek every sort of means in order to throw off the yoke of tyranny and to enjoy once more the precious gift of self-government"' (Beaton 2019, p. 58). Regarding 'the explosive tensions and ruptures that Greek intellectual society experienced in the three years preceding the revolution of 1821', see Iliou 1974, p. 580. Regarding the arguments upon which the modernist-critical activity of the Greek Enlightenment was organised and expressed, see Iliou 1978.

23   One example is enough to illustrate this situation: Hoffmann von Fallersleben (1798–1874), a professor at the University of Breslau in Prussia and poet, composed in August 1841 the 'Lied der Deutschen' (Song of the Germans) to a melody by Joseph Haydn:

Germany, Germany above all,
above all in the world,
When, for protection and defense,
it always stands together brotherly,
From the Meuse to the Nieman,
From the Adige to the Belt!
Germany, Germany above all,
above all in the world!

But a 'fraternally united' German consciousness (much less, territory) had yet to be formed; what did exist were the many German-speaking states, and especially the Christian (Protestant) absolute monarchy of Prussia, whose authorities considered Fallersleben's national message seditious, and removed him from the professorship. After World War I, the 'Lied der Deutschen' became the German national anthem. See Heinrich 2018, p. 255; also Heinrich 2019, p. 255. Henrik Mouritsen outlines the development of the national idea in the German-speaking world as follows: 'Partly under the influence of the Napoleonic occupation of Europe, the Romantic idea of the nation gained a stronger political aspect, giving rise to the new ideal of the nation state in which the nation realized its true potential and destiny. Thus, the natural aim of a nation was defined as political autonomy and self-governance. Only under those conditions could it fulfil its historical role and achieve perfection and freedom. The two latter were combined in Hegelian thinking, which endowed the formation of nation states with a deeper historical meaning as the fulfilment of history's hidden plan and purpose. The nation state represented a giant step forward for humankind towards the realization of God's will on earth' (Mouritsen 2009, p. 44).

4   The Priority of the Political Element: The Nation as
       State-Instituted 'Popular Will'

The theoretical debate on the nation entered a new phase with the publication in 1990 of Eric Hobsbawm's book *Nations and Nationalism from 1780 to
the Present.*[24] Hobsbawm's trajectory of thought transcends both the 'objective' and 'subjective' conceptions of the nation and builds a materialist theory
of the emergence and character of the nation as a process of *politicisation of the
popular masses* that leads to the formation of the *type of capitalist state* which
gradually prevailed in Europe (and beyond), from the events of 1789 in France
to the second half of the nineteenth century. This process includes apparatuses
of 'representation' of the masses in the state, namely, a new type of domination
of the ruling classes over the dominated, political rights and the transformation
of the subject into a citizen.

From Hobsbawm's analysis, concisely put, the following positions emerge:

(a) the nation is a *social relation* that was formed subsequent to the French
Revolution in Europe, in most cases in the nineteenth century, and (b) which
is a condensation and outcome of *nationalism*; (c) nationalism is produced
as a *politicisation of the masses*, a (d) politicisation which is connected with
the radical modification of the *mode of integration of the masses* (the social
classes subject to capitalist power and exploitation) *into the state*; (e) *nation
and* (*capitalist*) *state* do not coincide, but are inextricable, being two sides of
the same coin: the nation, as a derivative of nationalism, by definition constitutes a *demand for* and a *claim to* a state, while the nation as a 'people' is
also institutionally organised by the state ('popular sovereignty': the 'will of the
nation' that is expressed through the state and the institutions of 'democracy');
(f) nationalism is inherently characterised by a tendency towards racism.

(a)   Like most serious students, I do not regard the 'nation' as a primary nor
       as an unchanging social entity. It belongs exclusively to a particular, and
       historically recent, period;[25]

(b)   nationalism comes before nations. Nations do not make states and na-
       tionalisms but the other way round;[26]

---

24   The importance of this analysis by Hobsbawm is sometimes underestimated. The follow-
       ing assessment is paradigmatic of this: 'The *Invention of Tradition*, published in 1983, the
       same year as Anderson's book, is the British historian's most important contribution to
       the debate on nationalism, more important than *Nations and Nationalism from 1780 to the
       Present*. Not only for the originality of the idea, but also for the *response it met with*' (Liakos
       2005, p. 94, emphasis added).

25   Hobsbawm 1992, p. 9.

26   Hobsbawm 1992, p. 10.

(c) the state confronted nationalism as a political force separate from it, quite distinct from 'state patriotism', and with which it had to come to terms. However, it could become an enormously powerful asset of government, if it could be integrated into state patriotism, to become its central emotional component.[27]

(d) [The nation] is a social entity only insofar as it relates to a certain kind of modern territorial state, the 'nation state', and it is pointless to discuss nation and nationality except insofar as both relate to it;[28]

(e) The very act of democratizing politics, i.e. of turning subjects into citizens, tends to produce a populist consciousness which, seen in some lights, is hard to distinguish from a national, even a chauvinist, patriotism – for ... 'the country' is in some way 'mine';[29]

(f) the time when the democratization of politics made it essential to ... attach all to nation and flag, was also the time when popular nationalist, or at all events xenophobic sentiments and those of national superiority preached by the new pseudo-science of racism, became easier to mobilize.[30]

Nationalism (the nation) creates a rupture and a new situation within the capitalist social formations in which it develops, and profoundly rearranges the way populations (social classes) are subjected to power, while inaugurating the era of 'citizenship', as well as political and social rights. But this radically new era of rights and popular representation, the era of nationalism, is also an era of racism (which, under certain circumstances, may also lead to ethnic cleansing). For example, as Michael Heinrich documents, until the mid-nineteenth century in Prussia, there existed anti-Judaism (a religious criterion) rather than anti-Semitism (viewing Jews in terms of race and nation). This meant that any Jew who was baptised a Christian made himself eligible for any position in the state apparatus, even in the highest ones, from which he had previously been excluded on the basis of religious criteria.[31] In the era of nations, anti-Semitism, as racism, cannot be eradicated by forsaking one's religion.

It can also be concluded from the aforementioned that whilst the national idea is initially shaped by circles belonging to the 'intellectual elite' of a region or a social formation, nationalism and the nation cannot be spoken of with either exclusive or primary reference to the movements of those circles and

---

27   Hobsbawm 1992, p. 90.
28   Hobsbawm 1992, pp. 9–10.
29   Hobsbawm 1992, p. 88.
30   Hobsbawm 1992, p. 91.
31   Heinrich 2018, pp. 56 ff., 70 ff., 127; Heinrich 2019, pp. 50, 115, 206.

the texts they produce, much less to the date of their first appearance. Nationalism and the nation arise from the dissemination of national politicisation and the national idea amongst the dominated classes, something which implies a form of action or mobilisation related to this new consciousness ('identity') of belonging to the nation. Indeed, national 'secularity' is now distinguished from state politics, acquiring a degree of autonomy from the state.

In the next section of this chapter, I shall comment and attempt to expand upon some of Hobsbawm's theses. I find it appropriate at this juncture to point out that there have been other analyses that have emphasised the fact that the French Revolution inaugurated the era of nationalism and nations, and that pivotal to this process was the entry of the popular masses into the political foreground, for instance as propounded by George L. Mosse in 1993;[32] all the same, these analyses do not, contrary to that of Hobsbawm, identify the structural interconnection and complementarity (as two sides of the same coin) of the process of the reconfiguration of the (capitalist) *state* and the emergence of the *nation*. In certain cases, the nation is even defined as the (negative) 'countervailing force' of the (positive) state.[33]

---

32   In Mosse's *Confronting the Nation: Jewish and Western Nationalism*, we read: 'The French Revolution began a new age of mass politics, a visual age and one of the spoken word rather than one centered upon the printed page, the traditional vehicle of political thought. To be sure, the rise of the popular press provided an effective means of political propaganda, but such journalism was geared to produce an immediate effect and had few ties with traditional political thought. Political movements now had to project themselves upon the largely illiterate or semieducated masses, whose newly roused political consciousness had to be taken in to account' (Mosse 1993, p. 61). 'The general will of the people was mediated by the nation, and it was through the nation that the people were thought to express themselves' (Mosse 1993, p. 27).

33   In 1946, Hannah Arendt, discussing J.T. Delos's book *La Nation* (1944), criticises the author's views, arguing that the state has been transformed into a 'tool of the nation' and therefore into totalitarianism: 'A people becomes a nation when "it takes conscience of itself according to its history" ... The state on the other hand is an open society, ruling over a territory where its power protects and makes the law. As a legal institution, the state knows only citizens no matter of what nationality ... Nationalism signifies essentially the conquest of the state through the nation. This is the sense of the national state ... This was the first step transforming the state into an instrument of the nation, which finally has ended in those totalitarian forms of nationalism in which all laws and the legal institutions of the state as such are interpreted as a means for the welfare of the nation. It is therefore quite erroneous to see the evil of our times in a deification of the state. It is the nation which has usurped the traditional place of God and religion' (Arendt 1993, pp. 208–9).

5   The Nation of Capital: Further Points on a Theory of the Nation

We have seen that nationalism brings the masses to the political forefront, which the state then incorporates into its apparatuses as 'sovereign people'; in other words, nationalism is enmeshed within the political (state) element, which is then prioritised over the religious element. The religious element continues to play a clear, defining role, as it is often set as a prerequisite for being a citizen of the (first Greek) state; however, the main aspect of the new, 'modern' identity is political, to be Greek, Italian, etc. The religious 'belonging' that continues to coexist is eventually subordinated to the political (state) 'belonging'. The identification of the population is now with the nation state and not with the monarch or the religious leader. This is the basis upon which irredentism (the pursuit of the expansion of state territory, the conception of global contradictions as *national* differences, the demand for the creation of an independent nation state where one does not exist) develops.

A prerequisite for this political belonging is the evolution of broader ties of economic, administrative and cultural communication so as to connect and bind the rural populations with those of the urban centres, a development that was achieved with the expansion of capitalist relations and the (usually indirect – see subsequent chapter) subsumption of rural social relations under capital from the middle of the eighteenth century onwards, with all the ideological forms of 'freedom' (or demand for 'freedom': of trade, of the individual, etc.) that accompany it.

The nation therefore emerges within a *capitalist social space* or *social formation*, when capitalist relations *embody and connect* broader and more compact social aggregates.

At this point it ought to be mentioned that according to Marx's analysis in *Capital*, in Western Europe 'the capitalist era dates from the sixteenth century',[34] despite remnants of degenerated feudal or other pre-capitalist relations, and despite poverty and the decline in production (and in peasant income and consumption!) in the agrarian sector of countries like seventeenth- and eighteenth-century France.[35] Furthermore, Marx also notes:

> we come across the first sporadic traces of capitalist production as early as the fourteenth and fifteenth centuries in certain towns of the Mediter-

---

34   Marx 1990, p. 876.
35   Rubin 1979, pp. 91–105. The relation between capitalism and 'bourgeois revolutions', which in general took place in social formations in which capitalism had already prevailed, will be tackled in Chapter 8.

ranean ... In Italy, where capitalistic production developed earliest, the dissolution of serfdom also took place earlier than elsewhere. The serf was ... at once transformed ... into a 'free' proletarian, who, moreover, found his master ready waiting for him in the towns.[36]

In the theoretical and historical analysis contained in a recent book of mine,[37] I came to a conclusion similar to the one Marx presents in *Capital*. A series of imponderable historical contingencies, mainly related to economic antagonisms, the recurrent and destructive Venetian-Genoese wars starting in the thirteenth century, the crises in the Venetian colonial system and the plague, all served as the historical conditions and factors that eventually led to the prevalence of the capitalist mode of production in the Venetian social formation in the second half of the fourteenth century. More specifically, these conditions led to the formation, in the late fourteenth century, of huge, state-owned manufactures organised on the basis of the capital–wage labour relation (as the labourers were deprived of the access they had previously had to the ownership of the means of production through 'profit sharing' or 'associations'). In parallel, all non-salaried sources of income of the majority of seamen were drastically restricted, creating a proletariat of wage-earning mariners. In this case as well, money-owners auctioning off state-owned fleets, and shipowners commanding private ships, became capitalists, as 'the confrontation of, and the contact between' (Marx) them and the emerging proletariat took hold. Finally, in order to support the wars, a huge internal public debt was created, while at the same time, a secondary bond market was formed, developments which nurtured both advanced budgetary management and fiscal policies, and greatly expanded capitalist finance. By the end of the fourteenth century, Venice emerged as a capitalist social formation, practically introducing capitalism into Europe.

Naturally, it should be emphasised that capitalism as a social system is not just the wage relation, profit and the market. Wage labour existed, at times being considerably widespread, long before the birth of capitalism,[38] just as there were 'entrepreneurial' (non-capitalist) relations of monetary exchange

---

36   Marx 1990, pp. 875–6.

37   Milios 2018.

38   'By the end of the fifth century [B.C.], as we know from the Erechtheum accounts, wage rates of one drachma per day were common. The daily pay of sailors in the fleet was also between one drachma per day ... and half a drachma ... and the daily pay of dicasts was half a drachma from 425 onwards' (Ste. Croix 2004, p. 43). 'The poorer women of Athens and, presumably, of other cities also worked for wages' (Kyrtatas 2011, p. 105).

and respective 'money-begetting' modes of production, which, for example, Aristotle analyses in detail, as Marx points out.[39]

According to Marx's analysis in *Capital*, there exist a series of *fundamental* characteristics which, in their interconnectedness, distinguish capitalism from all other social systems:

> (a) wage labour; (b) monetization of the whole economy (money beget-ting money); (c) concentration of the means of production and dissoci-ation of the capitalist from the labour process as such; (d) free competi-tion and the fusion of individual capitals into aggregate-social capital; (e) the financial mode of existence of capital; (f) the formation of a specific juridical-political-ideological structure and a corresponding state form.[40]

These characteristics had developed in many countries of Europe – but also to some extent in areas of the Ottoman Empire (see Chapters 4 and 10) long before the age of nationalisms. Capitalism as the dominant system predates the age of nationalisms and nations by several centuries. Therefore, the general state-ment that 'A nation is ... a historical category ... belonging to ... the epoch of rising capitalism'[41] is relativised (and ought to be further analysed).

In closing this chapter, I will summarise as follows: the nation is a social rela-tion *within* capitalism that is necessarily bound to a capitalist state, but is not identified with the capitalist state and capitalism, nor is it exclusively and uni-

---

39   'The two peculiarities of the equivalent form we have just developed will become still clearer if we go back to the great investigator who was the first to analyse the value-form, like so many other forms of thought, society and nature. I mean Aristotle' (Marx 1990, p. 151). For a perspective on 'money-begetting' pre-capitalist modes of production, see Milios 2018, pp. 109–22: (a) The *money-begetting slave mode of production*, existing since antiquity and clearly distinguishing itself from the classical slave mode of production. As Marx writes: the 'transformation of the earlier, more or less patriarchal slavery into a sys-tem of commercial exploitation' (Marx 1990, p. 925); 'the transformation of a patriarchal slave system oriented towards the production of the direct means of subsistence into one oriented towards the production of surplus-value' (Marx 1991, pp. 449–50). (b) The *con-tractual money-begetting mode of production* that emerged in the Middle Ages in relation to financial schemes based on partnerships or associations. The 'contract' between the money-owner and the labourer, who in the latter case was free from all forms of personal servitude or bondage, entailed a complex form of exploitation. The labourer was in part a wage-earner, but also had (limited) access to the ownership of the means of production (of 'capital') through both 'profit sharing' and the right to trade merchandise on voyages. In other words, he was not a proletarian, even if part of his income came from wage pay-ment.

40   Milios 2018, p. 4, see analytically pp. 11–18.

41   Stalin 1913.

laterally 'constructed' by the capitalist state. The nation is equally tied to the 'initiative' of the capital-dominated classes and functions as a decisive vehicle for the 'modern form' of their subordination to the strategies of the capitalist state.

From what I have just stated it could be concluded that the nation historically contains both a 'tendency towards freedom' and a 'tendency towards totalitarianism'.

The 'tendency towards freedom' is discernibly linked to the demand for liberation from an empire or transnational state entity, which from a certain point in time onwards is experienced as a framework for national 'slavery' and the oppression of those belonging to the nation that is seeking independence. Moreover, it is for this reason that the process of national independence is almost always accompanied by the irrevocable decision of large sections of the population (of the nation) seeking independence to act on the words of the slogan 'Freedom or death', to sacrifice their lives for the sake of achieving an independent nation state.

The 'tendency towards freedom' is also linked to a demand for the abolition of a 'dynastic' regime, as it claims the transformation of a subject or liege into a citizen; that is, it is associated with the demand for the creation and extension of the political rights of the popular classes (institutional equality and egalitarianism, universal education independent of the Church and in accordance with the principles of the Enlightenment, priority of the principle of democracy over the principle of legality, etc., the right to vote and 'equality within the nation').

Nevertheless, alongside the 'tendency towards freedom', equally inherent in the process of every nation-building, the 'tendency towards totalitarianism' also emerges. This is the tendency to homogenise the 'interior' of the national territory, and to subject it as a *unified whole* to the rules and norms of the (new) state sovereignty and class power; that is, to subject it to a class power which is differentiated from other contiguous systems of class power according to its specific national characteristics.

In the texts pertaining to the declaration of Greek independence that we examined in the previous chapters, all Christian peoples of the Balkans are 'christened' Greeks, as descendants of the ancient Hellenes, as citizens of the Greece being formed. Obviously, such a thing could take place because the corresponding processes of nation-building in the other Balkan populations were still absent at the time. The only nationalism already formed, Greek nationalism, came in to fill the gap. Even after the establishment of the Greek state, as we shall see in subsequent chapters, the 'tendency towards totalitarianism' appeared in the form of the Grand Idea, the *Megali Idea*, i.e. an irredentist demand and strategy for the expansion of the borders of the Greek state within the supposed 'national boundaries', which ostensibly covered the Ottoman-dominated Balkans and Asia Minor.

We can thus recognise that the 'tendency towards totalitarianism', the tendency towards the national homogenisation of populations, does not only act 'inwards', within an administrative territory and the corresponding population (and any 'minorities' located in the territory where that population lives); it acts at the same time 'outwards', seeking to expand where it does not encounter considerable (national) resistance, to integrate and homogenise other population groups, subjecting them to a prospectively expanding nation state. In another formulation, we would say that the 'totalitarian tendency' contains not only an inward-looking trend, that is, the normalisation-homogenisation of a nation, but also an outward-looking trend, i.e. nationalist expansionism. 'History' (the ancestral 'national character' of the claimed or disputed territories), but also the existence of ethnic populations or minorities in the claimed territories, feeds this extroverted trend of the 'totalitarian tendency', even when it is no longer likely to prevail (see Chapter 8).

The national constitution of a people thus passes through nationalist conflict (which does not necessarily occasion war), whilst it is confronted with the homogenisation-expansion processes attempted by neighbouring nations. We shall see that the history of the Greek state since the mid-nineteenth century is largely characterised by its conflict with emerging nationalisms of other Balkan peoples, and in particular with Bulgarian nationalism. Within a few decades, the excerpts from the proclamation of Alexandros Ypsilantis or from the text of Theodoros Negris cited earlier herein were transformed from invitations to struggle, into paradoxes.

In any event, it is important to understand that when the process of the formation of a nation state is fulfilled, that is, after the much sought-after national independence is achieved, the 'totalitarian tendency' is established as the dominant aspect of ideological and political power relations.

CHAPTER 4

Romans and Greeks in the Ottoman Empire: From Pre-national Social Cohesion to a Greek Nation

1 Introductory Remarks concerning the Birth of the Greek Nation

It was argued in the previous chapter that the nation by definition is 'political', namely that from the moment of its inception it is set in the heart of a territorial state. In this sense, the nation is 'the people of a state'. At times it concerns the conversion-integration of subjects ('the people' under either a monarch or an aristocratic state entity) into citizens, or it may concern 'the people' of a 'state within a state' (*imperium in imperio*) that is being re-configured into a nation and demands 'freedom' (the formation of an independent state) and rights (as in the case with Greece).

As a nation state exists in order to express the 'will of the nation', the social differences that traverse society are obscured. More aptly put, the nation becomes a 'union of antagonistic classes', of those doing the exploiting and those who submit to the exploitation, of those dominating and those being dominated, while class conflict takes place beyond the visible realm.[1] In fact, when this class conflict eventually takes on manifest forms, they are often attributed by all parties involved to being characteristics of the nation: 'foreign-instigated sedition', 'oligarchy serving foreign interests', 'traitors', etc.

All of the foregoing highlights the fact that when one speaks of nationalism and the nation, one is not only speaking of 'ideas', but mostly of *'the sovereign people' and the state*, or of the totality of the social classes as it is homogenised within the institutions of a (quasi-) state. From this viewpoint, two additional conclusions surface:

(a) The appearance of the 'forefathers' of nationalism, that is, of the first circles of national(ist) intellectuals, or 'fraternities', nationalist publications, secret societies, etc., does not constitute proof of an already-accomplished national politicisation of the population towards which all these entities are directed, even if the semblance of speech and movements constitutes one of many pre-conditions for the final configuration of the nation. Put another way, Rigas's texts of 1797 (*New Political Administration* ... and the *Thourios*, or *Battle Hymn*) do not suffice in determining the moment of the birth of the Greek

---

1 See Marmora 1983.

nation;[2] nor is the activity of the Russian Decembrists throughout the 1820s helpful in pinpointing the genesis of the Russian nation.[3]

(b) One can speak of the origins of the Greek nation when the rural populations, who comprised the greater majority of the inhabitants of the region where the vision of the 'emancipation of Hellas' emerged, were integrated into the national(ist) processes of politicisation.

In the present chapter, I shall demonstrate that this national politicisation of the broader popular masses came about as a result of the disintegrating social relations that had held the 'ancien régime' together within the structural framework of the Ottoman Empire, and of the subsumption of the countryside, during the latter half of the eighteenth century, into capitalist economic and social relations that had already expanded into the urban areas and coastal settlements where Orthodox populations of the empire resided. Within the new socioeconomic context, far-flung geographical regions which in the past had been characterised as territorially limited, topical identities, were homogenised economically, politically and ideologically. Contributing to this process, without its being the determining factor, was the fact that Atticised Greek (*Katharevousa*) comprised the official language of the Orthodox Christian population in the Ottoman administration (both ecclesiastical and 'political' or economical), being as much a part of the religious apparatus as of the educational processes aimed at the Orthodox Christians of the empire, irrespective of their mother tongue or patois, be it Greek, Albanian, Bulgarian, Wallachian or any of the regional languages or dialects.

Following a brief presentation of the social and political relations of power in the Ottoman Empire, I will then expand upon aspects of the pre-national social and ideological cohesion that characterised the empire's Orthodox Christian populations, so that the origins of the Greek nation may thence be clarified.

---

2   There are indications that Rigas's *Battle Hymn* promoted nationalist sentiments to certain educated strata as early as the late 1800s: 'The twenty-one-year-old Lord Byron and his travelling companion John Cam Hobhouse first became aware of Korais, and the admiration in which he was held, while staying in the house of a local primate in the Peloponnese at the end of 1809. The very name of Rigas was sufficient to produce an "ecstasy" in their host. From Hobhouse's diary we know that the lines later translated and made famous by Byron were already being sung, to the tune of the "Marseillaise", in the Peloponnese, only eleven years after Rigas's execution:

   Sons of the Greeks, arise! / The glorious hour's gone forth, / And, worthy of such ties, / Display who gave us birth. / Sons of Greeks! let us go / In arms against the foe, / Till their hated blood shall flow / In a river past our feet' (Beaton 2019, pp. 66–7).

3   I remind the reader of the fate of the 'Song of the Germans' composed by Hoffmann von Fallersleben in Prussia in 1841, which was to become the German national anthem in the twentieth century (see Chapter 3).

2   Remarks on the Structure of the Ottoman Empire

Ottoman suzerainty in the former Byzantine territories exhibits significant parallels with the kind of social organisation and 'governance' extant during the Byzantine Empire, especially until 1204.

The Ottoman state consisted of an 'Asiatic'-despotism.[4] 'Asiatic' not as a synonym for 'barbarian', that is, as an hierarchical-classificatory judgement against some supposedly superior 'western' feudalism, but in the sense as it is extrapolated from Marx's analyses: as a mode of production different from the feudal, i.e. a pre-capitalist mode of production that is characterised by collective forms of the organisation of power, as well as of labour.

The structural elements characterising the Asiatic mode of production (and distinguishing it from the contemporaneous feudal societies) were: a) the absence of *private* property in the means of production, and b) collective organisation of the labouring class in village or urban communes. The land supposedly belonged to God, who had assigned it to the ruler (the sultan), who personified the state. The land in the form of *timars*, i.e. territories paying *tributes* to the state, was granted to state officials, the timariots, who possessed it without holding any form of private ownership rights on it. All agrarian or urban communities paid tributes to the state.[5] Contrarily, those who manned state apparatuses[6] did not pay tributes or taxes.[7]

---

4 For further analysis, see Godelier 1964; Mandel 1971, pp. 120–45; Milios 1988, 1997, 1999; 2018, pp. 97–103, İnalcık 1978, 1997; Sugar 1983.

5 Marx distinguishes 'Asiatic landforms' from all other pre-capitalist production forms: 'Amidst oriental despotism and the propertylessness which seems legally to exist there, this clan or communal property exists in fact as the foundation, created mostly by a combination of manufactures and agriculture within the small commune ... A part of their surplus labour belongs to the higher community, which exists ultimately as a person, and this surplus labour takes the form of tribute etc., as well as of common labour for the exaltation of the unity' (Marx 1993, p. 473). Marx argued that the tribute is a historically specific form of surplus, which should be distinguished from rent, i.e. it should not be 'erroneously include[d] in this economic category' (Marx 1990, p. 890). The notion of the Asiatic mode of production is obviously not compatible with the evolutionist four-stage scheme (primitive communism – slavery – feudalism – capitalism) codified by Soviet Marxists. As Ernest Mandel notes: '[T]he mechanistic and anti-Marxist straitjacket of the "four stages" which all mankind was supposed to have necessarily passed through ... This straitjacket had compelled writers who claimed to be Marxists but who wanted to be accepted as "orthodox" by the Communist parties to assemble under the heading "feudal society" a most variegated collection of socioeconomic formations' (Mandel 1971, p. 119).

6 Those who manned the state apparatus were: 'the Janissary army, the *timar*-holding *sipahis*, the ulema and the bureaucrats' (İnalcık 1997, pp. 12–13).

7 'Under the Ottoman regime the population was divided into two main groups. The *askeri*,

The ruling class therefore attained the *ownership relation* (the power of expropriation of the surplus product) collectively, organised as a state.

At the same time, the *possession* of land (the management of the production process, the responsibility of putting the means of production into operation), as well as the *use* of it (the ability to undertake the act of production, per se) belonged to the Asiatic communities. The individual farmer possessed and cultivated the land solely through his (or her) affiliation with the community. Both ownership and possession of land was thus collectively organised.[8]

The Ottoman conquest of Byzantium led to a suppression of feudal forms that had developed there, especially from the thirteenth century (until 1453):

> By reversing this tendency toward feudalization of the Balkans, the Ottomans established a strong centralized regime, similar to certain states of Western Europe in the fifteenth century. During this centralization process, the Ottomans restored to state proprietorship, or control, the bulk of the lands found in the hands of local lords or families and monasteries. In many cases, it is true, they reassigned part of these lands to their previous owners, but these local lords were now made Ottoman *timar*-holders under strict state control.[9]

Notwithstanding the fact that the sultan existed as the direct representative of God and Mohammedanism on earth, adherents of other religions were also protected by the state.[10] However, the population was divided based on its religious faith into the 'faithful and the faithless', and were integrated into the state accordingly. The greater part of the 'faithless' of the Ottoman Empire were the Christian Orthodox. The Orthodox Patriarch of Constantinople was charged

---

the military or administrative class ... was thereby officially exempted from all taxation. The second group, the *reaya*, the merchants, artisans and peasants (literally the "flock"), pursued productive activities and therefore paid taxes' (İnalcık 1997, p. 16).

8   Asdrachas 1978, 1982; Milios 1988; Mutafchieva 1990. Nikolaos Moschovakis maintains that the origins of the community system were Byzantine, something that could be considered as true, *to the extent* that in the Byzantine Empire, until at least 1204, but also in some regions until the Ottoman conquest, the Asiatic mode of production prevailed: 'The communities ... are patently of Byzantine origins ... in 1458 we find that Athens surrendered to Omar under the explicit condition that community privileges be retained, that there be alongside the Ottoman administrator a council of archons or elders' (Moschovakis 1882, p. 76).

9   İnalcık 1997, p. 15.

10   'Once the lands had become tribute-paying territories, the non Muslim inhabitants assumed the status of *ahl al-zimma*, i.e. protected subjects of the Muslim state in accordance with Islamic Law' (İnalcık 1997, p. 14).

with all manner of religious jurisdiction in addition to juridical and educational responsibilities over the entire Orthodox population of the empire. His
jurisdiction was in fact extended over a wider population base compared to
what it had been in the latter centuries of Byzantium.[11] At the same time, the
Orthodox Church acquired extensive timars, that is, the right to exact tributes. Furthermore, Greek-speaking laymen held high political positions in the
Ottoman administration, the former of whom, for the most part, had origins
in the old Byzantine Empire and were referred to as *Phanariotes*.[12] This uniform religious, educational, as well as administrative institutional organisation
of the Orthodox populations of the Ottoman Empire under the ruling hand
of the Patriarch was exclusively Greek-speaking. The administrative region of
the Balkans where the corresponding Orthodox populations dwelled was called
Rûmelia or Rûm-éli,[13] where éli means region, while Rûm (from Romans) was
generally translated by Westerners as *Graeci* (Greeks).[14]

In the framework of the Ottoman system, the timar constituted an economic
and in tandem political and military unit within the framework of the Asiatic
state. It thus served as the basic administrative link in the power system. The
entire system was supported, on the one hand, by the local authorities (in the
context not only of timars, but of each Asiatic community), and on the other by

---

11   Paparrigopoulos 1971, Vol. 14, pp. 56 ff.

12   See Chapter 5, note 1.

13   İnalcık 1993, p. 82. Other administrative districts were: Anatolia (Asia Minor), Eastern
      Anatolia, Hungary, Syria and Palestine.

14   Typical of the identification of the Rûm with the so-called *Greci* (*Graeci*) in the West is the
      following passage by Heath W. Lowry in reference to the mother of the sultan Suleiman
      the Magnificent (1520–66): 'As to who she was, here the answer is contained on the Kitabe
      (dedicatory inscription) which adorns her türbe (tomb), whereon she is called a Bânu-
      i Rûm ("Greek lady")' (Lowry 1993, p. 22). As Johannes Koder observes: 'The Byzantines –
      and following the Ottoman conquest in the 15th century, accordingly, the Greeks – defined
      themselves as *Romans*. In the languages to the east of Byzantium, the terms were adopted
      and adapted: Romans to Rumi and Romania to Rum ... Conversely, in western mediaeval
      Europe the Byzantines were called Graeci or Greci, seeking, amongst other things, the
      delegitimisation of their rights in Roman imperial ecumenicalism' (Koder 2018, p. 75). In
      any event, beginning in the thirteenth century or even earlier in Byzantium, 'traditional
      ancient Greek stereotypes of a cultural superiority are adopted against the barbaric ele-
      ment' (Koder 2018, p. 84), something which leads to the gradual abandonment of the
      previous categorical identification of the term Hellene with pagan. Regarding the latter
      question, see, e.g. the missive by Mikhail Psellos (1018–78) to 'the king and master Mikhail
      Doukas', which mentions as regards the Chinese: '[T]he Chinese indeed inhabit the most
      eastern reaches of the world; they are all Hellenes in doctrine', cited in Papadopoulou 2018,
      p. 95, where one can also find a presentation of the evolution of the meanings of the terms
      genus, race, nation, etc.

the existence of the potential for intervention by the central military apparatus. The *pasha* (Paşa), the Ottoman 'governor' of a province, exactly as the timariot, did not possess any form of rights of individual property or inheritance over the timars, but simply functioned as an 'employee' of the state. He was appointed by the sultan and his control over the farmers was determined exclusively by the *firmans*, which were sovereign edicts, issued by the sultan.

The most common form of tributes was the tithe, in other words, one-tenth of the agricultural or craft (and/or artisan) production, which was delivered in kind to the timariot. Aside from the tithe, the unfaithful would pay the timariot a 'head tribute' in monetary form. At some point during the fifteenth and sixteenth centuries the head tribute reached approximately a third of the total value of the tributes paid by the non-Muslims to the timariot.[15] There were also other forms of tributes that were paid in monetary form, as, for example, tributes on sheep, etc.[16]

Communities (Orthodox communities included) constituted basic structural elements of the Asiatic social order, as much on the economic plane (collective possession of land, organisation of production, disposal of what remained of the surplus product – following the tributes paid to the timariot – to the benefit of the community and its lords), as on the ideological-political plane. As structural elements of Asiatic society, communities strengthened and consolidated the principal role of the political and ideological (religious) level: they were built based upon an internal hierarchy that was governed by a body of lords-primates (*proestoi* or *kotsambasides* – *aghas* in Turkish). This communal power (in which the Orthodox primates certainly participated) in essence bound the community to the timar and subsumed it under the domain of the timariot; there were certain exceptions to this, of course, where the communities circumvented the timariot's power by maintaining their own direct representative in the central Ottoman state apparatus in Istanbul.[17]

---

15   Asdrachas 1978, pp. 14 ff.
16   Aside from the timars of the sultan, there were also the *vakuf*, which were timars that belonged as much to the Ottoman religious apparatus as to that of the Christian Orthodox. One difference concerning property relations in rural areas appears in the so-called *mulk* lands, which nevertheless played an entirely marginal role, at least until the outset of the eighteenth century: they were lands conceded by the sultan to certain officers as a form of private property in return for substantial services to the state. The *mulk* continued to fall under the state and were thus obliged to pay the pre-determined tributes. That notwithstanding, their proprietors had the right to concede these holdings or pass them on as an inheritance to their descendants, while at the same time they were in possession of increased powers over the labourers, resulting in the emergence of forms of serfdom and/or wage labour.
17   Paparrigopoulos 1971, Vol. 14, p. 134.

In addition to this, a regional military apparatus, the *armatoloi* (*martolos* in Turkish), was integrated into the state institutional structure of the provinces and timars. This was an armed corps under a commander who on occasion (e.g. in Mainland Greece) maintained full autonomy from the authority of the timariots and primates, functioning as a mechanism of 'keeping the order' in a particular area.[18] The *armatoloi* would every so often demand (depending on their military strength at the time) increased financial and political privileges that would then incite tension with the local or central Ottoman authorities. Whenever the Ottoman authorities intervened contrary to their interests, these armed bands would cross over to being *klephts* ('thieves'). Until the full-fledged crisis of the Ottoman Empire, the *klephts* were not predominantly plain robbers or bandits, nor were they revolutionaries. They were largely a politico-military group that would lay claim to a position of authority in the framework of the Asiatic power relations (war aristocracy), in spite of the fact that whenever they clashed with the authorities, they would resort to robbery and looting.[19] These armed units would criss-cross between being bandits, *klephts*, and military rulers-*armatoloi*. The *klepht*, 'whose activity is found in the practice of robbery ... [O]nce he has achieved a certain degree of strength, aims at engaging in the stuff of *armatoloi*'.[20] Needless to say, the very existence of the *klephts* bespeaks a tendency towards destabilisation on a local level within the Ottoman political system.[21]

The social system of the Ottoman Empire had begun to degenerate in the middle of the seventeenth century into a phase of crisis and disintegration, symptoms and effects of which were the movement and re-settlement of large populations in the western regions of the empire, the concomitant restructuring of the communal system that comprised the foundation of Asiatic social relations, the wars to the east and the displacement of areas of trade to the west, the significant development of foreign trade, a series of changes in the functioning of the state apparatus that allowed for the upgraded role of the *Phanariotes* in it, etc. All of the manifestations of these transformations were

---

18   See Asdrachas 2019, pp. 157–94, Kotarides 1993, pp. 21–90.

19   'The *post hoc* false praising and embellishment and aggrandisement of the klephts as patriots marked the historiography of previous periods' (Hering 2004, p. 73).

20   Asdrachas 2019, p. 149.

21   'Those Klephts who abstained from conducting raids and agreed to maintain law and order in the countryside of a territory assigned to them ... were exempted from taxes, received a salary from the communities of their captaincy and sometimes military equipment. The Turkish army ... was not allowed to enter the areas protected by them' (Hering 2004, p. 67).

a part of the process of destabilisation and dissolution of Asiatic communal relations in the countryside.

The social transformation, however, followed two radically different paths.

On the one hand, at the crux of the escalating decline of the communities, and of benefit to the timariots, forms of extensive land ownership were being formed (the timariot evolved into a landowner), whereupon to a great extent relations of villeinage developed. Such forms started to dominate in the Northern Balkans and central and northern regions of what is today Greece.[22]

On the other hand, the strengthening and relative independence (from the control of the timariot) of some other (mainly mountainous, but also coastal) communities led to another type of transformation of relations that bound the community together: relations of collective possession (and use) of the land were inclined to become private relations of possession and ownership of the land; the role of the primates tended to take on the form of political protection of the tillers of an area as well as their political representation against central state authorities, while at the same time the cultivators were increasingly subsumed under (commercial) capital via the market. Primarily the regions of southern Greece and the islands, where the Revolution had taken hold, followed this course.

So, in the majority of territories where the Revolution of 1821 had broken out and taken hold (in the Peloponnese, on the mainland and Aegean islands), the disintegration of Asiatic social relations meant the attainment of broader economic and political autonomy from the central Ottoman authority. The Asiatic order was delegitimised in those regions, the Ottoman state having already become an 'impediment' of sorts to the new way of life, and to the economic activity with which it was affiliated (see the subsequent sections of the present chapter).

This issue is a key one, as national identity is only moulded upon the delegitimisation of earlier identities; or, as claims Eric Hobsbawm, when 'all these traditional legitimations of state authority were ... under permanent challenge'.[23]

Before penetrating the issue more deeply, which is pivotal to my line of reasoning, I see it fit to lay emphasis on the non-national character of the social relations underpinning the populations of the Ottoman Empire up through the end of the eighteenth century, something which has been systematically obfuscated by nationalist ideologies.

---

22   Stoianovich 1980.

23   Hobsbawm 1992, p. 84.

3   Language and the 'Universalist Hermeneutics' of Nationalism

According to the positions just discussed, documents, movements, educational initiatives, etc. that aimed at penetrating distinct religious principles or identities, and/or armed movements that attempted to 'upgrade' religious communities and local power structures, are not necessarily integrated into an era of nationalism (of nations).

Be that as it may, the nationalist ideology that emerged later, accommodated *post hoc* all of those texts, documents and real or alleged events into the manufactured 'history of the nation'.

Nationalist ideology, alternatively stated, functions 'universally', subsuming into a 'national history' whatever it can refer back to as some of the 'purported' identities or characteristics of a nation. As Siniša Malešević astutely observes:

> Whereas in the early nineteenth century only a very small number of political, cultural and economic elites developed a strong sense of national attachments, in the twentieth and early twenty-first centuries nationalism has become a mass phenomenon that impacts on the thoughts and actions of billions of individuals globally ... [T]here is simply no way to avoid nationalism in a world whose legitimacy resides in the principle that the nation state is the only legitimate form of territorial organisation. It is here that the nation states differ from pre-modern forms of polity where there was no place for nationalism as their rulers invoked very different sources of rule justification, mythologies of kinship, the divine origins of kings, specific religious traditions, civilising missions and so on. Thus there is no modernity without nationalism. While this ideological doctrine might escalate only intermittently, it nonetheless dominates persistently.[24]

In the present section, I shall point to an example that illustrates what was mentioned in the previous chapters as regards the perspectives that 'Bulgaria' constitutes a part of 'Greece', but as well to the *post hoc* 'national' interpretation of non-national contradictions.

Paisios (1722–73), whose mother tongue was Bulgarian, initially a monk and then deputy abbot of the Hilandar Monastery at Mount Athos, and who in 1962 was canonised by the Bulgarian Orthodox Church, penned in Bulgarian the *Slavo-Bulgarian History* (*Istoriya Slavyanobolgarskaya*) in 1762 at the Holy Pat-

---

24   Malešević 2019, pp. 4, 5.

riarchal and Stavropegiac Monastery of Zographou (the Zograf monastery) of Mount Athos, where he dwelled. In this work, Paisios champions the language and history of the Bulgarian-speaking populations and decries their (linguistic) Hellenisation. Panagiotis Kanellopoulos notes:

> The prevalence of Greek learning not only at Mount Athos, but in Bulgaria itself, where until 1835 there were but only Greek schools (for Bulgarians and Greeks alike) incurred the reaction of the monk Paisios.[25]

Paisios addresses himself to Bulgarian-speaking intellectuals and lettered clergy whom, being graduates of schools and seminaries (where the language was the archaic Greek – *Katharevousa*), he reprimands and exhorts to speak, write and master the Bulgarian language, of which they should feel proud, as it is the language (and they themselves are the descendants) of an esteemed and excellent genus, creators of great works in the past:

> It is necessary and useful for you to be cognisant of everything that is known about the deeds of your forefathers ... some, however, prefer not to learn anything about the Bulgarian genus ... they lack interest in their Bulgarian language, they learn to read and speak Greek, and are ashamed to be called Bulgarians. O, senseless and foolish one! Why be ashamed of being called Bulgarian and why not speak and write in your own language? ... Of all Slavs the Bulgarians were the most glorified genus; it was they who first called their leader a tsar, it was they who first had their own patriarchate, and it was they who first became Christians and had conquered many lands ... But why, foolish soul ... do you defect to a foreign language? He will say, however, that the Greeks are wiser and more learned, while the Bulgarians are naïve and silly and have no words of refinement ... Just look, though, you foolish one, there are many a people, who are wiser and more glorious than the Greeks. Does a Greek, nevertheless, abandon his language ...? You, Bulgarian, do not be led astray, become acquainted with your genus, your language and educate yourself in your own language.[26]

In Paisios's sermonising there is not a single trace or reference to a 'future Bulgarian state' and the impending 'freedom' of the Bulgarians; even more,

---

25   Kanellopoulos 1982, pp. 58–9.
26   Cited in Kanellopoulos 1982, pp. 59–60.

there is no hint of, nor a single allusion to, the duty of sacrifice for country (and religion), no thought of 'freedom or death'. And not only that. In Paisios's appeal to the Bulgarians for the configuration of a Bulgarian-speaking hieratic-educational network, for 'learning in their own language', there was *not a single response for several decades*. As we are informed by Daniela Kalkandjieva:

> The interest of Orthodox Bulgarians in higher theological education appeared in the course of *their national movement (1820–1870) for establishing a Church, independent from the Patriarchate of Constantinople*. These demands, however, could not be realized without an enlightened hierarchy. Until the beginning of the nineteenth century Bulgarian clerics were trained in monastery schools ... The situation changed at the beginning of the nineteenth century, when many Bulgarians *went to the prestigious theological school on Chalki Island and at the ecclesiastical seminary in Athens*. Nine of their graduates were among the first metropolitans of the Bulgarian Exarchate, established in 1870 ... [*T*]*he theological schools on Chalki and in Athens were engaged with the Greek nationalistic propaganda*. Soon they lost their attractiveness for Bulgarians, who were fighting for the restoration of their medieval church. *In the second half of the century*, Bulgarians preferred to receive their theological training in Slav ecclesiastical seminaries.[27]

From the aforementioned excerpt it is worth noting that the Bulgarian higher clergy continued their learning in the Greek language, on Halki as well as in Athens, until the middle of the nineteenth century, when for the first time they began to be troubled by Greek nationalism. *Ergo*, the assertion that a certain church-backed Bulgarian 'national movement' actually began in 1820 is problematic, and bears upon the generalising nationalist ideology that prevails to this day.

What is even more remarkable is that while Paisios is described as a purveyor of 'anti-Hellenism' by Greek nationalists,[28] concerning Bulgarian nationalism

---

27 Kalkandjieva 2005, pp. 229–30, corrected and emphasis added.
28 'These anti-Greek sentiments presented in Paisius' writing, characterized the Greeks as some kind of Bulgarian national enemies' (Wikipedia source: https://en.wikipedia.org/wiki/Paisius_of_Hilendar). To the contrary, Panagiotis Kanellopoulos, whose views on the 'distinct popular consciousness' of each Balkan peoples were presented in Chapter 2, criticises the viewpoint that Paisios 'was of anti-Hellenic disposition' with the following points: 'We do not recognise in others ... the right to a patriotism commensurate to our own patriotism. Paisios ... was not a Greek patriot. He was a Bulgarian patriot ... Only in one own's language can a people model their own education' (Kanellopoulos 1982, pp. 59–60).

he is thought to be a leading figure in the Bulgarian national awakening![29] In closing this section it should be emphasised that the terms Greek (*Graecos*: Гръцки) and Bulgarian (български) contextually for the monk Paisios point to language groups, and not to nations in the contemporary sense.

The Greek-speaking populations of the Ottoman Empire defined themselves as 'Romans', not only during the 1760s, but for at least the subsequent three decades of the eighteenth century. I remind the reader that in all three lexicons of the Balkan languages published before 1821 (*Protopeiria* by Theodoros Anastasios Kavalliotis, 1770, *Introductory Teaching* [*Eisagogiki Didaskalia*] by Daniel Moschopolites, 1802, and the *Lexicon of the Roman and Colloquial Arvanitiki Languages* by Markos Botsaris, 1809; see Chapter 2), the (Greek) language is defined as 'Roman' or 'Romaic'. In fact, Daniel Moschopolites exhorts those speakers of other languages: 'And prepare yourselves, all of you to become Romans'.[30]

It has also been seen that when the term *Hellene* entered the revolutionary jargon of 1821 carrying a distinct national significance – as with Rigas's texts, *Hellenic Nomarchy*, etc. – it did not fully displace the term *Graecos* (and the corresponding *Graecia*), which derives from the western *Greco*, etc. (recall Alexandros Ypsilantis's proclamation: 'Greek Men, those sojourning in Moldavia and Wallachia!').[31]

Though its formation was early relative to the majority of European nations (the case of the Bulgarian-speaking populations, who were essentially politicised into nationalism beginning in the mid-nineteenth century, for example),

---

29 'It is generally accepted that Bulgarian nationalism began to take shape in the middle of the 18th century, and that its most representative early manifestation was the Slavonic-Bulgarian History (История славяноболгарская, 1762) by Paisius of Hilendar. This was then expanded further in the 19th century and continued to develop thereafter ... It is as if the nascent nationalism, constructing / re-constructing memory for a Bulgarian state followed by a desire for its recovery ... Noticeably, all of these frameworks were coined outside Bulgarian space' (Aretov 2014, pp. 174–5). Other historians are of course more cautious when promoting the written history of Paisios of Hilendar as the departure point for Bulgarian nationalism: 'Up until the 1870s, the mainstream of the Bulgarian national liberation movement limited its demands to the establishment of a separate Bulgarian church or millet, which would grant to the Bulgarians cultural autonomy and political representation' (Detrez 1997, p. ii).

30 See Chapter 2, note 37.

31 Besides, as is well-known, Adamantios Korais argued on behalf of the term *Graecos* / Greek, and not Hellene. In his work *A Dialogue between two Greek inhabitants of Venice when they learned of the illustrious victories of the Emperor Napoleon* (1805), we read: '– I hear you always calling us Greeks; and why not Romans, as we have been called until now? ... – Our forebears were called Greeks; thereafter they took on the name Hellenes, not from a foreign nation, but from a Greek again, who had as his main name, Hellene

the Greek nation had not yet been formed at the close of the eighteenth century (see below). Hence, the question at this point is: what was it, beyond
religion, which had previously held the populations together, populations that
were later politicised nationally and mobilised by the Revolution? Moreover, of
what nature were the earlier insurrections, as, for instance, the 'Orlov Revolt'
of 1769 in the Peloponnese? The answer to such questions will afford us, as
earlier noted, an enhanced understanding of the process behind the origins
of the Greek nation.

4   The *Chronicle of Galaxidi*, or a Pre-national, 'Roman' Historical
       Narrative of the Period 981–1703

If a configured nationalism consistently bears the baggage of an eternal 'national history', it will be worth examining the rare, 'historiographical' text of the
period before nations, which, on the one hand, mentions or describes (more
or less known) historical events that unravelled over a period of eight centuries, and, on the other, and more notably, evaluates and critiques these events
according to the ideological trappings imparted by its author in 1703, the year
the document was written.

From the manuscript in question: '*J. Chr., a history of Galaxidi drawn from
old manuscripts, vellums, registries, authentic Chrysobulls [imperial edicts],
wherever they may be found, and exist and have been saved in the Vasilikon
Monastery of Christ the Saviour, built by he who was once lord and despot Master Mikhail Komnenos, in eternal memory. Amen.* Penned by the hieromonk
Efthymios, in the year MDCCIII (1703), in the month of March'. The text was
published for the first time in 1865 as *The Chronicle of Galaxidi* by Constantinos Sathas (1842–1914), who edited and wrote an extensive introduction and
notes. This text, by the hieromonk Efthymios, is articulated in 14 brief sections,
each of which refers to events of a particular date, of a particular year, or of a
broader time period.[32]

In the upcoming sections I shall cite and comment on certain excerpts
from the *Chronicle* which I regard as useful in considering the question at
hand, the idea of pre-national social cohesion in the Greek territory. This will

---

... One of these two, now, is the true name of the nation. I preferred Greeks, as all of the
    enlightened nations of Europe called us thus' (Korais 1805, p. 37).

32   The titles of the sections are as follows: 'AD 981 or 996', 'AD 1054, July 6', 'AD 1059', 'AD 1081',
    'AD 1147', 'AD 1204', 'AD 1259', 'AD 1222–1259', 'AD 1310', 'AD 1397', 'AD 1397–1404', 'AD 1571–1574',
    'AD 1660', 'AD 1690'.

be done so as to more lucidly draw a contrast between pre-national social cohesion and national politicisation, the era of nationalism. Where necessary, I shall provide the historical context relevant to the passage in question.

4.1   'Christian-Hostile Men, Called Bulgarians, Destroyed the Christians'

The *Chronicle* begins with the devastation of Galaxidi wrought by the armed bands of General Samuel, later Tsar of Bulgaria (see Chapter 2), during the years of conflict with the Emperor Vasileios II (the 'Bulgar-slayer'), 977–1014. It considers that the attacks were made by 'Christian-hostile men' who 'destroyed the Christians', although the Bulgarians, as was known, were Christian Orthodox, as they had already been proselytised from the second half of the ninth century.

> AD 981 or 996. In the time of the reign of King Constantine Romanos, glowering and Christian-hostile men, called Bulgarians, invaded Greece and by sword and staff destroyed the Christians and drew straight for the Morea ... The *non-believers* came to Galaxidi, which was built in the old times and was surrounded by a beautiful castle, having both a fleet of ships and a multitude of houses ... [The] Galaxidians, seeing such immense soldiery, armed with long poles, and with many an arrow and helmet, which shone like the sun, they embarked the ships and in the city there remained only several old men for whom there was no space on the ships ... After fifty years, the land became quiet, and the wrath of the Lord destroyed the Bulgarians, and the Galaxidians went ashore, and the houses of Galaxidi were again built, which were all ashes and ruins, and woods, and thickets up high again sprouted.[33]

The perception of the 'enemy' as necessarily being 'non-believers', 'Christian-hostile men' who turn against the 'Christians' of Galaxidi makes it clear that when the *Chronicle* was written in 1703, the population mainly identified with being Christian. It is also worth noting that Galaxidi was already regarded as a naval town by the end of the tenth century, with a ship capacity that the chronographer regards as being capable of transporting almost the entire population of the town.

---

33   Efthymios 1996, pp. 200–1.

4.2   '[A]nd ... by the Grace of God, They Were Obliterated and the Nation Was Liberated'

The *Chronicle* makes reference to the raid of the Turkish-speaking Mohamme-dan *Ouzoi* in the Galaxidi region as follows:

> AD 1059. As time passed, other pirates came, clothed in skins like bears, and eating uncooked flesh, like beasts, and roasting men alive on the spit; and they conquered all of Hellas, which was called Romania; and the anti-christs enslaved the land in a most inhumane way, and tormented it; and they destroyed the churches, and seized whatever silver and gold that they could find, and tortured the Christians ... and persisted in looting and exterminating them for two years; and then the royal troops came against them, and there was a terrible battle, and being helped by the grace of God, they were obliterated and the genus was liberated.[34]

The state of the Oghuz (*Oğuz*) or *Ouzoi*, *Uzes* or *Turkomans*, has existed since AD 750 in present-day Kazakhstan. In 1059, they invaded the Balkans, and fol-lowing their defeat by the Byzantine army in 1065, survivors were incorporated into the Byzantine army and assimilated into the Byzantine order.[35]

The geographical use of the term 'Hellas' is of interest as a synonym for Romania, in other words, of Byzantium ('Ρωμανία'), as well as the reference to 'genus', which is patently a reference to the Christian population of Galaxidi, but also of other areas that had been 'enslaved' in 1059 by the *Ouzoi*.[36]

4.3   'Sir Emmanuel ... Possessed by a Demonic Spirit'

With the conquest of Constantinople by the Fourth Crusade in 1204, Galaxidi fell under the sovereignty of the Despotate of Epirus, that is, of one of the three Greek-speaking states arising from the aftermath of the demise of the Byz-antine Empire by the crusaders (the others were the Empire of Nicaea and the Empire of Trebizond). In 1222, Theodoros, the Despot of Epirus, waged battle against the Latin Kingdom of Thessalonica (that was under the sovereignty of the Latin Empire of Constantinople), and, being victorious, captured the city.

---

34   Efthymios 1996, p. 203.
35   As 'narrated by Mikhail Attaleiates [a Byzantine historian of the eleventh century, J.M.], the Ouzoi and some *Petsenegi* (*Pechenegs* or *Patzinaks*; *Peçenekler* in Turkish) during the era of Constantine Doukas were assimilated into the Byzantine army and some of them in fact reached high-ranking positions' (Papadopoulou 2018, p. 94).
36   'In particular, genus affirms the origins from a specific town or from a broader geograph-ical area or from a particular people' (Papadopoulou 2018, p. 91).

He renamed the domain under his control the *Empire of Thessalonica* and was crowned 'Emperor of the Romans', a title also held by the Empire of Nicaea, the latter of whom eventually seized Constantinople in 1261 and restored the Byzantine Empire (the Empire of Romania).[37] The *Chronicle* describes as follows the complicity of the Galaxidians in the war against the Latin 'Empire of Constantinople':

> AD 1259 ... At that time their lord was Sir Emmanuel,[38] brother of Sir Michael. He, being *possessed by a demonic spirit, was always eager to seize lands*; and gathering exceptional soldiery, the finest of Rumeli, he started his campaign, and passing through Thessalonica, he reached Byzantium, and the Frankish king went out to battle; and Sir Emmanuel, after receiving many and innumerable gifts from the Franks, ceased the war; then he dissolved the army, and gave them many gifts, and *to some he gave land*; as he also had in his army two hundred and fifty Galaxidians, who showed great bravery and order, he bestowed many gifts upon them, ensuring that Galaxidi should not pay any tribute to Sir Emmanuel, and that he alone should be called their lord, and that when he was on campaign that they should follow him.[39]

The feudal character of the Empire of Thessalonica becomes plain in this passage, with its subordinating manorial systems (*'and to some he gave land'*) or the (semi-)autonomous towns (*'ensuring that Galaxidi should not pay any tribute ... and that he alone should be called their lord, and that when he was on campaign that they should follow him'*). What is also plain is the absence of any national sentiment in the sense of how it is contemporarily perceived. The 'ethnic' community of Galaxidi harbours no trace of national-irredentist ideology, considers neither Thessalonica nor Constantinople as 'its' affair, nor does it identify with the invasive proclivities of the Despotate of Epirus or the Empire of Thessalonica: 'Sir Emmanuel ... being *possessed by a demonic spirit, was always eager to seize lands'*.

---

37   Theodoros's strategic aim was the conquest of Constantinople, in competition with two other claimants, the emperor of Nicaea and the Bulgarian tsar. This rivalry on occasion would take the form of military clashes, and now and then alliances would be formed, with the one pitted against the other for the Byzantine throne. See Vasiliev 1952, pp. 518–34.

38   'Mistakenly written in lieu of Theodoros' (note by the editor of the *Chronicle*).

39   Efthymios 1996, p. 208, emphasis added.

4.4 *'Izar Bey Went to Salona, and the Galaxidians Were Truly Saddened, for He Was a Good Man'*

We encounter the same absence of national universalist-irredentist ideology (the enslaved country or the subjugated nation, the people-nation, the longing for an independent state, etc.) in the *Chronicle* as regards all historical accounts pertinent to the period of Ottoman suzerainty:

> 1397–1404 ... When the Turks seized Galaxidi, it was under their authority and in the charge of the Bey, who was in Salona [Amphissa]; and then, when the Turks captured Epachtos [Nafpaktos], which the Venetians ruled, the Bey came and stayed in Galaxidi; *this Bey, who was called Hatzi-Baba, was a good man*; and when this Bey decided to build a mosque and a minaret, he very much displeased the Galaxidians, who did not wish to have a mosque near their churches; and after a thousand entreaties, promises and offerings, *they persuaded Hatzi-Baba not to build a mosque and minaret, and the Bey received much money, and did not build a mosque and a minaret*; and this Bey stayed four years in Galaxidi, and died of a severe illness; and the Galaxidians were truly heartbroken. And *they buried him with an official ceremony, as if he had been a Christian, as he had been a good man* ... And there came another Bey, who was called Izarbey, a very good man, and he built at his own expense the stone canal, which brings down fresh water from the monastery of the Holy Trinity to the vineyards; and he also built a fountain, where his name still appears in both Turkish and Romaic letters ... there came a royal command that the Bey should leave Galaxidi, and go to Salona; and so *Izar Bey went to Salona, and the Galaxidians were truly saddened, for he was a good man. And not a single Turk stayed in Galaxidi*; only every year three Turks came and gathered the Haraji [the tribute, J.M.], which Galaxidi was obliged to pay, as continues to this day.[40]

What can be observed is not simply (a) the (at times) smooth relations of the community (of a naval town) with the Ottoman authorities ('And *they buried him* [the Bey, J.M.] *as if he had been a Christian, as he had been a good man*'), but also (b) the negotiative power of money central to the Ottoman Asiatic system ('*and the Bey received much money, and did not build a mosque and a minaret*'), and (c) the autonomy of the merchant-naval communities ('*And not a single Turk stayed in Galaxidi; only every year three Turks came and gathered the Haraji, which Galaxidi was obliged to pay, as continues to this day*').

---

40 Efthymios 1996, pp. 215–16, emphasis added.

4.5   *Armed Conflict: '[A]nd the Romans Raised Arms against the Turks'*
Even in the event of armed clashes between Greek-speaking Christians and
Ottomans, such frays were not considered (in 1703, by the author of the *Chron-icle*) as indicative of either a struggle for independence or even as righteous
insurrections:

> 1397–1404 ... At the time when a Turk, called Prilebes, ruled over Lidoriki,
> Galaxidi and the other villages and the country of Epachtos [Nafpaktos],
> a contention between Romans and Turks arose, and *the Romans raised
> arms against the Turks*, and struck down many of the Zorbas, where *there
> was no end to their evil deeds and crimes*; and many bands of Turks were
> sent against them, and the Lidorikians and many Salonians hastened to
> Galaxidi and pleaded with the Galaxidians, *who had ships, to allow them to
> sail with the ships to Frankish regions*, and to flee from the Turks; and there,
> while they were talking about this, there came an official statement from
> the lord of Salona, the Turk, who told them that he would not harm either
> the Salonians or the Galaxidians or the Lidorikians, only that they should
> return to their family homes ... and the Bey took oaths on the Koran and
> to Mohammed, in whom he believed, that they should be forgiven and
> remain unharmed and return to their homes and be allowed to resume
> their work. And so this upheaval ended in joy, and they avoided the ter-
> rible danger that had awaited them.[41]

It can be noted that the chronographer speaks: (a) of *armed attack* (and not
'resistance', as modern Greek nationalism would have one believe), (b) of the
Romans (not of Hellenes-Greeks) against the 'Turks' (*'the Romans raised arms
against the Turks'*), (c) which it interprets (justifies) with reference to the 'evil
deeds' of certain Ottoman 'Zorbas' (= irregular Muslim armed bodies: *'where
there was no end to their evil deeds and crimes'*). Beyond the likely issues of local
power (the amount of tributes, control over regions, etc.) which are not referred
to in the *Chronicle*, (d) the only discernible distinction is religion, as the insurgents ask the authorities of the naval town for assistance in their escaping to
Christian territories. Of note as well is, (e) the peaceful resolution of a dispute
following negotiation and mutual oaths.
    Even on the singular occasion (prior to 1703) when a more extensive insur-
rection against the Ottoman Empire in the region of Galaxidi had taken place
with the participation of *Maniates* (inhabitants of Mani) and other Pelopon-

---

41   Efthymios 1996, pp. 214–15, emphasis added.

nesians (in 1571), it may be characterised as having had the religious tone of a more widespread anti-Muslim ('crusader-like') campaign:

With the initiative of Pope Pious v, the Liga Sancta (a sacred Christian union) was introduced in 1571 in order to intercept the advance of the Ottomans into Europe. That same year (1571), the naval battle of Lepanto (Nafpaktos) took place, in which the fleet of the sacred Christian union (that had been formed by Spain, Malta, Venice, Genoa and the Papal States) overcame the Ottoman fleet and checked the Ottoman advance. Venice held the principal role in the naval battle, having contributed 110 of the total 208 warships of the union, and her admirals headed the Christian fleet. Capitalising on the outcome of the naval campaign and their presence in the Ionian and Aegean Seas, the Venetians incited rebellion amongst the Christian populations in the Peloponnese and Mainland Greece.[42] The *Chronicle* recounts the events as follows:

> 1571–1574 … In what I am recounting to you, I will also tell you about *an evil, born of the faithlessness of the Franks, who are always at odds with the Roman faith*. When the Franks succeeded in defeating the Turkish armada, they *exhorted all Christians that they should raise arms against the Turks*, and that they would provide them with support. Hearing such consoling words, the Christians with great joy and very secretly prepared to strike the Turks. Many a Morean came to Galaxidi … one Bostitzian [betrayed] the secret to the Turks … And all the Moreans who had risen went to Mani, and there they raised a campaign, slaughtering the Turks. Three Moreans, coming secretly to Galaxidi … and Lidorikians, [and] Vitrinitzians came to Galaxidi as well, decided to take up a campaign, and to kill the Turks, relying on the aid of the Franks, and there gathered three thousand and went up to Salona … and outside Salona they saw the Turkish army, who, having heard the news, went out to fight against them. There *came the messengers, with news that not one of the Venetians had raised arms* … Hearing these tidings, others displayed cowardice and fled, and *the army of the Romans* disbanded in a disorderly way. After two days had passed, letters came to Galaxidi from the Bey … The first twenty-three primates of Galaxidi, together with the Vitrinitzians and the Lidorikians, set out and went to Salona, and the Bey hosted them with honour and false joy; and after *relaying to him how they had been deceived by the Franks and raised arms, but that no harm was done,* the Bey …. in the evening

---

42 'The Venetians, as enemies of the Turks, were in contact with the Greeks, and during the Venetian-Turkish wars, armatoloi served in their ranks, of whom some later received land in the occupied territories' (Asdrachas: 2019, p. 21).

ordered that they should be seized one by one, and bound with chains, and put into a dark dungeon, and there they slaughtered them all with swords, all eighty of them, without missing one ... did you hear that! ... all dead for the motherland and religion, all of them, forgiven of all their sins![43]

What becomes evident from the foregoing excerpt is the following: (a) the 'crusader-like' (Christian-anti-Muslim) element of the Venetian intervention (*'they exhorted all Christians that they should raise arms against the Turks'*), to which the Galaxidians and other Orthodox paid heed, (b) the designation of the populations that took up arms as 'Romans' (*'the army of the Romans* disbanded in a disorderly way') and (c) the disposition towards conciliation and reaffirmation of subordination to the Ottoman order when Venetian aid ultimately did not appear (*'relaying to him how they had been deceived by the Franks and raised arms, but that no harm was done'*). Despite the prominent and influential position of the Orthodox Church within the apparatuses of the Ottoman state,[44] it must not be forgotten that it was the church of the 'unfaithful' (who, whilst indeed monotheists, and as such were amongst those not persecuted, yet they were inferior, being not followers of the 'true' religion – *ahl al-zimmah*: *people of the covenant* – and were thus unworthy of being assimilated into the central Ottoman state apparatus). This resulted in the preservation of a field of conflict between the populations and Orthodox institutions of Rûm-êli and the Ottoman authorities.

Moreover, it is worth pointing out that at the time of the naval battle of Lepando (Nafpaktos) and the insurrection that is described in the *Chronicle*, a sizeable segment of the subjects and combatants of Venice and her possessions were Greek-speaking Orthodox,[45] as Venice maintained extensive commercial relations with Venetian Crete as well as with a considerable number of coastal towns of the western Greek-speaking mainland.[46]

---

43   Efthymios 1996, pp. 217–18, emphasis added.

44   'The Patriarch ruled in accordance with the same ways of the Great Vizier, using the code of Justinian. He had the right to dispatch those found guilty to the Shipyard (or the well-known galley), accountable to no one ... The janissaries formed his honorary bodyguard, dependent upon him and carrying out his orders to the letter' (Philemon 1834, p. 33).

45   'Venice waged many wars on land and by sea with Cretan galeotti, a large part of the naval battle at Nafpaktos was the work of these galeotti ... alongside the Cretans, the Corfiotes and Pargians and Kefallonians fought as well' (Sathas 1986, p. 104).

46   Crete, 'was excessively frequented by local and other merchant fleets. Indeed, our analysis for the year 1514 ... shows that Candia was connected by sea with Canea (Chania); towns in the Peloponnese: Coron under Ottoman rule, Monemvasia, Napoli di Romania [Nafplion];

The phrase 'for the motherland and religion' that appears, as regards the doings of the Galaxidians and other notables, should not be interpreted out of its chronological context, according to present-day terminology. The motherland for the chronographer (and for the other Galaxidian 'Romans') was in fact a narrow geographical area: it consisted of Galaxidi and the immediately surrounding areas under the jurisdiction of the church apparatuses of the 'Romaic faith', which, in turn, operated under Ottoman sovereignty. As the chronicler himself points out: 'This is the true story of this land, being my motherland, and for her sake I laboured many a night poring over old books'.[47]

4.6   The Local Romaic-Orthodox Identity

In closing this section, one further remark should be noted. Galaxidi was a self-governing naval-commercial town, as after 1404 there were no longer any Ottomans or Ottoman authorities present (*'only every year three Turks came and gathered the Haraji'*). If we search in the *Chronicle* for elements of 'belonging' in a wider population base beyond the area of Galaxidi and the environing settlements, then without a doubt the only indication of such that appears is the 'Romaic faith'. Any mention of the (Roman) genus has to do with the single religious-administrative unit of Orthodox Christians in the Ottoman Empire, the Rûm, as has already been mentioned.

No version whatsoever of the concept of a nation exists. Of note, any reference to *significant historical events* in neighbouring 'Greek' areas is *absent*, as, for example, the *occupation of the entire Peloponnese by the Venetian state* a few years prior to the writing of the *Chronicle* (the sixth Venetian-Ottoman War: 1684–87), something that would be inconceivable in the framework of a *national* historical narrative.

And a final point: as a naval-commercial town, Galaxidi was dominated by money-begetting activities[48] directed largely abroad. The *Chronicle* never once refers to such activity, nor to the effects of such activity on the formation of the

---

and the islands of Stampalia (Astypalaia), Skiros, Naxos and Sifnos in the Archipelago' (Gluzman and Pagratis 2019, p. 149). Regarding the commercial relations of Venice with the Christian ports of the Ottoman Empire, Bruce McGowan writes: 'Thus although none of these ports was large, the cumulative importance of the new Adriatic ports was considerable; besides Durazzo/Durrës ... we must place the names Missolonghi, Galaxidi, Arta, Prevesa, Valona and Dulcigno/Ulcinj' (McGowan 1981, pp. 31–2).

47   Efthymios 1996, p. 224.

48   As already noted in section 3.5 (see, e.g. note 39), by the term 'money-begetting activities', I mean those monetary economic activities whose surplus product takes the form of money; or, put differently, production processes whose function (and 'aim') is the production (of more than the initial sum) of money – in the case examined here, the 'contractual

'identity' of those involved: shipowners, captains, seamen, workers in the local shipyards, wholesale dealers, etc. The chronicler likely belongs to the 'simple people' of stockbreeders and farmers, whose existence enwreathed the seafaring community. In only one instance does he allude to a seafarer, 'captain Metros Varnavas, who was a god-fearing man and world-traveller, having gone to many Frankish regions',[49] and that was occasioned by the 'vision' that the seaman had seen in his sleep that prompted him to become a monk, 'and he went with a Frankish ship to Jerusalem, where he was [re]born as Hatzis'.[50]

However, as has already been put forth, the birth of a nation is nothing more than the national(ist) politicisation of the 'masses', something which did not exist in 1703.

5   Two Events Non-national in Character

5.1   *The Orlov Revolt*

In this section I shall comment on the widespread belief that the Revolution of 1821 was not historically the first *national* (Greek) revolutionary movement, and that there were earlier ones, the most significant of which was the insurrection called the *Orlofika*, or the Orlov Revolt.[51]

The Orlov Revolt unfolded during the Russo-Ottoman War of 1769–74, when, accompanied by the presence of the Russian fleet in the Peloponnese, an uprising of the Christian population took place under the command of the brothers Alexei and Fyodor Orlov.

In truth, the Orlov Revolt, as with similar armed conflicts or uprisings that are related to names such as Lambros Katsonis or Nikotsaras, were movements associated with local warlords (*armatoloi* and *klephts*; see above): armed action to reinforce the position of the Orthodox 'military' rulers of the Ottoman regime, which ushered in violence and banditry at the expense of the local population. By the same token, the military action was *Christian* in nature, and was not akin to national movements.

---

mode of production' and the capitalist mode of production. For further analysis, see Milios 2018, Ch. 7.

49   Efthymios 1996, p. 224.
50   Efthymios 1996, p. 224.
51   This viewpoint is not a novel one, nor has it been exclusively integrated into the centre of Greek national historiography. Friedrich Engels, with regards to the Revolution of 1821, wrote in 1890: 'No wonder, then, that the Greeks, who had twice revolted since 1774, should now rise again' (Engels 1890, https://www.marxists.org/archive/marx/works/1890/russian -tsardom/index.htm).

The Orlov Revolt had been organised by the Russian state as an alleged move towards the emancipation of the Orthodox Christians (not of the 'Greeks'!) of the Ottoman Empire, and though it constituted the most significant insurrection prior to 1821, it did not take root in the Christian population. As noted by Papadia-Lala:

> The propagandist missions in the Balkans, and more particularly in Greek territory, of agents, such as Papazolis and Sarros, paved the way for the reception of the plans of [Empress] Catherine, which appeared to be veiled under the ideological cloak of the liberation of the subjugated Orthodox by the great power of the same religious doctrine ... The arrival of a squadron from the Russian fleet under Theodor Orlov in the port of Oitylos on 28 February 1770 (according to the Gregorian calendar) would create amongst the villagers unbridled enthusiasm; enthusiasm that would rapidly dissipate, as the Greeks, particularly the *Maniates*, would note as much the low numbers of the Russian forces, as well as the difficulty in collaborating with their leaders. The few initial successes, as with the occupation of Mystras, would be clouded by the acts of violence that followed and would be smothered by the numerous failed operations.[52]

The revolt in the Peloponnese was quashed by armed bands of Albanian-speaking Mohammedans. Yet these forces went on to engage in systematic slaughter and pillaging throughout the region, which resulted in the Ottoman army turning against them. In fact, during this stage, the Greek-speaking *klephts* and *armatoloi*, amongst who was Constantinos Kolokotrones, father of the pre-eminent leader of the 1821 Revolution, Theodoros Kolokotrones, fought alongside the Ottoman army against the armed Albanian bands. Theodoros Kolokotrones describes the events in his memoirs as follows:

---

52   Papadia-Lala 1984, p. 138. Constantinos Paparrigopoulos describes the 'acts of violence' referred to by Papadia-Lala as follows: 'At the end of February 1770, the first squadron of the Russian fleet sailing from the Baltic to the Mediterranean under Theodoros Orlov anchored at Oitylos ... At first relatively few Maniates obeyed his proddings ... [T]wo corps of a scant few were put together, named the legion of *east and west Sparta*, of which the western, consisting of 200 Greeks and 12 Russians ... and they seized Kyparissia, but [the event] turned into a great deal of plundering not only of Turkish villages but of Greek as well' (Paparrigopoulos 1971, Vol. 14, pp. 248–9). Regarding the supposedly 'national' character of the Orlov Revolt, R. Beaton notes: 'The *Orlofika* ... are often remembered as a kind of proto-national revolution. But self-determination for the Christian inhabitants of the Peloponnese or the islands was never on the table' (Beaton 2019, p. 18).

The revolt in the Peloponnesus took place in 1769 ... My father ... was leader of the Armatoloi in Corinth. ... While the Turkish army was advancing upon Tripolitsa in order to besiege the Albanians ... The Albanians saw that it would not be possible for them to hold Tripolitsa ... They rushed into the fields, and the cavalry cut them down on the plain as reapers mow the wheat. The horsemen fell upon them and reaped them, the cavalry on the one side and my father and his troops on the other.[53]

It is also telling of the Orlov Revolt that the authorities and population of Hydra, whose role in the Revolution of 1821 and in the founding of the first Greek state was pivotal – as, on the one hand, it was considered one of the few free Greek territories prior to the decisive (for Greek independence) naval battle of Navarino (see Chapter 6), while on the other, the Hydriote shipowners were the principal financial backers of the Revolution[54] – refused to participate in the *Orlov Revolt*, as well as in the later movements, something which eventually resulted in the bombardment of the town of Hydra by then officer of the Russian army Lambros Katsonis.

In refusing to participate in the revolt during the period of the Orlov in 1770 in the Peloponnese, the Hydriotes gained the exceptional favour of the [Sublime] Porte, they benefitted to the greatest extent in the growth of their navy from the Treaty of Küçük Kaynarca (1774), as they did from the affiliated trade agreement of Paris (1783). Yet at the end of the eighteenth century they endured much under Lambros Katsonis, with whom they did not consent to collaborate in his maritime operations in the struggle against the Turks, as they had [also suffered] under arch-pirate William

---

53   Kolokotrones 2013, pp. 125–26, corrected according to the Greek original. Constantinos Sathas mentions that following the victory of the Ottoman army, its commander, Hasan Bey, issued an order that the corpses of the Albanian-speaking contingent be made into 'a pyramid of four thousand heads cemented together with sand and lime' (Sathas 1869, p. 528).

54   'The shipowners who became rich during the Napoleonic wars contributed ships and provisions and wages. The extent of the offerings is judged by a single number: According to official documents, they amounted to 10.000.000 old drachmas from Hydra, 5.700.000 from Spetses and 4.430.000 from Psara ... Yet if one takes into account ... that the total amount of money received by the state from Greeks throughout all the years of the Revolution, according to the official declarations of the Accounting Committee to the assembly of Argos, did not exceed 23 million piastres [= approximately 38 million old drachmas, J.M.], it must be acknowledged that the offering made during the Campaign by the three islands would today equal a billion' (Andreades 1925, p. 10).

from Malta ... Both [of these latter] bombarded Hydra and attempted a landing operation of 500 men, under the leadership of armatolos Androutsos, father of Odysseus [a well-known figure of the 1821 Revolution, J.M.], who was collaborating with Katsonis, which was aborted on account of the brave resistance of the inhabitants.[55]

Thus, any assertions by nationalist historians (see Chapter 9) that a 'national' (Greek, Serbian or other) revolution took place before 1821 cannot be substantiated.[56] Equally unsubstantiated are, as will become clear in the next two chapters of this book, the viewpoints of certain historians who conflate the Greek Revolution with other, non-national uprisings in the Balkans during the first two decades of the nineteenth century, which are portrayed as outcomes of the geo-political initiatives of the Great Powers.[57]

The existence of the *Greek-speaking* ecclesiastical and administrative apparatus of the Ottoman Empire was not enough to justify the formation of a commensurate *national* consciousness in the Christian populations, in spite of the conviction to the contrary of the revolutionaries of 1821, who, as seen in Chapters 1 and 2, hastily presumed to consider the entire Christian population of the empire as Greeks.

---

55 Paschalis 1933, p. 590.

56 The same is true for all other insurrections which were later labelled national revolts or revolutions. An example: 'The revolt of the Serbian *knezes*, or peasant leaders, in 1804, has often been seen as the first of the "national" revolts that would lead to the creation of the modern Balkans. But that is the interpretation of hindsight. A typically vicious set of tit-for-tat killings in Belgrade province had been sparked by the janissaries asserting their own authority over that of the Sultan's representatives. In the conflict that followed, the Orthodox Christian population found itself fighting *for* the Ottoman Sultan against his internal enemies. The revolt of 1804 was eventually crushed, though it took nine years and in the meantime the situation had become further complicated by Russian involvement. A second Serbian revolt, in 1815, succeeding in establishing, for the first time, an Orthodox Christian warlord, Miloš Obrenović, in charge of an Ottoman province' (Beaton 2019, pp. 52–3). Regarding the insurrection in Sfakia, Crete, during the Orlov Revolt Beaton writes: 'Patriotism begins at home, in Sphakia, and from there extends to the rest of the island. There is no sense of a wider "national" identity in this account' (Beaton 2019, p. 37). And he adds: 'there is little evidence for anything that could be called revolutionary sentiment during most of the eighteenth century' (Beaton 2019, p. 42).

57 For example, Siniša Malešević, downplaying the dynamics of the Greek Revolution, writes: 'the largest conflict of this period, the Greek War of Independence (1821–29), had little to do with clearly articulated nationalist aspirations and much more with Ottoman internal instabilities coupled with the wider geo-political pressures of the Great Powers' (Maleševiç 2019, p. 177).

5.2   The 'Ionian State'

Nevertheless, nor was the first Greek-speaking state in the nineteenth century, the short-lived 'Ionian State' (also known as the United States of the Ionian Islands, or the Septinsular Republic) (1800–15) ever considered 'Greece', or in any sense of the meaning a *national* Greek state. The Ionian State, which had previously existed as a part of the Venetian domain, was created following the occupation of Venice by Napoleon in 1797, and as a result of the alliance of powers (and corresponding agreements) between France, Britain, Russia and the Ottoman Empire. 'This was an extraordinary step. At a stroke, for the first time in modern history, it gave a Greek-speaking population control of its own administration, and that under the provocative title of "republic"'.[58]

In the first constitutional charter of the 'Ionian State', which was ratified in 1803, the terms 'nation' or 'national' are used to indicate, first and foremost the citizens of the state, and secondarily to those belonging to a religious creed:

> Article 4. The prevailing religion of the state shall be Greek Orthodox. The Roman Catholic religion is recognised and protected. Any other [form of] worship is tolerated ... The law defines the privileges of the *Hebrew Nation* that is settled within the state.

> Article 32. The Electoral Body shall elect: the Representatives of the Legislative Body and the members of the Executive Branch, or otherwise of the Senate ... These members of the two Powers, are not considered as Representatives or Deputies of each Island separately, but as *Representatives and Members of Parliament of the Nation in its entirety.*[59]

When the constitutional charter of the Ionian State was voted upon in 1803, the *Thourios* and other texts by Rigas had already been printed. Nonetheless, the conceptions surrounding Greek nationalism and the related claim for the foundation of an independent state comprising the entire Greek nation does not seem to have influenced the framers of the constitutional charters of the state.[60]

---

58   Beaton 2019, p. 47.
59   *Constitutional Charter of the United States of the Ionian Islands,* emphasis added.
60   See also Mavrogiannis 1889.

6 The Ottoman Empire and the Birth of the Greek Nation

In this section I shall argue that the process of configuration of the Greek nation essentially began after the French Revolution, at the outset of the nineteenth century, with the development and dissemination of the national(ist) idea (and the corresponding political-organisational initiatives: secret societies, publications, etc.) aiming at an independent Greek (national) constitutional–republican state, by overthrowing Ottoman rule. The wide dissemination of the national(ist) ideology, beginning mainly with the Greek-speaking urban communities beyond Ottoman borders, was made possible amongst the masses both in urban centres and rural areas of the later Greek territory on account of the pronounced economic and social processes that had taken place since the end of the eighteenth century through the dominance of capital relations and the hegemonic role of Greek-speaking capitalists and buyers-up, which directly impacted the corresponding trade and money networks, as well as intellectual and learning circles.

6.1 The Permeation of Money-Begetting and Capitalist Relations and the Acceleration of Linguistic Hellenisation

During the second half of the eighteenth century, as much within Europe as within Ottoman borders, economic and social processes of great significance were taking place.

The indirect subsumption of the agricultural or household production by communities or individual farmers and craftsmen under the commercial capital of the cities by way of the 'buying-up' of their products was typical of the new era.

While the communities had lost their old, 'closed' and in part self-sustaining character, individual producers thereafter began to achieve economic independence. That being said, the craftsman or farmer could only remain an independent commodity producer as long as he or she was in a position to sell their products in the local market or to different merchants. The evolution of the division of labour, the differentiation in demand and the specialisation and diversification of production, the increase in productivity, and, finally, the need for the product to be directed towards not only the local market, but (and mainly) to more remote markets, led to the dependence of the producer upon but a single merchant, who would become the *buyer-up* of the total production of the craftsman or farmer. As it was the buyer-up who positioned the product on the various markets, they determined both the type and quantity of the products that every farmer or household-manufacturer that worked on his or her behalf would produce, essentially controlling the production process of the individual producers. The merchant – buyer-up determined the product orders to be produced by the producers now dependent on him, who were ever more frequently being supplied by the very same buyer-up with the necessary raw materials.

In this way, the buyer-up fundamentally *acquired control over the production process* of the individual producers, in other words, *of their means of production*. It is he/she who took decisions on the scale of production and the degree of diversification of the products within production. It is also he/she who decided on the division of labour between the separate producers under his/her control, in accordance with the established aims-criteria of productivity-profitability, market conditions, the increase in demand, etc., matters that were under their responsibility. They could therefore fix the prices of commodities that they bought (up) from the direct producers, resulting in their being remunerated (by the buyer-up) – even though they formally retained their economic independence, that is, the formal possession of their tools or the land cultivated by them – with an income, which at best equalled a worker's salary: a form of piece-wage, something that could be compared to the modern system of outworking.

The indirect subsumption of labour under capital was thus characterised by the absence of the standard wage contract, and by the fee of the conventionally independent worker in forms of piece-wages.

This concerned an indirect-early form of subsumption of labour under capital, which fed the development and expansion of mature capitalist relations (the direct subsumption of labour under capital: salaried labour – big capitalist enterprise). What took place is what Rubin refers to as the:

> cottage industry (the so-called domestic system of capitalist industry). It made especially rapid headway in those branches of production, such as cloth manufacturing, which worked for specific markets or for export to other countries.[61]

---

61   Rubin 1979, p. 24. 'In the scientific classification of forms of industry in their successive development, work for the buyers-up belongs to a considerable extent to *capitalist manufacture*, since 1) it is based on hand production and on the existence of many small establishments; 2) it introduces division of labour between these establishments and develops it also within the workshop; 3) it places the merchant at the head of production, as is always the case in manufacture, which presupposes production on an extensive scale, and the wholesale purchase of raw material and marketing of the product; 4) it reduces those who work to the status of wage-workers engaged either in a master's workshop or in their own homes ... This form of industry, then, already implies the deep-going rule of

The long-distance tradesman or 'free merchant', the labourer who was indirectly subsumed into long-distance trade (the cottage industry-worker, farmer, craftsman – all various forms of piece-wages), constituted the fundamental 'figures' of pre-industrial-merchant capitalism, together with the intermediary-buyer-up, who mediated between the labourer and the 'free merchant'. Other 'figures' included the wage-earner in the manufactures or the commercial enterprises in long-distance trade, on the merchant ships, etc. (here again, early forms of wages that were associated, e.g. with forms of 'cooperatives' of shipowners-seamen on commercial ships, etc. were preserved[62]).

From the moment that the new (capitalist) social relations ruptured the local (communal) Christian community, and even more so from the moment that long-distance trade became international (export) trade, a process of linguistic 'Hellenisation' was set into motion, not only amongst the merchant-capitalists, but amongst social groups and classes that were subsumed under the capital of a position of the dominated-subject for exploitation.

The Christian merchants of the Ottoman Empire, without their necessarily having been through the Greek-speaking educational system promoted by the church and other apparatuses, were oriented towards the Greek language, even if they were not descendants of Graecophones. Greek was not just the language of the Orthodox Church at that time, but of the Christians who had attained some rank in the Ottoman state apparatus, a fact of indisputable significance to the Greek-speaking merchant class. The local Christian tradesmen, if not already speakers of Greek, had important administrative-political, technical and cultural reasons to learn the Greek language.[63]

To begin with, merchant-entrepreneurs were in need of a reliable means of communication (language) and of stable relations with the Ottoman state apparatus. A language was needed that would facilitate and allow their business activity with the Christian authorities of the Ottoman Empire (the Patriarchate,[64] officers, *Phanariotes*) to be furthered unhindered, *as well as* enable them to be in touch with one another whenever protection against arbitrary dealings of the Ottoman authorities was required. The only language satisfying those conditions was 'official' Greek (*Katharevousa*). The Christian

---

capitalism, being the direct predecessor of its last and highest form – large scale machine industry' (Lenin 1977, Vol. 2, pp. 434–5, emphasis added).

62   See Milios 2018, pp. 114–21.

63   See also Todorov 1986, pp. 287 ff.

64   'In 1766/77 the Ecumenical Patriarchate succeeded in ... the absorption of the Archbishops of Ipekios and of Achrida [Orhid], acquiring thus the monopoly of the ecclesiastical jurisdiction to the Orthodox populations of the Ottoman Empire' (Kostis 2013, p. 44).

townspeople of the empire thus from early on turned to the Greek language. Victor Roudometof remarks:

> In Belgrade, for example, Serbian townsmen dressed in the Greek style, the Belgrade newspapers included the rubric Grecia (Greece), and, at least according to Stoianovich (1994: 294), the local Christian 'higher strata' were Grecophone until 1840. In South Albania and Greece during the late eighteenth and nineteenth centuries, thousands of Orthodox Albanians and Vlachs became completely Hellenized (Skendi 1980: 187–204). In the Bulgarian lands, during the second half of the eighteenth century, the domination of cultural life by the ecumenical patriarchate led to the promotion of Grecophone culture in liturgy, archives, and correspondence (Markova 1980).[65]

In his book *The Age of Revolution 1789–1848* published in 1962, Eric Hobsbawm draws a connection between the process of linguistic Hellenisation in the financially and culturally 'advanced' parts of the Ottoman Empire (that is, the social classes and groups that emerged out of the dissolution of the old regime and the expansion of bourgeois social relations) with the distinctive role of the Greek-speaking elite of the Ottoman Empire:

> Most Greeks were much like the other forgotten warrior-peasantries and clans of the Balkan peninsula. A part, however, formed an international merchant and administrative class also settled in colonies or minority communities throughout the Turkish Empire and beyond, and the language and higher ranks of the entire Orthodox Church, to which most Balkan peoples belonged, were Greek, headed by the Greek Patriarch of Constantinople. Greek civil servants, transmuted into vassal princes, governed the Danubian principalities (the present Rumania). In a sense the entire educated and mercantile classes of the Balkans, the Black Sea area and the Levant, whatever their national origins, were hellenized by the very nature of their activities. During the eighteenth century this hellenization proceeded more powerfully than before, largely because of the marked economic expansion which also extended the range and contacts of the Greek diaspora.[66]

---

65   Roudometof 1998, p. 13.
66   Hobsbawm 1996, pp. 140–1.

Certainly, as much as the linguistic Hellenisation of the Christian financial and administrative elite contributed to the formation of the Greek nation, the two processes, as we have repeatedly stressed, should not be confused, as they appear to be in the aforenoted passage by Hobsbawm (see Chapter 8). Roderick Beaton describes the social cohesion of the Orthodox population in the eighteenth century as the 'Orthodox commonwealth':

> That is to say, a sense of commonality was based on a shared religion and a shared education in the Greek language. This 'commonwealth' had no single geographical centre. Its heartland could be described as the southeastern corner of Europe, known today as the Balkans, but it was sustained by links deep into Russia in one direction and into Anatolia and parts of the Middle East on the other ... There are two transforming achievements associated with this commonwealth during the eighteenth century. One of these is the development of education, along with the circulation of printed books in modern Greek and the dissemination of secular learning adapted and translated from the West. The other is the expansion of trade.[67]

6.2 The Dominance of Greek-Speaking Capitalists in the Ottoman Empire at the End of the Eighteenth Century: Its Spread Into Central Europe and Russia

In line with what was elaborated upon in the previous section, societies of Greek-speaking merchant capitalists quickly dominated the Christian areas of the Ottoman Empire. The money-begetting activities of the empire were in essence divided between the Graecophones and the Ottomans until the middle of the eighteenth century, including tax rental.[68] Until the mid-1700s, large, foreign companies were the principals conducting foreign trade in the Ottoman Empire with the West. This changed with the permeation of the new money-begetting activities into the agricultural regions of the empire, where the networks of buyers-up, or 'middlemen', would concentrate the products of a multitude of direct producers – simultaneously orienting production by

---

67 Beaton 2019, pp. 20–1.
68 'To provision Istanbul, great quantities of rice, wheat, salt, meat, oil, honey, fish, wax, etc., were imported by sea, and those engaged in this trade were among the city's wealthiest merchants, who were organized in various associations. In the midseventeenth century, the first of these were shipmasters transporting their cargoes in their own ships ... they were divided into the "captains of the Black Sea" ... numbering 2000, and the "captains of the Mediterranean" ... numbering 3000. They were Muslims or Greeks' (İnalcık 1967, p. 120).

the latter towards the demand from abroad. Under these new conditions, the Greek-speaking[69] 'free merchants' acquired a clear advantage.

It was difficult for the foreign 'free merchants' (from countries outside of the Ottoman Empire) to prevail in the networks of this 'domestic system of capitalist industry' (Rubin, op. cit.), unless they could continue to enjoy the privilege, granted by their governments, of exclusivity of trade with their respective countries.

Were such a privilege to be abolished, transactions would pass into the hands of the local (Graecophone) merchants, as they were the ones who enjoyed direct relations (due to linguistic relevance, indigeneity, friendship, kinship, exchange, etc.) with the 'mediation links' (brokers and buyers-up), but also with direct producers (farmers, craftsmen, artisans, collectives) in the pre-industrial capitalist chain of production.

The 'free merchant' who conducted trade abroad was at the top of that multi-level pre-industrial capitalist system of production.

Even while discrimination of European governments on behalf of their citizens continued to be practiced, the 'free merchant' could be an Ottoman subject who had bought the 'barat' – in other words, the title of 'interpreter' to some foreign authority, which then provided them with the rights and opportunities of other foreign (European) nationals. As noted by Félix Beaujour, consul general of France in Thessalonica from 1787 to 1797:[70]

> The buyers are commercial factors, settled at Sérès, or factors sent by the Frank merchants resident at Salonichi. These factors must be well provided with money, because they are obliged to pay, before delivery of the goods, three-fourths of the cottons in advance. They purchase the commodities without seeing them, and go into the villages only for the

---

69   When I refer to 'Greek-speaking' or 'Graecophones', be they merchants or other capitalists, clergy, etc., I also include those who, while having a different mother tongue (Wallachian, Albanian, etc.), spoke in tandem the Greek *Katharevousa* for professional-financial, educational or administrative-political reasons – so as to be integrated into the ecclesiastical or administrative apparatus of the Rûm of the empire.

70   'We call patent *drogmans* the Greeks and Jews who purchase a *barat*, or patent, of drogman, not with a view to discharge the office of an interpreter to ambassadors and consuls, but in order to enjoy the privileges attached to that office. The *barat* withdraws the Ottoman subject from his proper jurisdiction, in order to place him under that of the Franks. These species of protections are sold like merchandizes; and it is the ambassadors and consuls who carry on this singular kind of traffic. The dearest barats are those of France and England. I have seen them sold for as much as ten thousand piasters' (Beaujour 1800, p. 430).

purpose of packing and carrying them away. It is thus that immense transactions are commenced, which are concluded without [a] broker, without writing, without contracts to make good the purchases, but solely by verbal agreements, always faithfully performed.[71]

Lastly, the buyers-up were also associated with (often in relations of exchange) with an array of local men of power and/or administrative officers (timariots, primates, etc.), who ensured, on the one hand, the direction of the production of certain products demanded by the buyer-up (and by extension, by the exporter or 'free merchant' of long-distance trade), and on the other hand, the *exclusive disposal* of production for the buyers-up in question.

The Graecophone merchants who conducted the export end of trade were, then, more 'productive' than their foreign competitors precisely because they could unite and mobilise the manifold mediation networks, through which (merchant) capitalism was spread and expanded, dissolving or transforming pre-capitalist relations of social cohesion and consensus. Kinship, indigeneity, linguistic relevance (forged on the basis of those new relations) no longer served as mediators of the Asiatic-communal-state hierarchies of *aghas* and *traditional primates*, but of the circuit of money and manufacture and commercial capital, upon which the Ottoman system of tributes positioned itself as a foreign body.

It is characteristic that Beaujour refers to 'the manoeuvres of the Greek merchants in whose hands the exchange is',[72] and hastens to add that those merchants, 'being *secretly confederated together*, always know how to regulate it according to their own interests'.[73] A more vivid representation of the issue is the report of the French Consul François Claude Amour, the marquis de Bouillé in Arta, written on 1 April 1750:

> I have repeatedly pointed out the unjust damage brought upon French navigation by those Greek consuls and vice consuls subject to the Sultan,

---

71   Beaujour 1800, p. 43. Naturally, foreign merchants had also been using the buying-up method since at least the seventeenth century: 'The French, before the year 1789, had always bought in common, which is what they call *uniting together* ... The advantage of the *union* was, that of presenting only one buyer to the venders, and consequently of not raising the price by agreement' (Beaujour 1800: 104). In an epistle by the consul du Broca to the merchants of Marseille, Arta 13 July 1705, which S. Maximos (1973: 50) cites, we read: 'If you so desire, gentlemen, you may give an order, via Naples and Messina, for buying up; send both money and ships together, for the loading'.

72   Beaujour 1800, p. 290.

73   Ibid, emphasis added. See also Kremmydas 1980, p. 48 ff.

natives of Ioannina and Arta where they have their merchant homes, their relatives as partners in business and friends and all the others *who are affiliated with them by blood and friendship, such a multitude of people* who naturally most willingly give preference to other flags rather than ours ... Here, all trade is conducted by Greeks with other Greeks established in Messina, Naples, Livorno, Malta. If I had to contend with foreign consuls, those of the Austrian Empire, the English, Neapolitans, Dutch, Ragusians and others, I am certain that the French flag would have consistently enjoyed preference where it was due. What can I do, however, against *such a multitude of people that these Greek consuls have about them*?[74]

Via mediation, brokerage and buying-up networks, all of which directed foreign trade into the hands of local Greek-speaking, long-distance merchants and shipowners by crowding foreign nationals out of the picture, the whole of society was transformed.[75]

The prevalence of commercial capital had already, in fact, transformed production. The technological level and competitiveness of 'Greek' manufacture in certain sectors was at the cutting edge internationally. Beaujour writes:

It is from Greece that we have borrowed the art of dying cotton red. Some Greek dyers came to settle, towards the middle of this century, at Montpellier, and dyed cotton there, after the manner of their country. Their processes were soon copied by the French dyers; and it is thus that the dying of the Levant has been communicated to our manufactories of Languedoc and Béarn, and to those of Rouen, Mayenne, and Chollet.[76]

And concerning the Society of Ambelakia, a large spinning manufacture and financial corporation based on a developed cottage network in Thessaly, he notes: 'Never was any society established on more economical principles, and never were fewer hands employed to direct affairs of so great an extent'.[77]

---

74   Cited in Maximos 1976, pp. 69–70, emphasis added.
75   'A broad network of intermediaries, which were bestrewn throughout all the ports of the Eastern Mediterranean and Black Sea, allowed the Greeks over time to establish virtually full maritime and commercial supremacy' (Todorov 1986, p. 98). 'At the end of the [eighteenth, J.M.] century, Greek commercial capital assumed a distinctive position in all the markets of the East and connected them with the rest of the Mediterranean and Europe' (Maximos 1973, pp. 15–16).
76   Beaujour 1800, p. 196.
77   Beaujour 1800, p. 191.

Trade in the 'East' fell largely into the hands of the Greek-speaking subjects of the Ottoman Empire, as it was not just Graecophones who became merchants, but *merchants* (the manifold and multifaceted mediation networks of money exchange characteristic of merchant capitalism) *who became Graecophones*. It was in this framework that the ideas of the Enlightenment around 'liberty, equality and the sciences' were propagated, which lay the ground for the national politicisation of the masses (the rise of nationalism). As noted by K.Th. Dimaras,

> in this incipient period of the Enlightenment, and, or, let us say, pre-Enlightenment, the abrupt and rapid economic and intellectual upsurge in the territories of 'what lies to our East' [the Balkans and the Levant, J.M.], will have ... direct consequences on the bearers of this prosperity: on the merchants and on the lettered class. The world of commerce, which is overlaid with the Phanariot world, tends towards social dominance.[78]

The domination of Greek-speaking merchants in the Ottoman Empire was reinforced by the after-effects of the French Revolution and the succession of wars in its wake. Graecophone merchants controlled a large segment of the trade in Marseilles at the time, founded branch offices in all cities in central Europe with significant commercial trade centres, such as Vienna, Trieste, Marseilles, etc., all the while investing in the European banking system. They actively operated in the Russian Empire as well.[79] From the end of the eighteenth century, the commercial capital of Greek-speaking subjects of the Ottoman Empire boasted a particularly notable dynamic. As Angeliki Inglesi writes:

---

78 Dimaras 1989, p. 27.
79 Beaujour presents numerous examples of merchants who dominate the maritime export trade, or long-distance trade, of certain products. A typical example follows: 'The best furs come from the interior of Russia. It is the Greeks who go to purchase in the southern provinces of that empire in the markets of the Ukraine and of Poland, and who come afterwards to sell them again in the markets of Selimia and Ozengovia, whence they are dispersed through all Roumelia' (Beaujour 1800, p. 319). Gelina Harlaftis writes of the Graecophone shipowners of the period: 'Their success lay in the business networks already established throughout the Mediterranean by Greeks for the transport of maritime trade from East to West, which ensured reduced costs in the running of their shipping operations and thus competitiveness in the international market of the Mediterranean' (Harlaftis 2013b, pp. 242–3. See also Harlaftis 2013a, Harlaftis and Laiou 2008).

... [T]he most influential Greek community in Central Europe arose in Vienna and evolved into a cultural-political centre ... before the Revolution of 1821 ... The fortuitous juncture that enabled the prevalence of the Greek element in the trade of Central Europe with the East was due to the absence of a native commercial class with adequate experience, as well as in the concession on the part of Austria of privileges to Ottoman subjects for the establishment and practice of their trade.[80]

The subsequent period would see the development of Greek nationalism in this social, economic and cultural climate.

6.3   In the Wake of the French Revolution: National Politicisation

The new economic and social relations that would carve out the economic and social space of the capitalist relations of production hailed a new way of life (in which money played a definitive role) and, as a consequence, new ideological forms and identities.

The demand for economic freedom birthed a demand for personal as well as political freedom, the latter of which transformed the terms of acceptance of religion (as a partially secularised identity). This framework of a way of life and perspectives became a host to the ideas of the Enlightenment as apparent 'truths' that were in harmony with the practices and way of life of the strata affiliated with capitalist social relations.[81]

For reasons related to the broader social environment, these ideologies were first politicised in the Greek-speaking communities beyond Ottoman borders.

It was *following the French Revolution*, which 'fertilised' these ideologies by leaps and bounds,[82] that the ideological characteristics of liberalism and nationalism were assumed. As Hobsbawm observes in *The Age of Revolution*:

> It was among this cosmopolitan diaspora that the ideas of the French Revolution – liberalism, nationalism and the methods of political organization by masonic secret societies – took root ... Their nationalism was to some extent comparable to the elite movements of the West. Nothing else explains the project of raising a rebellion for Greek independence in the Danube principalities under the leadership of local Greek magnates;

---

80   Inglesi 2004, p. 7.
81   Dimaras 1989, Dimaras 1992, Kitromilides 1996, 2013, Noutsos 1999.
82   Vournas 1989.

for the only people who could be described as Greeks in these miserable serf-lands were lords, bishops, merchants and intellectuals. Naturally enough that rising failed miserably.[83]

That notwithstanding, the demand for economic, as well as political and personal, *freedom* – for the abolition of the constraints and forms of coercion of the ancien régime, the demand for political equality and self-determination – had been disseminated widely amongst the masses in the southern and coastal regions of the contemporary Greek geographical space as well; that is, wherever the capitalist relations of production had formed a suitable social and ideological coherence. The demand for freedom by the Christian populations of southern, coastal and island Greece became, then, identical with the enlistment into the national idea of Hellenism, the foundation of an 'enlightened' independent state.

At this point it is worth citing a passage from a text by Friedrich Engels which refers to the Greek Revolution. Without his having ever systematically studied social relations in the Ottoman Empire or the Greek Revolution, Engels observed in 1890 that on the one hand, Asiatic ('Oriental') domination, which relied on 'self-government' on a local level, differed radically from feudalism, while the Greek Revolution can only be cognisable in relation to the dissolution of this Asiatic domination for the benefit of capitalist social relations. He writes:

> The Greeks ... were a commercial people, and the merchants suffered most from the oppression of Turkish Pashas. The Christian peasant under Turkish rule was materially better off than anywhere else. He had retained his pre-Turkish institutions, and complete self-government; so long as he paid his taxes, the Turk, as a rule, took no notice of him; he was but seldom exposed to acts of violence, such as the peasant of Western Europe had had to bear in the Middle Ages at the hands of the nobles. It was a degraded kind of existence, a life on sufferance, but materially anything but wretched, and, on the whole, not unsuited to the state of civilisation of these peoples; it took therefore a long time before these Slav Rajahs discovered that this existence was intolerable. On the other hand, the commerce of the Greeks, since Turkish rule had freed them from the crushing competition of Venetians and Genoese, had rapidly thriven, and had become so considerable that it could now bear Turkish rule no longer.

---

83   Hobsbawm 1996, p. 141.

In point of fact, Turkish, like all Oriental rule, is incompatible with Capitalist Society; the appropriated surplus-value is not safe from the hands
of rapacious Satraps and Pashas; the first fundamental condition of prof-
itable trading is wanting – security for the person and property of the
merchant ... [T]he Philhellenes who collected funds, sent volunteers and
fully armed corps to Greece, what were they but the Carbonari and other
Liberals of the West?[84]

One indicator of the starting point of the process of national politicisation was
the mushrooming of secret revolutionary societies and, specifically, the appearance of the Friendly Society. According to available sources, within two years
of the founding of the Friendly Society, at the beginning of 1817, only two members had been initiated, 'Xanthos in Constantinople and Anthimos Gazis in
Milies, Pelion'.[85] As is seen in the *Historical Essay on the Friendly Society* by
Ioannis Philemon,[86] who also made use of the personal archives of Alexandros
Ypsilantis, the Society began to flourish amongst the masses in 1818.[87] From the
catalogue of the 667 members of the Friendly Society cited by the author in a
subsequent work of his,[88] the same conclusion can be extracted, as well as the
fact that those who were initiated within the Ottoman Empire numbered no
more than a third of the total, most of whom were located in Constantinople
and the Peloponnese. It is reasonable to assume that Greek nationalism evolved
on a mass scale during the second decade of the nineteenth century, until the
outbreak of the Revolution.

Greek nationalism, i.e. the Greek nation, is therefore one of the oldest in
Europe (and globally), having emerged at least three decades before the other
Balkan nationalisms. As Eric Hobsbawm has aptly argued in regard to the pro-
cesses of national politicisation of the majority of European 'peoples':

What were the international politics of the years from 1848 to the 1870s
about? ... [I]t was about the creation of a Europe of nation states ...
Whatever else it was, 1848, the 'springtime of peoples', was clearly also,

---

84   Engels 1890.
85   Philippou 2015.
86   Philemon 1834.
87   'They nonetheless succeeded in recruiting a membership just over half of whom were
      merchants, with significant numbers of doctors, teachers and, in the somewhat special
      case of the Peloponnese, landowners and members of the Church hierarchy' (Beaton 2019,
      pp. 70–1).
88   Philemon 1859.

and in international terms primarily, an assertion of nationality, or rather of rival nationalities.[89]

Notwithstanding a portion of exaggeration, given that the American and French revolutions had already inaugurated the era of nationalisms,[90] the following statement by Roderick Beaton seems to aptly describe the early, in international comparison, formation of the Greek nation: '[I]n 1830, the first of the new nation states of Europe came into existence. Within a few decades, national self-government would have become the norm throughout the continent'.[91]

6.4 Nationalism as a Socio-political Rupture and a Change in an Historical Phase of Society

I shall conclude the present chapter with an observation that I consider fundamental to my line of reasoning: the nation (nationalism) has a *political nature*, it shapes a political-state identity, an identity of the 'citizen' (to be), under which a religious identity is subsumed. The new identity in this case is *Hellenic*-Christian, having displaced the earlier *Christian*-Hellenic identity that had been promoted by the Orthodox Church since the end of the eighteenth century.[92]

This was a tremendous ideological-political rupture, affiliated with unprecedented institutional and state-related changes: institutions of representation and novel ways of integrating populations into the state, political parties, constitutional order (or the prospect thereof), irredentism and national 'cleansing', etc. With the national politicisation of populations (the domination of nationalism), 'modern times' entered a new phase which at first glance appeared irreversible; in other words, it appeared to have slipped past the 'point of no

---

89   Hobsbawm 2006, p. 103.
90   'With the French Revolution ... Greek-Orthodox intellectuals reconceptualized the Ortho-dox Rum millet. They argued for a new, secular "Hellenic" national identity. Still, their visions of a future state included all Balkan Orthodox Christians' (Roudometof 1998, p. 11).
91   Beaton 2013, p. 346.
92   As Ioannis Zelepos points out, when referring to the religious attack against the Enlightenment at the end of the eighteenth century: 'Amongst the many "miracles" numbered as proof of religious truth, what is also mentioned is that *Hellenism was transformed into and became Christianity, with the collaboration of the Lord*' (Zelepos 2018, p. 357). In truth, what the revolutionaries of 1821 aimed for and in part achieved was that Christianity be transformed into (independent of language and 'tradition'), and become, Hellenism. It was a case of an inversion, brought on by nationalism (whereby the element *Hellene* subsumed the Christian element), and not about any 'substantial identification' with the past, as Zelepos seems to claim.

return'. 'If we were to declare that we do not recognise any Finnish nation ... that would be sheer nonsense. We cannot refuse to recognise what actually exists', wrote Lenin in 1919.[93]

Nevertheless, as paradoxical as it may seem at first glance, an idiosyncratic version of 'non-recognition' of a nation is the nationalist doctrine of its eternal existence. Were all of history a 'national history', a story of 'national struggle and adventure', then what happened with the 'awakening' of the nation was more or less to be expected, and, in any event, not a radical *social shift*, but simply some change within the *continuity* of the existence of the nation.

It is at such perspectives that I shall take a critical look in Chapter 9 of the present book; but first I shall address the effects of the Revolution and the institutional ruptures that it induced.

93   Lenin 1974, Vol. 29, p. 174.

PART 2

The Revolution and its State

∴

The First State of the Revolution: The Victorious Period (1821–1824)

1   Constitutions and Institutions: The Formation of a Bourgeois State

A revolution is not judged by the evaluative assertions and the 'memoirs' of its protagonists – especially a national revolution such as the Greek one, which places the onus of an interpretation based on a nationalist perspective onto its protagonists, cloaking their specific policies and personal positions, political and social conflicts, etc. under the guise of 'national interest' and 'destiny' of the nation and motherland. The Greek Revolution may be assessed and interpreted by its character and by its dynamics, beginning with the institutions that it created, the regime that it (attempted to) impose[d], and, naturally, by the official documents that were voted upon in the National Assemblies as guiding principles of that regime. And while it is true that 'the subject itself of the Revolution was anything but homogeneous',[1] as one might easily gather from just the events of the civil wars of 1823–24 (see below), still, its leading and, eventually, prevailing tendency during the period of armed conflict (1821–27) was formulated with clarity in those official texts and resolutions.

From the moment of its outbreak, the Greek Revolution promulgated its radical, Enlightenment-bourgeois character; and from the very beginning as well, it formed corresponding bourgeois-representational institutions, with the expectation of the formation of a (capitalist) constitutional state. As Dimitris Dimoulis observes:

> A reading of the first Greek constitutions engenders, from a standpoint of terminology and content, impressions similar to those taken from reading any modern European constitution. The first acts of legal organisation of the Greek state are entirely 'modern'. This is due to the fact that they express the three distinguishing characteristics of modern constitutionalism. They establish (popular) sovereignty, are totally regulatory in nature and use universal linguistic formulations. The composition (and

---

1   Kotarides 2017, p. 11.

to a major extent, the triumphal passage) of these texts would have been inconceivable in any European country at the beginning of the eighteenth century.[2]

As far back as when the proclamation entitled 'Fight for faith and mother-land' was printed by Alexandros Ypsilantis in Moldavia (see Chapter 1), we read: '[T]he assembling nation wants to elect its Elders'. The nation, which is nothing but the people of the nation in action, is the source of state power and is represented by leaders ('Elders') whom it itself elects. The very same (ideo)logical schema was formulated in the three regional structures of state power that were consolidated within a very short period of time after the declaration of the Revolution: the *Peloponnesian Senate* under the leadership of Petrobey Mavromichalis (28 March 1821, the official proclamation being 26 May 1821), the Assembly of *Western Mainland Greece* under the presidency of Alexandros Mavrokordatos (7 November 1821) and the Assembly of *Eastern Mainland Greece* (or the Areios Pagos) under the presidency of Theodoros Negris (15 November 1821).

At the First National Assembly of Hellenes (the National Legislative Assembly, or the General National Assembly), which took place following the aforementioned at Epidaurus (20 December 1821–16 January 1882), the precepts, according to which 'Hellas is destined to be governed', were formulated, and which 'the various peoples of Hellas' were obliged to observe. In the constitution (General Provisional Polity, or Political Constitution of Hellas) that was ratified by the First National Assembly on 1 January 1822, it is stipulated that 'those inhabitants native to the Territory who believe in Christ, are Hellenes and [are to] enjoy without any distinction all civil rights'. Aside from the 'natives', however, were those who 'were the same as the autochthonous inhabitants before the Law', the 'foreign-born' (Christians of the Ottoman Empire who sought refuge in the territory of liberated Greece) and those 'foreigners' (in other words, citizens of a foreign country), who 'possess the desire to become Hellenes'.

With the constitution, human rights and the right to own property are guaranteed, Asiatic (Ottoman and ecclesiastical) law is abolished, French commercial law is adopted, the distinction between executive and legislative powers is institutionalised, while two political bodies, the Parliamentary and the Executive, are defined, and 'the non-enactment of the office of a head of state reflects the radical severance with the monarchic-despotic past'.[3] What was being

---

2 Dimoulis 2000, pp. 37–8.
3 Dimoulis 2000, p. 54.

configured, in other words, was a typical bourgeois institutional framework, which further constituted a common strategic terrain for all of the socio-political forces that had participated in the Revolution.

> All Hellenes are equal before the law without exception or degree, class or office ... All Hellenes have the right to [participate in] all offices and hon-ours, granted to them based only on the merit of each ... The property, honour and security of each Hellene, is protected by law.[4]

The constitution confirmed principles that had been set out in previous con-stitutional-like texts, as, for example, in the Areios Pagos (the Organisation of Eastern Mainland Greece)[5] on 16 November 1821, in which the original defini-tions of the Greek citizen were given, as well as the criteria for differentiating the Greek from 'foreigners', or 'foreign nationals'. The basic criteria for integ-ration into the Greek nation (into the body of Greek citizens) was (a) the *Christian religion* of the native, and (b) *the will* of the Christian 'foreigner' to be assimilated as a citizen into the Greek state and thus become a Greek.[6]

The electoral law that accompanied the constitution stipulated that the people 'in every village' elect representatives who, on a second tier, elect the

---

4 'Provisional Constitutionalist System of Hellas according to the First National Assembly of Epidaurus, 1822', in Mamoukas 1839, Vol. 2, pp. 16–17. Even prior to the ratification of the first constitution, on 25 May 1821, Petrobey Mavromichalis, addressing American Philhellenes on behalf of the Messenian Senate, a first Peloponnesian administration before the formation of the Peloponnesian Senate wrote: 'You were the first to declare those rights and again you were the first to recognise them ... What now remains is for you to further your glory all the more, by assisting us in cleansing Hellas of the barbarians, who for four centuries have been polluting her' (cited in Vagenas and Dimitrakopoulou 1949, p. 11).

5 The Organisation of Areios Pagos declared, at the time of its founding, that they were obliged to take care of 'schools, orphanages, hospitals in the towns to be built' (cited in Stasinopoulos 1970, p. 42).

6 'Thus the Greek state consists of Christians who are recognised politically in the bourgeois-revolutionary ideals of independence and the organisation according to the rule of law. True "Foreigners" are only the Muslims, the obvious "enemies". The position that the nation is con-structed via state apparatuses, which create a consciousness in "their" citizens of a uniform integration, especially through a linguistic and cultural conflation that constructs a common lineage, is confirmed in the circumstance under consideration. From all this a particularly sig-nificant conclusion can be drawn. In revolutionary Greece, the term nation does not indicate language or origins, that is, the "ethnological" provenance, but the common formation/integ-ration/subsumption of a particular population of a state. The integration in this particular case presupposes a belief in Christ and in the political Revolution. Thus, the total number of inhabitants of an independent Christian state that recognises "natural rights" is character-ised as a "nation". The term people functions as a synonym, although it has a more intensely "ethnological" hue to it, than the term "nation"' (Dimoulis 2000, pp. 51–2).

members of the Parliamentary body (the 'Parastates', or 'Attendants'), who must be 'native' Greeks and own some form of real estate.

> The electoral law of 1822 introduced into Greece *ab initio* the general and indirect electoral right of legal consolidation, without ascribing importance, as was accustomed in Europe at that time, to the criteria of profession, property and educational level. Political 'openness' would be institutionally relativised by the stricter terms of political participation for the non-'native', and by the restrictive conditions for electability that legally reflect [the fact] that in the legislative bodies primates, military leaders and intellectuals were almost exclusively elected. Neither the legal nor practical relativism, nevertheless, diminish the political significance of the introduction of the direct vote.[7]

Needless to say, as was common in the constitutional texts of the period of both the American and French Revolutions, women were excluded from the electoral process, but in the case of Greece, those embracing other religions, such as Muslims and Jews, were excluded as well. And while concerning the former, the measure was on the face of it understandable, as long as there continued to be a degree of identification on the part of Muslims with the Ottoman authority against which the Revolution was turning, the exclusion of Jews makes clear the power-related-homogenising function that is intrinsic to the nation (nationalism).

Upon completion of the tasks at the First National Assembly on 30 March 1822, with the fifth resolution, the National Assembly,

> Having considered the existence of a number of dependent Administrative bodies, for instance Senates, the Areios Pagos, etc., harmful by way of being a great impediment to the advancement of the Public Economy and having considered the present circumstance conducive to their demise; they voted for the following. All the partial Administrative bodies of the Departments of the Territory shall henceforth be abolished, and the various peoples of Hellas [shall] directly depend upon national Governance.[8]

With this decision, a process of the elimination of local powers was launched, hence dramatically weakening the pre-revolutionary form of power of the *primates*. Despite the fact that the primates, as we developed in the previous

---

7 Dimoulis 2000, p. 57.
8 Mamoukas 1839, Vol. 2, p. 98.

chapter, had been transformed into links in the new bourgeois relations, in the subsumption of the peasants and artisans into commercial capital, all the same, the political influence that they continued to possess as local lords meant the fragmentation of political power and, correspondingly, of the territory, a fragmentation in local powers, which could potentially take on the form of a federal-type of state governance. I refer here to a (potential) federal-type of state governance and not simply to 'local authorities' or regionalism, as since its proclamation, the Revolution (and even since the initiation of many of its leading figures into the Friendly Society) aimed at the foundation of an 'Hellas', of a constitutional Greek state, embracing regions far beyond those of the former local or regional powers, as was, for example, the Peloponnesian Senate.[9]

In any event, the resolution of 30 March 1822 put into motion a process of the abolition of the primates as a distinct social group, a process which would be completed in the succeeding time period by way of the civil wars that took place during the Revolution. As we shall see below, in the course of two civil wars during the period 1823–24, the primates ceased to embody a relatively autonomous regional political authority and were integrated into various social and political roles: they either functioned as leading personalities of political trends and parties that were formed during the final years of the Revolution, and/or they assumed leadership positions in the framework of a unified Greek state.

The institutional framework and state structure that was approved in the First General National Assembly were ratified by the Second National Assembly that took place between 30 March 1823 and 18 April 1823 in Astros. With the resolutions of the Second National Assembly, freedom of the press was recognised, serfdom and slavery[10] were abolished, and torture was ban-

---

9   I will here disagree with Nikos Rotzokos, who considers the 'motherland' for the Pelo-
     ponnesian primates as exclusively focussed on the boundaries of the Peloponnese as an
     'historical-social unit': 'According to the perspective and logic of the primate, what is
     meant by the term "motherland" is a specific place, where the primates' authority is exer-
     cised, as well as its human potential. Thus, concern for one's country is nothing but the
     safeguarding of that place, of its people and of the relations of power that hold it together.
     The Peloponnese, with its provinces, institutions and hierarchies, in other words, not as a
     geographic unit but as an historical-social unit' (Rotzokos 1997, p. 134).

10   Prior to the Revolution, slavery was constitutionally valid even in Wallachia, which was
     under the administration of *Phanariotes*. In the *Legislative Constitution on the Orderliness
     and Duty of Each of the Judges and Officers of the Principate of Wallachia*, 'formulated by the
     ruler of all of Hungaro-Wallachia, Master Sir Ioannis Alexandros Ioannis Ypsilantis, Voe-
     vodas [Prince], in the year of the saviour 1780', we read: 'When gypsies [Roma] are sold,
     the relatives of the master of those gypsies should be preferred' (*Legislative Constitution
     ...*, p. 225).

ned.[11] Further, certain provisions in the constitution were amended to correspondingly strengthen the legislative (Parliamentary) body over that of the executive. In tandem, in the naturalisation of the 'foreign-born (Christians)' as Greeks, it was required that they had 'the Hellenic voice of the motherland'. The non-Greek-speaking 'foreign-born (Christians)' could be naturalised after five-year permanent residence in the Greek territory, while in order to be eligible to stand for election, 10 years will have had to have passed following their naturalisation. While the right of soil (*Ius soli*) by definition was not upheld for those coming from areas outside the Greek territory, language was then introduced as a criterion for Greekness. And again, there were still exceptions to those who provided significant 'services to the needs of the state', that is, foreign or non-Greek speaking, non-native combatants who had participated in the Revolution. The criterion of language introduces 'a clearer, "ethnic" designation of the Greek, which does not influence, nevertheless, the fundamental validity of ius soli: natives continued to attain the status of "Greek" irrespective of the language spoken'.[12]

The Second National Assembly generalised the general electoral right of adult men, while 'in practice every private residence was recognised as real estate'.[13]

The ratification of the constitutions of 1822 and 1823 (as well as that of 1827, see subsequent chapter) makes the bourgeois nature of the Revolution abundantly clear, something that subsequent (and contemporary) nationalist literature has difficulty recognising and refuses to accept for reasons that will be explored in Chapter 9. The constitutions and the processes of (electoral) representation of the people that were established by them clearly signify the formation of a new, *Greek capitalist* state in those territories of the Ottoman Empire where the Revolution prevailed.

2 Lords, Politicians and Military Corps: The Political Uplifting of the Masses

The Revolution of 1821 was declared by the noble strata of the areas that rebelled; that is, by the *primates* (in the Peloponnese, on the south-eastern mainland and the islands) and by the *warlords-armatoloi* (on the greater part

11   Stavropoulos 1979, Vol. I, pp. 410–13.
12   Dimoulis 2000, p. 58.
13   Hering 2004, p. 86.

of the mainland).[14] The liberal intellectuals (the 'politicians') who rushed into the regions under rebellion when the Revolution first broke out played an influential role in those areas of the mainland as well.

The Revolution in the Peloponnese, on the mainland and the islands was to a great extent successful during the first three years of the struggle on account of the enlistment of a large portion of the population of both rural areas and towns. On 23 September 1821, Tripolitsa, the capital of the Peloponnese, was occupied; it was followed by Arta on 13 November 1821 and Missolonghi on 23 May 1822. On 28–29 October 1822 the flagship of the Ottoman fleet was set ablaze off the island of Tenedos, Napflion was occupied on 3 December 1822, on 13 March 1823 the Greek government announced a naval blockade of all Ottoman coasts and of those Aegean Islands still 'under Turkish yoke', from Crete to Thessalonica; on 2 May 1823 the Ottomans surrendered the fortress at Kissamos to the commissioner of Crete appointed by the Greek government, Manolis Tombazis, and on 28 August 1824 the Greek fleet beat the Ottomans at the naval battle of Gerontas, near the island of Leros.

The successes of the Revolution and the formation of the new Greek state would have been inconceivable without the wide dissemination of nationalism and affiliated ideas of the 'Enlightenment' of the constitutional-republican (bourgeois) state amongst the masses in the rural areas and towns alike. As argued earlier, the birth of a nation – nationalism – signifies, above all, the politicisation of the masses for their integration, as citizens, into a state that will be 'theirs', as it will 'safeguard their rights'. Such political conscription is apparent in the substantial participation of the male population in the armed conflict.

Evidence of this participation can be drawn from the 'logistics' of the Revolution, i.e. from the budgets of revenues and expenditures of the revolutionary government, as the Revolution was not limited to military encounters: the formation of the first Greek administrations, the national assemblies and the ratification of the first constitutional documents – that is, everything associated with the building of a state – all entailed the corresponding economic

---

14   'Under the power ... of the military aristocracy in Mainland Greece, especially in the Western [mainland] part, strong communal self-government that would be found in the hands of the primates could not be developed, as opposed to in the Peloponnese, where the equivalent, with the armatoloi, rural field guards and civil guards, were salaried employees of the community with limited responsibilities and were appointed by the provincial lords' (Hering 2004, p. 68). The primates, even those in the Peloponnese, had diverging tendencies and it was not rare for disputes to break out amongst them.

management of 'public funds'. The collection of these funds was a condition for carrying out the armed struggle, while it rendered necessary the registration of arms-bearers brigaded into the revolutionary corps both on land and sea, whose life and action was financed (on salary) to a significant degree by public funds: by Greek government offices.

According to statistics presented at the Second National Assembly at Astros (30 March–18 April 1823) by the committee that was charged with the budget (further analysed below), on land:

> Hellas maintains three kinds of troops: the 1st Troops for laying siege to various strongholds ... = 18,300 men. 2nd Troops for domestic purposes = 6,050 men. 3rd Troops for military campaigns = 26,650 men. [Total] 51,000 men.[15]

To these fighters, those who served in the naval operations should be added, on whose numbers we do not have any consolidated data. In March 1822, the 'Maritime Ministry' was established, but even so, 'the communities on the islands had the actual management of ships, each separately'.[16] According to the number of ships,[17] but also to the maintenance of the 60 ships that the government

---

15   Andreades 1904, p. 8.
16   Papazoglou 1933, p. 292.
17   'The pre-Revolutionary Greek ships numbered about 700 and belonged to the communities of Hydra, Spetses, Psara and Kasos' (Papazoglou 1933, p. 291). Of these, at least 200 are recorded as having participated in the naval battle operations, whilst the rest continued their commercial activity. Athanasios N. Vernardakis reckons that in 1815, the 'Greek merchant marine numbered 615 ships, with a capacity of 153,580 tonnes, with 37,526 seamen and 5,878 cannons' (Vernardakis 1990, p. 211). See also Skarpetis 1934, p. 201. According to Thomas Gordon: 'Pouqueville asserts, that the marine of Hydra counted in 1813 120 vessels of the mean bulk of 375 tons, carrying 2400 pieces of cannon, and manned by 5400 sailors; in 1816 they had 40 ships of from 500 to 600 tons burden, built in their own yards. Spezzia possessed 60 vessels of the mean bulk of 325 tons, and 2700 seamen. Psarra had also 60 sail of greater burden, their mean bulk being 425 tons, but with smaller crews and fewer guns; their sailors amounted to 1800. Of these 10,000 mariners, one-third at least was recruited from other points of the Archipelago' (Gordon 1872, Vol. 1, p. 166). Roderick Beaton comments as follows on the national characters of these seamen and fleets in the decades before the Revolution: 'In precisely what sense these merchants and crews were "Greek" at this time is debatable: most of the inhabitants of Hydra and Spetses spoke Albanian as their mother tongue, but now began to add Greek endings to their family names. Since their own language had no written form, all their records were kept in Greek, which was also the language of their Church' (Beaton 2019, pp. 25–6).

was called on to bear the costs of in 1823,[18] a rough estimate of the seamen who took part in the Revolution could number 15,000–16,000.[19]

According to the assessment of the National Assembly and other available sources, the 66,000 combatants that participated in the Revolution is a considerable number for the period: it composed 18 percent of the male population of the first Greek territory (of a total population of 750,000 in 1828),[20] and 10.5 percent of the male population of the total area that revolted. There were also those who indirectly contributed to the Revolution, for instance those engaged in the production of gunpowder and other war material, the purveyance of food, clothing, etc., as well as in the maintenance and repair of ships.

The ways of the traditional local warlords (*armatoloi* and *klephts*) more or less characterised those of the armed corps (the 'army'), both politically and ideologically, and rested on practices such as violent 'hostage'-taking, slave trade and rapine. This harboured an element of the Ottoman 'tradition', which was to be expected to persist into the dawn of the new era. Kolokotrones, in his *Memoirs*, describes as follows the battle leading to the seizure of Tripolitsa:

> The Turks who had been left in Tripolitsa sallied out to skirmish for the purpose of preventing the Hellenes to aid the besiegers. The soldiers, however, whom I had dispatched on that service attacked the enemy from above and crushed them ... The greater part of the Turkish army ... procured six hundred mule loads of provisions and horses and infantrymen; the provisions were at the side ... The Hellenes gave themselves up to pillage, and so the Turks were saved because they did not go after them. I threatened the men with my sword, I tried flattery and cajolery to move them, but they did not heed me. And so the Turks were saved. In this battle the Turks numbered six thousand and the Hellenes one thousand, all Karytaina men.[21]

---

18   Andreades 1904, p. 8.

19   Ioannis Loukas arrives at the same conclusion: 'It appears that the total Greek naval forces came to 206 ships with 4,000 cannons and 15,000 men' (Loukas 1998, p. 62). As regards the pre-Revolutionary period, the author (Loukas 1998, p. 45) adopts the assessment of A.N. Vernardakis (see note 17 above), without referring to a source.

20   Hering 2004, p. 65. According to Athanasios N. Vernardakis, the population of Greece was 875,150 people in 1821, 741,950 in 1828, 752,077 in 1838 and 986,731 in 1848 (Vernardakis 1990, p. 2). N.I. Svoronos estimates differently: 938,765 inhabitants in 1821, 753,400 in 1828, 823,773 in 1839 (Svoronos 1934, p. 224).

21   Kolokotrones 2013, p. 169, corrected according to Greek original. Soldiers took the plunder as private property, and sold a portion of it. Andreades (1904, p. 10) notes, regarding this: 'One of the more honest men of the struggle, D. Ypsilantis, tried to implement as a rule that

Regarding the captives and slaves, Kolokotrones writes:

> The family of Sechnetzi Bey remained with me, twenty-four people in all;
> Giatrakos took Kiamil Bey, and Kehayas was also taken prisoner, and with
> the harems taken by Petro Bey ... After ten days had elapsed all the Hel-
> lenes carried off their spoils and went to their different districts with their
> slaves, both male and female. In those ten days which had been granted
> to the Hellenes to secure their spoil we had a council which Ypsilandis,
> Petro Bey and other, being the leaders, attended.[22]

Nevertheless, this traditional warlord element was now gripped by nationalism and the pressing need to be subsumed under a constitutional state that
would represent the nation. What is distinctive is that the soldiery from the
lower strata were the principal proponents of the constitutional institutions
and representative assemblies and, further, were the ones who strived for the
formation of a *national representational body* and a *unified government* for the
entire liberated territory, something which the primates of the Peloponnese did
not want at the time that the Revolution began, and attempted to stave off: 'A
national parliament or a central government was not a part of their plan'.[23]

   With the question of 'a national parliament' unresolved, the primates initially clashed with Demetrios Ypsilantis, brother of Alexandros, who had arrived in the Peloponnese in June 1821. When the confrontation became known,
the armed corps rose up against the primates[24] and, in fact, in October 1821, the

---

a portion of the spoils be allocated to the public purse. He earned nothing but laughter
and ridicule'. And Gunnar Hering writes: 'Kolokotrones displayed such zeal for getting rich
during the war that they gave him the nickname Captain Booty' (Hering 2004, p. 107).

22   Kolokotrones 2013, pp. 171, 173, corrected according to Greek original. On 20 March 1822,
Lykourgos Logothetis, who was tasked with the defence of Chios, sent a missive addressed
'To the 2nd Assembly of Hellenes' in which he states, amongst other things: 'We set out on
the eighth of the present March against the tyrants of Chios ... we defended the town and
with our first assault we shoved the entire enemy into the fortress, we are holding them
neatly secured and hope of course to crush them ... And yet the worst of all. Ch. Ant-
onios Vournias, a Chian, taking with him some of similar convictions, declared himself
Commander-in-Chief of Chios ... goes round and round, plundering, looting and strip-
ping everything bare, and snatches at whatever he finds without reflecting on whether it
is a Christian or Turk he has seized ... We beseech you however with your deep intellect
to assess our circumstances hither and his actions and *write to him with resolution to settle
down*' (*Chiakon Archeion* [*Chian Archives*] 1924, pp. 44–5; emphasis added).

23   Hering 2004, p. 76.

24   'That was the pretext for the riots, during which the militiamen and people of the lower
strata, mostly peasants, vented their anger against the lords' (Hering 2004, p. 76).

former did not hesitate to threaten the latter with annihilation, believing that the primates challenged the prospect of a representational constitution.[25] In December 1821, before the First National Assembly of Epidaurus, whose projects had begun on 20 December 1821 (see above), armed combatants once again threatened to execute the primates because they thought that 'they do not want to hold an Assembly'. Writes Kolokotrones:

> We were quite agreed in making a government, but we quarrelled about the place where it should be held. The soldiers who were gathered there made a petition to me asking for my consent to their killing all the primates. Someone had provoked them by spreading the rumour that the primates thought that it was not necessary to hold an assembly, and instead they deluded the people. At noon I went and argued with them. 'What are you doing now', I asked. 'Take your oaths ... and then you can go to a place where you can begin the assembly' ... The People had always intended to kill the primates and took offence at the slightest prompting. The politicians went to Epidaurus and began to frame their laws and we, the military, departed for Corinth.[26]

Furthermore, as immediately following the Revolution the Greek government proclaimed the Ottoman lands as 'national lands', the intervention of the masses and combatants during the Second National Assembly nullified any prospect of the lands being sold, the goal being that the regime preserve the possession of the land for the peasants-small producers themselves (and the correlative relations of family agriculture whose products would be destined for either the local market or the buyers-up). In this way, as Professor Andreas Andreades details, the prospect of forming extensive land ownership in the liberated regions was thwarted, while at the same time the 'collateral' for the contract of a foreign loan was secured on the part of the government:

> The sale of public lands could potentially yield much, as the fallen Turks had left infinite cultivable and substantial urban tracts of land in our hands. But the assemblies rightly aimed for what would be one of the main resources of the future and as the most secure collateral for a foreign loan, they prohibited from the outset the sale of national lands and

---

25   In October 1821, 'the rumour was spread amongst the troops that the lords, and even more so the government, wanted to secretly assassinate all of the prominent military personnel so as to later subjugate the insurrectionists' (Hering 2004, p. 77).

26   Kolokotrones 2013, p. 175, corrected according to Greek original.

rendered most difficult the sale of perishable estates ... The lands would be sold for much lower than their intrinsic value; they would be bought solely by those who had some funds at their disposal, that is, by foreigners, expatriate Hellenes and primates. In that way the state would collect little, and a new caste of timariots would be formed ... The danger of such a timar system of lords replacing aghas had been denounced by the 'camp of the common folk' at the Assembly of Astros, which is why they had prohibited the sale of national lands.[27]

The masses, and in particular those who were armed, having acceded to nationalism (the national idea), were also set up as a quasi-political force that would safeguard and support the radical-liberal institutional framework of the revolutionary state. From their ranks there arose new political leaders, beyond the primates, *armatoloi* and intellectuals, and especially in the military, where a new leadership emerged from the armed brigades of the Revolution, which in many cases served to undermine the warlords that had sprung from the armed brigands, the *armatoloi*.

The leaders of the armatoloi had had similar experiences with the rulers of the Peloponnese: the war provided many obscure persons the opportunity to distinguish themselves, and one new corps of warlords that had ascended rapidly did not want to submit to the old factions of armatoloi. In the person of the national hero of the Greeks Makriyannis (1797–1864) we meet a representative characteristic of this new group of officers, who had become great and exacting only on account of the war ... As regards the precipitous advancement we shall allude as an example only to the fact that, within approximately one year, a total of 260 [210, J.M.] militiamen were promoted to high-ranking officers and specifically 27 became generals, 11 major generals, 56 chiliarchoi [commanders of battalions of 1000 men], 34 lieutenant commanders of chiliarchias, 50 brigadier generals, 32 ekatontarchoi [commanders of battalions of 100 men].[28]

---

27   Andreades 1925, pp. 8, 37; see also Maurer 1976, pp. 345 ff.
28   Hering 2004, pp. 78–9. Georgios Psyllas (1794–1878) writes in his memoirs of his conversations with Nikitas, a fighter of 1821: 'And at one point he [Nikitas] told me that the Governor should endow the warlords with vast expanses of national land ... "as I am no longer that Nikitas of the first years of the Revolution, but now Général Nikitas, whom distinguished foreigners visit, and I must have an open residence and servants and all the rest in accordance with my rank"' (Psyllas 1974, p. 61).

Where the 'traditional' 'ways of the warlord' – of the *armatoloi* and *klephts* – fit neatly into the new era of nationalism and civil rights was in the practices of the eradication of the 'Other': in other words, any person who cannot be integrated into the nation must be necessarily expelled from the national dominion and erased from national memory by the new 'homogeneous' society that claims a 'national historical destiny'. Characteristic of this was the seizure of Tripolitsa, where all non-Christians, Muslims and Jews were indiscriminately slaughtered – men, women and children alike. Kolokotrones describes the massacre of occupied Tripolitsa as follows:

> The Hellenic contingent which entered it, cut down and were slaying men, women and children from Friday until Sunday. Thirty-two thousand were reported to have been slain, one hour around Tripolitsa. One Hydriot killed ninety. About a hundred Hellenes were killed. But the end came: a proclamation was issued that the slaughter must cease ... My horse from the walls to the palace never touched the earth.[29]

The scenario at Tripolitsa may be considered as the most bloody, yet it is by no means the only such event. In nearly every seizure of a town or capturing of a ship, the fortune of the Ottomans was the same: the indiscriminate slaughter of all men, women and children. As Nikos Poulantzas points out apropos to the *national* capitalist state:

> The capitalist State marks out the frontiers when it constitutes what is within (the people-nation) by homogenizing the before and the after of the content of this enclosure. National unity or the modern unity thereby becomes *historicity of a territory and territorialization of a history* – in short, a territorial national tradition concretized in the nation-State; the

---

29   Kolokotrones 2013, pp. 170–1, corrected according to Greek original. Thomas Gordon decries the slaughter with the following words: 'A scene ensued of the most horrible description: The conquerors, mad with vindictive rage spared neither age nor sex – the streets and houses were inundated with blood and obstructed with heaps of dead bodies. Some Mohammedans fought bravely, and sold their lives dear, but the far larger proportion was slaughtered without resistance ... Flames blazing out from the palace and many houses, lighted up a night spent in rapine and carnage, and the return of day brought with it no remission ... [T]heir insatiable cruelty knew no bounds and seemed to inspire them with a superhuman energy for evil, which set lassitude at defiance. Every corner was ransacked to discover new victims and the unhappy Jewish population (even more than the Turks, objects of financial hatred) expired amidst torments which we dare not describe' (Gordon 1872, Vol. 1, pp. 244–5). See also Pouqueville 1824, pp. 279–80, 291.

markings of a territory become indicators of history that are written into the State … Genocide is the elimination of what become 'foreign bodies' of the national history and territory: it expels them beyond space and time.[30]

The creation of the Greek state politicised the popular masses, bolstered their bargaining position with the former lords – along with the new role they attained in the framework of the emerging capitalist modern Greek state – and provided them with 'power' over the lives and the conditions of existence of the 'enemy' and 'foreigners': 'May no Turk stay in the Morea, nor in the entire world', according to the folk song of the period![31]

3   Political Trends and Civil Wars

Of the social forces that were assimilated into the Revolution, and in relation to the institutional-state order that was formed, three political currents emerged:

The 'federalist current', as we have seen, was articulated mainly by the primates of the Peloponnese, who, at the outset of the armed conflict, formed the Peloponnesian Senate and were initially against the convening of a unified national parliament. The primates, serving as important links in the economic networks of the region, exerted influence over extensive parts of the population in the Peloponnese. So as not to jeopardise this influence, but also in order to ease tensions with the armed bands, they took a stand in favour of democratic institutions from the beginning with the founding of the Senate, and were first and foremost in favour of universal suffrage for men for the annual election of mandates,[32] who would subsequently elect the 'general ephors', those responsible for the governance of each province. 'The General ephors shall elect from amongst the members of their ephorate the most worthy [man], and to send him as a member of the Senate of the Peloponnese'.[33] This proposal, which was

---

30   Poulantzas 1980, pp. 114–15.

31   Roderick Beaton writes on this issue: 'By the end of 1821, the countryside throughout the Peloponnese and the southern part of Roumeli had been subjected to what today would be termed "ethnic cleansing"' (Beaton 2019, p. 82).

32   'May the people of each province, both of the villages and of town elect the most worthy of its members' (Mamoukas 1839, Vol. I, p. 12).

33   Mamoukas 1839, Vol. I, p. 13. 'The constitutions imposed [by the primates, J.M.] were amongst the most liberal on a European level. Spyridon Trikoupis, historian of the war of independence … rightly denies that the lords wanted to introduce an oligarchic system of governance' (Hering 2004, p. 85).

ultimately adopted, was countered by Demetrios Ypsilantis, 'dispatched by the General Commissioner of the Authority', who proposed the election of the ephors solely 'from [amongst] the primates of each town'.[34]

The emergence of the armed corps as a new, determinative pole of power forced the primates to concede to the prospect of a 'national parliament' and their integration into the unified administration of the liberated areas. At the same time, however, they sought to preserve increased autonomy from the central government, as well as from the governing bodies and decisions coming from the central authority,[35] in the tradition of the pre-revolutionary autonomy that had been enjoyed in the Peloponnese.[36]

From this point of view, one of a certain regionalism, the 'federalist current' could be considered to constitute a conservative tendency within the Revolution. A figure central to this current was Petrobey Mavromichalis.

With the strength of the armed forces behind them, two other political currents emerged that were beyond the conservative-federalist one: schematically speaking, they could be described as the *centralist-conservative* trend, which was under Theodoros Koloktrones, and the *centralist-liberal* one, under Alexandros Mavrokordatos. 'The united front against Turkish rule, against the Moslem state, had until then incorporated all social strata of the Christians ... Thus to the extent that the common enemy was driven out, fresh conflicts arose'.[37]

The way in which the war had been conducted favoured 'centralist' wings, that is, those that sought the unification of the state apparatuses, military planning and governmental power.

Regarding the centralist-conservative current: Kolokotrones attained considerable political might as leader of the 'army' of the Peloponnese, especially following the seizure of Tripolitsa on 23 September 1821. He was in alliance with Demetrios Ypsilantis, who had clashed with the primates precisely upon the issue of central government and a united parliament (see the previous section of the present chapter), yet also in relation to a restriction of the electoral body to the primates (sought by Ypsilantis). Also, Ypsilantis 'wanted in fact to impose pre-emptive censorship of the Press in all the liberated regions'.[38]

---

34 Mamoukas 1839, Vol. I, p. 9.
35 See Paparrigopoulos 1971, Vol. 15, pp. 51ff.
36 'Constantinople conceded not only to the Maniates, but to the entire Morea, a kind of pan-Peloponnesian autonomy with an articulated self-government of the provinces and communities' (Hering 2004, p. 66). 'When the Peloponnese was under Frankish rule, it acquired its own historical identity. Thenceforth, its historical course has been largely self-contained' (Sakellariou 1978, p. 39).
37 Hering 2004, pp. 72–3.
38 Hering 2004, p. 85.

The political aims of this new political current were thus not restricted to the necessity of unifying political power. For the centralisation of power, this wing considered requisite the restriction of liberal institutions and the bourgeois representational system introduced by the Revolution. 'Kanellos Deligiannis mentions that at the assembly of Kaltezes [when the Peloponnesian Senate was formed, J.M.], Kolokotrones had petitioned for a 'governo militare'; Deligiannis claims that it was then that he heard that phrase for the first time'.[39]

Despite this, by the end of 1821 the primates in the Peloponnese had managed to maintain primacy over Kolokotrones. The Peloponnesian Senate that convened in Argos on 27 December 1821 elected mostly primates as representatives to the First National Assembly, whereby the by-laws of the Senate stipulated 'the primacy of political leadership over military governance, and the humiliated Ypsilantis had to settle for the presidency of that governing body'.[40]

Regarding the centralist-liberal current: in contrast to the Peloponnese, where the military leadership under Kolokotrones succeeded in attaining political power on the strength of the armed forces, the armed corps on the mainland were subsumed under various warlords, with oft-conflicting aspirations and practices. This allowed political leaders Alexandros Mavrokordatos and Theodoros Negris, both former *Phanariotes*, to prevail over the dissenting forces of the regions,[41] and to unify, by November of 1821, the two regional governments, with parallel constitutions. 'And both Constitutions mention a future National Parliament and left no doubt as to the subordination of military officers to the elected political body'.[42]

At the First National Assembly of Epidaurus, the primates dominated the representation of the Peloponnese, though they were only 10 of the 59 representatives; they constituted, that is, a minority against the 27 representatives from the eastern mainland and 13 from the islands of Hydra, Spetses and Psara (the remainder being eight from the western mainland, one from the island of Kasos). Alexandros Mavrokordatos was elected president of the executive body, while Theodoros Negris was appointed as 'Secretary-General of the Dominion', 'Minister of Foreign Affairs' and 'President of the Board of Ministers'. Demetrios Ypsilantis was elected president of the parliamentary body, and

---

39   Hering 2004, p. 72.
40   Hering 2004, p. 82.
41   'The caste of the armatoloi in Mainland Greece could not keep its force with such continued intensity, and required the political leadership and co-ordination of two politicians: Alexandros Mavrokordatos in the west, and Theodoros Negris in the east ... [who] endeavoured ... into a regional parliament, to integrate the clergy, military officers, political primates and the lettered class' (Hering 2004, p. 80).
42   Hering 2004, p. 81.

Sotirios Haralambis, member of the Peloponnesian Senate and amongst the most notable of the primates of the Peloponnese, as vice president. From these two bodies, the *Dikastikon* (the Judiciary) was established as an independent body.

Following the First National Assembly, tensions escalated between the politicians (of the government and executive body) and the military corps of the Peloponnese under 'Commander-in-Chief' Kolokotrones, which to a great extent pertained to the institutionalised authority of the government to manage military operations.

At the Second National Assembly (29 March–18 April 1823) 'two political camps that convened in different settings'[43] were formed. Petrobey Mavromichalis was elected president of the executive body and Alexandros Mavrokordatos as general secretary, whilst Ioannis Orlandos, of the liberal political faction, was elected president of the parliamentary body. The decisions of the National Assembly even further enhanced the powers of the central government. Thus, amongst other things, it was decided that officials from other provinces be appointed as the administrative officials of the provinces so as to avert the potential for influence of local powers and interests. In tandem, the position of 'Commander-in-Chief', which was held by Kolokotrones, was rendered obsolete. 'The modern, liberal elite managed to strengthen the Parliamentary body with respect to the Executive and to broaden the catalogue of human rights in the new constitution. The Peloponnesian warlords pushed for a counter-assembly in Silimna on 18 May 1823'.[44]

Kolokotrones refused to hand the fortress of Nafplion over to the government, arguing that it should remain in the hands of the Peloponnesians. In November 1823, when the Parliament unseated two members of the executive body for unlawful activity, Panos Kolokotrones attempted, at the behest of his father Theodoros, to manoeuvre a sort of coup d'état in the Parliamentary body, from which 23 members escaped to Kranidi and established a new executive body, with Hydriote Georgios Kountouriotes as president, who had the support not only of the islands but of politician and warlord Ioannis Kolettis, from Mainland Greece (Roumeli). The first civil war of the Revolution thence broke out, and for a period of time two governments existed in tandem: one was in Tripolitsa, the president of which was Petrobey Mavromichalis, and the other was in Kranidi, under Georgios Kountouriotes. The primates of the Peloponnese, along with the warlords, were split between the two factions.[45] When

---

43   Hering 2004, p. 87.
44   Hering 2004, p. 90.
45   See Hering 2004, pp. 95–7.

on 7 April 1824 Kountouriotes seized Tripolitsa, Theodoros Koloktrones commanded his son, Panos, to surrender Napflion, thereby securing amnesty for himself and his followers at the end of the civil war.

Nevertheless, in the immediate aftermath of the first civil war, the Peloponnesian primates realised that they had in no way benefitted from the changed situation. The presence of the primates had been restricted in the newly-formed government, while in October of 1824 troops from Roumeli were sent to the Peloponnese to safeguard the collecting of taxes that had been delayed. The primates then allied with Kolokotrones, and the second civil war broke out. The liberal wing, which controlled the government, managed to prevail once more, thanks to the intervention of the warlords from the mainland and support from the islands.

> But the government was stronger than ever ... Around the end of November and the beginning of December in the custody of Ioannis Kolettis, the government sent the strongest infantry force in Greece, that is, the Roumeli battalions under Karatasos, Gouras, Karaiskakis and Tzavellas ... So that is how the eastern Peloponnese was subdued; other Roumeli battalions ascended from Vostitsa to Kalavryta and from there went down into Messenia, dispersing and suppressing the insurrectionists in the western Peloponnese.[46]

The second civil war concluded in December of 1824 with the defeat of the Peloponnesians. Alexandros Mavrokordatos was elected as secretary of the executive body, while Kolokotrones surrendered to the government and was imprisoned on Hydra.

> We went to Tripolitsa; there was a committee there composed of Skourtes, G. Mavromates, and K. Zapheiropoulos, and they gave me to understand upon their oaths that I could go there safely ... I trusted them, and went to Nauplia. There I saw that in two or three days they had driven away all my men, and had left me alone, in arresto [under arrest], until they got hold of the others. They embarked us on the sloop Gorgo, Skourtes was also there and they took us to Hydra ... We remained there four months. Twenty days after we were seized, Ibrahim came into the Peloponnesus.[47]

---

46   Paparrigopoulos 1971, Vol. 15, pp. 137–8.
47   Kolokotrones 2013, p. 203, corrected according to Greek original.

The defeat of the alliance of the Peloponnesian primates and the conservative centralist wing of Kolokotrones in the second civil war also meant the end
of the autonomous political role of the (former) primates in modern Greek history, as mentioned in the previous section. The regionalist-federalist rationale
that the primates represented had been obliterated.[48] At the beginning of 1825,
Kolokotrones was granted amnesty so as to be available for the strengthening
of the Revolution against the invasion of the Peloponnese by Egyptian forces
under Ibrahim pasha, but his counsel was not enough to change the scenario.
I shall deal with those issues in the upcoming chapter.

4 Regarding Class Antagonisms within the Revolutionary Forces

The Revolution consolidated an alliance on a social level of the capitalist class
(merchants, shipowners, large-scale buyers-ups and manufacturers, tax tenants on a broader regional or national level), of liberal intellectuals, of the
middle strata that had been integrated into the new bourgeois relations under
development (amongst whom were both short- and middle-range buyers-ups
and other intermediaries and local political mediators-primates), of peasants,
of the proletarian classes (seamen, etc.) and other poor strata of the period, all
under the hegemony of the bourgeois nationalist strategy and the liberal ideas
of the Enlightenment.

Regarding these ideas, i.e. the ideological and political effectiveness of the
Enlightenment, Eric Hobsbawm aptly points out the following:

> In theory its object was to set all human beings free. All progressive,
> rationalist and humanist ideologies are implicit in it, and indeed came
> out of it. Yet in practice the leaders of the emancipation for which the
> enlightenment called were likely to be the middle ranks of society, the

---

48   The regional-federalist logic to which I refer does not have to do with 'localism' per
      se, more specifically with the traditions of communal organisation that were affiliated
      with the 'ancien régime', and which had survived for decades only as marginal social
      forms in the newly-formed state (see section 7.4, Chapter 7). It concerned tactics that
      aimed at the preservation of the regional powers and the corresponding *federal* insti-
      tutions of representation *within the new state*, in the way the same strategy was articu-
      lated in the wake of the proclamation of the Revolution in the Peloponnesian Senate,
      Areios Pagos, etc. As Gunnar Hering remarks, '[I]n the second civil war the idea of a
      centralist state prevailed over its initially distinct federal structure in the formation *of
      a Greek collective*' (Hering 2004, p. 98, emphasis added). See also note 9 in the present
      Chapter.

new, rational men of ability and merit rather than birth, and the social order which would emerge from their activities would be a 'bourgeois' and capitalist one.[49]

After Napoleon's defeat in 1815 and the restoration of the House of Bourbon in France, Greece-in-formation was in fact the only revolutionary centre in Europe, attracting radical activists and fighters not only from Europe, but from the Americas and elsewhere. According to statistics cited by Anna Karakatsouli,[50] the number of 'Philhellenes' that fought in the Revolution (not including those soldiers of the Great Powers who had meddled in the hostilities) fluctuated around 1,200, more than one third of whom were native German speakers.[51] 'Philhellenes' are also described as all those who supported the Greek Revolution in foreign countries by organising committees of solidarity with the 'Greek cause', raising and sending funds to the revolutionary Greek government and contributing articles or works of art.[52]

The 'class alliance' described above was articulated through state-related forms that were created by the Revolution (the government, assemblies, electoral procedures, etc.) by way of armed bands, conspiratorial societies and the political parties that emerged towards the end of the armed conflict. Whilst the struggle between the distinct class interests within this social alliance was expressed in manifold ways, all the same, it consistently manifested as having been mediated through the 'homogenising' function of nationalism, which dominated as much in the political factions as in the politico-military formations on a local level (in the Peloponnese, on the mainland and the islands).

Be that as it may, what actually lay veiled behind class conflicts would often surface, even prior to the Revolution.[53]

---

49   Hobsbawm 1996, p. 22.
50   Karakatsouli 2016, p. 15.
51   According to the entry in the Greek Wikipedia for the term 'Philhellene', 'the recorded number of philhellenes reached 940', out of which during the Revolution 313 were either killed or died.
52   Characteristic is the case of Percy Bysshe Shelley, who on 1 November 1821 penned the poem 'Hellas', in which we read: 'I hear! I hear! ... The crash as of an empire falling'. Shelley dedicated the poem 'To His Excellency Prince Alexander Mavrocordato late secretary for foreign affairs to the Hospodar of Wallachia the drama of Hellas is inscribed as an imperfect token of the admiration, sympathy, and friendship of the author' (Shelley 1874, p. 174).
53   'On Hydra ... clashes were brewing between shipowners and merchants on the one hand, and the unemployed, the majority of whom were seamen, due to the economic recession and the fall of Napoleon, on the other; these conflicts forced a rapid and active intervention in the war of independence' (Hering 2004, pp. 81–2).

The defeat of the 'federal trend' (that of the primates of the Peloponnese, a trend that was expressed principally in the Peloponnesian Senate) has already been examined, a defeat which had originated in the opposition of the masses (peasants, seamen, etc.) to the primates and other toparchs. This opposition of a class nature was not unique, however:

> Another example is the distinction between high-ranking commanding military officers on the one hand, and middle- and lower-ranking military officers on the other. At Missolonghi, the latter founded the Brotherhood of Philodikaion [Advocates of Justice] out of discontent with the arbitrary dealings and abuse of power by the higher-ranking officers; belonging to this circle was [Johann Jakob] Meyer, publisher of the *Hellenic Chronicles*:[54] ... [The] charter of the Brotherhood from 26 November 1825 ... foresaw that amongst the members there would be the principles of solidarity and equality without any distinction of degree; above such principles there would be only laws ... The brotherhood did not have the consciousness of a secret society; on the contrary, it wished to publicly propagate its ideals. Before formally accepting the candidate, they would subject him to a three-day initiation. The Brotherhood in Missolonghi until November of 1825 numbered 2000 in members. Its activity came to a halt with the negative turn of the war.[55]

---

54   Johann Jakob Meyer (1798–1826) was a Swiss radical who joined the combatants of the Greek Revolution in March of 1822, having already graduated as a pharmacist and having received instruction in certain subjects as a student of medicine in Switzerland. He served as a doctor during the siege of Patras, learned the Greek language and settled in Missolonghi where, with money he had secured initially from his Greek wife's family, and subsequently from Lord Byron and (following the latter's death on 7 April 1824) from Alexandros Mavrokordatos, published the *Greek Chronicles*, the most radical newspaper of the Revolution, between 1 January 1824 and 20 February 1826 (a total of 226 issues). Meyer, his wife Altani Inglezou and their one-year-old son were killed during their escape from Missolonghi, 10–11 April 1826. The *Greek Chronicles* were later reprinted, in Meyer 1858.

55   Hering 2004, p. 95. As Dinos Konomos writes, in Napflion secret societies affiliated with the Carbonari were active, in which just as many foreign radicals ('Philhellenes') participated as Greeks did. On 1 May 1825, the masonic-revolutionary secret society bearing the appellation 'The Philolaos Society' [Society of the Friends of the People], led by Ioannis Kolettis, with leading members Andreas Metaxas, Ghikas Karakatzanis, Panagiotis Dimitrakopoulos, Ioannis Theotokis, Adam Doukas and Theodoros Vallianos, was founded in Napflion, and later constituted the model for the so-called French Party. In the founding text of the society we read: 'Looking down into the abyss of loss, into which the Hellenic nation has managed to be swept, from the senseless rage of factions and the ghastly abuses ... I swear on the most dulcet name of beloved Hellas to contribute and collude with all my might towards the eradication of every self-serving, sordid, self-injurious

It could be argued that the democratic radicalism of the Assemblies (that was formulated in the language of the constitutions of the period), along with that of the (secret) societies, expressed to a great extent the class dynamics of the masses, who, in considering the outcome of the two civil wars,[56] created at the same time various reclassifications on a social level. As with what occurred on the occasions of other bourgeois-national revolutions, such popular dynamics were hegemonised following (and quashed by) the institutional-state formation of the new authority. In the circumstance that took shape after the first civil war:

> Following the expulsion or arrest of the major Peloponnesian lords, the lower strata saw the opportunity to control the system of tax collecting by themselves. Amongst the new groups of interests and views was the Society of the Brotherhood, a secret association that had been formed in Tripolitsa, and to which mostly craftsmen and, likely, professionals of the towns in the main belonged ... [T]he Executive [body] neutralised the coup d'état attempt, relocating peasants from the surrounding villages into the town.[57]

Regardless of the fact that at the Assemblies and in the societies no consciousness whatsoever had been formed around class interests and differences, their activity served to embody *tendencies* that *challenged the political and state-related form of existence of the capitalism of the era*: to begin with, the absolutist, or 'constitutionally limited' state, but the aristocracy of wealth and powers of the nobility as well. As Georgios Zoitopoulos (Zioutos) observes:

> But the working class is not yet mature enough to found, in this era, a political organisation (party), which will be the instrument of this historical turning point. The revolutionary elements of the period rally around secret, conspiratorial societies, which act in accordance with the organisational and political traditions of Freemasonry, of companionage, of the Carbornari, Jacobinism and other secret (closed) political organisations that are formed in France, in Germany, in Bohemia etc., especially dur-

---

system in Hellas, and towards the support of the true prosperity and political existence of the Hellenic nation' (Konomos 1973, pp. 46 ff.).

56   On the significance of the civil wars, see also Pizanias 2011.

57   Hering 2004, p. 95.

ing the 18th c. and the beginning of the 19th c. ... The first quarter of the 19th c. is characterised in particular by a plethora of secret, conspiratorial organisations. We know that in the framework of these organisations our 'Friendly Society' also belongs.[58]

The radical republicanism of the pre-industrial capitalist period led to a *convergence*, according to Zioutos, of the dynamics that the working class had developed through class conflict and national liberation movements:

> With the foreign invasion in France, the restoration of the Bourbons, who try to turn back to the ancien régime, is realised. Each and every progressive action is persecuted. Political rivals take refuge in secret, conspiratorial societies. Nevertheless, despite the backlash, national liberation movements break out in various countries: Spain (1820), Italy, Greece (1821), Russia (December 1825). The progressive forces are not quashed and in 1830 an expansive revolutionary movement begins, one that embraces many countries. In July of 1830 a republican insurgency breaks out, with the full participation of the masses and operative action on the part of the workers ... During the period of 1810–1816 uprisings take place accompanied by the destruction of machinery and factories in all the industrial centres of England ... In order to quell them, the English capitalist class passed a new law in 1812 that imposed the death penalty on workers who destroyed machinery. With this barbaric law 18 workers were tried and executed in 1813. The voice of Byron was heard in the House of Lords against this law, as he passionately defended the rights, the right to life, of the workers. And in 1816 Byron composed a song for the 'Luddites'.[59]

---

58 Zioutos 2009, pp. 75–6.
59 Zioutos 2009, p. 67. The poem is contained within an epistle sent by Lord Byron to Thomas Moore on 14 December 1816: *Song for the Luddites.*
    I. As the Liberty lads o'er the sea / Bought their freedom, and cheaply, with blood, / So we, boys, we / Will die fighting, or live free, / And down with all kings but King Ludd!
    II. When the web that we weave is complete, / And the shuttle exchanged for the sword, / We will fling the winding sheet / O'er the despot at our feet, / And dye it deep in the gore he has pour'd.
    III. Though black as his heart its hue, / Since his veins are corrupted to mud, / Yet this is the dew / Which the tree shall renew / Of Liberty, planted by Ludd!

The political enlistment of Lord Byron, to which Zioutos refers, is distinctive: he expressed support for the Luddites and endorsed the Greek Revolution, and was conscripted into the latter in July of 1823.[60]

With the entry of the Egyptian troops of Ibrahim Pasha into the liberated Greek territory in February of 1825, the military relation of forces in the war rapidly deteriorated for the Revolution, a fact that would play a catalytic role in the political and social alliances within it, as we shall see in the subsequent chapter.

---

60   Before joining the Greek Revolution, Byron travelled to Italy and in 1819 wrote the poem *The Prophecy of Dante*, in which he advocates the 'political liberation' of Italy. According to Roderick Beaton, 'although he seems not yet to have realised the significance of his discovery, Byron had stumbled into one of the most potent ideologies that would come to dominate the next two centuries in Europe: nationalism' (Beaton 2013, p. 72). Once in Missolonghi, Greece, he told his friend Pietro Gamba in January 1824: '[T]hose principles which are now in action in Greece will gradually produce their effect, both here and in other countries ... I am not ... come here in search of adventures, but to assist in the regeneration of a nation' (cited in Beaton 2013, p. 273).

CHAPTER 6

The Ebb of the Revolution, the Intervention of the 'Great Powers' and the End of Constitutional Republicanism (1825–1833)

1   The Unfavourable Turn in the War

The military relations of power between the revolutionary Greek state and the Ottoman Empire took a turn at the beginning of 1825, when Ibrahim Pasha, son of Muhammad Ali, the Albanian-tongued Ottoman 'despot' of Egypt and the Sudan, launched a campaign with a large naval squadron from which 17,000 troops alighted to attack the Peloponnese in order to assist Ottoman forces in the crackdown of the Revolution. As early as May of 1824, Ottoman troops had landed in Crete and suppressed the Revolution there, while in June 1824 the Egyptian army devastated the islands of Kasos and Psara, and in August of the same year it occupied the island of Kos. The Revolution, however, entered a truly difficult phase when the Egyptian army disembarked at Methone (Modon) in February–March 1825 and overcame Greek troops in the area of Neokastro, on the island of Sfakteria and at Palaiokastro in April 1825.

Despite a handful of victories of the Greek troops under Georgios Karaiskakis, Ioannis Makriyannis and Demetrios Ypsilantis, the Ottoman forces, in which the army of Ibrahim Pasha factored, had, by the end of 1826, seized Messenia, Tripolitsa, Argos, Monemvasia and Ileia. In April 1826 Missolonghi was taken as well, after a siege lasting nearly a year, from 15 April 1825 to 10 April 1826.

If the revolutionary Greek state managed to be salvaged notwithstanding the adverse military alliances that had been forged, it was because of the new international-political relations that were taking shape during that period, in large part due to the impact that the theretofore course of the Revolution had had on the adversarial relations amongst the 'Great Powers'. Even so, the military defeats and the downswing in the course of the Revolution, as well as the resolution of the 'Greek question' within those very relations between the Powers, contributed to the eventual domination during that period of an absolutist version of a state. This absolutist state was established in 1828 and lasted, with just a small pause, until 1843, its initial form being a Bonapartist regime (1828–31), and then subsequently an absolute monarchy (1833–43).

2   International-Political Relations and Diplomatic Recognition of
        the Greek State

2.1   *The 'Congress of Verona', a Harbinger of Changes in the Foreign*
        Policy of the Great Powers

From the moment of the outbreak of the Revolution, Greek authorities sought
recognition of their sovereignty as an independent state entity from the 'international community' (see Chapter 5, note 4). They distributed translations of
the proclamations that were published by the Assemblies to the foreign diplomatic missions and the foreign press, petitioning for the recognition of Greece
as an independent state and for assistance from the Powers for its struggle.[1] The
Messenian Senate, an early local administration before the formation of the
Peloponnesian Senate, was the first to make an appeal, in 24 March 1821, solicit-
ing succour from the USA, Britain and Russia.[2] All the same, the Great Powers,
as part of the Holy Alliance – the pact formed in 1815, after the Second Treaty
of Paris that followed the final defeat of Napoleon – remained hostile towards
the Revolution. Only Russia held a slightly different position, in her 'traditional'
role as 'protector of the Orthodox' (and not, naturally, of revolutions): in July
of 1821, Russia severed diplomatic ties with the Ottoman Empire, a move occasioned by the hanging of the Ecumenical Patriarch Gregory v, who was held
responsible for not having prevented the insurgency of his 'flock', although he
had, of course, condemned the Revolution and had excommunicated its leaders.

When the Congress of Verona convened (October–December 1822) with del-
egates from the states of the Holy Alliance,[3] the revolutionary Greek government addressed the Congress with a declaration and dispatched a delegation
to deliver it to congress participants. *Inter alia*, the following was declared:

> From the onset of the war until now, Hellas twice raised her voice through
> her lawful attendants, soliciting succour and the understanding of the
> Christian Kings of Europe, or, finally demanding fulfilment, and rightly so,
> of their full neutrality throughout the course of the holy war being con-
> ducted ... Rivers of blood flowed until this day, yet nevertheless the flag
> of the life-bestowing Cross, raised, is already fluttering over the fortified

---

1   *Philhellenism* ... 1936, p. 370.
2   Hering 2004, p. 155.
3   Representatives from the following states attended the Congress: Russia, Austria, Prussia, Bri-
    tain, Sardinia, Sicily, the Duchies of Tuscany, Modena and Parma, as well as a representative
    of the Pope.

walls of the Peloponnese, of Attica, of Euboea, of Boeotia, of Acarnania, and in the greater parts of Epirus and Thessaly, in Crete and on the islands of the Aegean Sea ... [The] provisional Government of Hellas hastens to declare in a responsible manner via the present, that she in no way wishes to accept any treaty, as beneficial as it may appear, as long as the lawfully sent envoys do not succeed in getting a proper audition, having defended the rights of Hellas and having expounded upon what she reasonably demands as well as what her needs and most sacred interests are.[4]

The Congress barred the Greek delegation from participating, as that would in fact have been a sort of *de facto* recognition of the Greek state. Further, the Revolution was considered, and quite justifiably, as 'subversive to the status quo' by all of the participants, and as such was condemned in the Encyclical of the Congress that was issued on 2 December 1822.[5] It was, however, made clear that the 'Greek question' was already considered to have played a catalytic role in the actuation and transformation of the clashing interests between the Great Powers. Tsar Alexander of Russia juxtaposes this:

Nothing was of greater benefit to Russia, nor more desirable to the Russian people, than a hasarded campaign occasioned by the Greek revolution; yet I abstained from this effort, as I considered that in this struggle there were marks of a subversive revolution of the social classes ... In England, public opinion would compel the government to deal with the issues of Greece in earnest ... The Greek question shall be put forth in England as being commensurate in fate with the slave trade; for this reason, rather than propose myself a plan to the allies that would ameliorate the political situation of Greece, I prefer to await the English court.[6]

---

4   Thanos Kanakaris, citation translated from the Greek Wikipedia entry: Congress of Verona, https://el.wikipedia.org/wiki/Συνέδριο_της_Βερόνας, cited from: 'In Argos on 29 August 1822; in the absence of the President of the Law-giving body; The vice president Thanos Kanakaris'.

5   In the Encyclical, we read: 'What the subversive spirit of societies began on the western peninsula, what it tried to effect in Italy, it accomplished in the eastern outposts of Europe. While military revolts in the kingdoms of Naples and Sardinia were quelled by force, the revolutionary torch was cast within the Ottoman Empire. The lords, being steadfastly decided to reject the principle behind the revolution in whichever place and in whatever form it appeared, hastened to condemn it by agreement, and engaged unwaveringly in the work of their shared concern, thwarting everything that might divert them from their course' (Thanos Kanakaris, cited in and translated from the Greek Wikipedia entry https://el.wikipedia.org/wiki/Συνέδριο_της_Βερόνας).

6   Cited in Kyriakopoulos 1929, p. 155.

The assessment of the Tsar of Russia as regards Britain patently rested on, beyond any subjective interpretation, an event that had taken place a few months earlier which appeared to forejudge a change in the British stance towards the formally declared public position of the Holy Alliance: when the revolutionary Greek government announced its naval blockade of the Ottoman ports on 25 March 1822, the British government declared Britain's 'neutrality', something that meant that it recognised the 'state of war' (belligerency) between Greek and Ottoman forces, thereby 'recognising' Greece's authority and its international status. In fact, on 30 April 1822, British authorities considered the hostage-taking by the Greek fleet from neutral, private, commercial ships that had managed to break the blockade as lawful (and not as 'piracy'), while the English fleet did not even attempt to protect private ships under English sovereignty in the Ionian Islands.[7]

In actuality, British foreign policy had been gradually abandoning its strategy of safeguarding the integrity of the Ottoman Empire, as the Greek Revolution had made it clear that such a strategy was no longer feasible, and Britain sought simply to promote a solution to the Greek problem that would favour its interests rather than Russian foreign policy interests. In this context, the formation of an independent Greek state could be acceded, according to assessments of British foreign policy, providing that the Greek-Ottoman conflict and disputes would end in that way, and the two countries would have a joint stake in standing up to Russian expansion towards the West.[8]

In contrast, Russia, anticipating, as we have seen, the prospect of the Greek state being recognised by Britain, and by extension, by the international community, hastened to submit, on 28 December 1823, the plan of the 'Three Departments' in order to resolve the Greek question. This involved the establishment of three semi-autonomous principalities (Eastern Hellas, Western Hellas and Southern Hellas, the latter of which would include Crete), all of which would be 'subject to tribute taxes' to the Ottoman Empire, would recognise the sovereignty of the sultan and would maintain Ottoman garrisons in their territory, modelled after the prototype of Moldavia and Wallachia.

Russia anticipated that these principalities would be tethered to its foreign policy, while simultaneously constituting a permanent 'trouble spot' within the Ottoman Empire. The proposal was rejected by the Greek government, which would not accept any form of plan that did not recognise the complete inde-

---

7   Rubin 1988, p. 214.
8   See also Hering 2004, pp. 157 ff.

pendence of Greece; but it was also rejected by the sultan, who refused to accept any form of challenge to his absolute suzerainty of the area.

2.2 Foreign Loans and Their International Political Significance: Discounting the Viability of Greece

The decisive step for the international recognition of Greece was taken, however, when the money markets discounted the country's chances of prevailing in the war with the Ottoman Empire, whereupon the banks of London concluded loans with the Greek government.

The Greek revolutionary government under the leadership of Mavrokordatos had rightly perceived, by 1823, the conflicts brewing in the Holy Alliance, gauging from the change in British policy commencing in 1822, when George Canning assumed the position of Foreign Secretary, and could thus, in 1824, secure the necessary terms for the first foreign loan to the Greek state, rendering possible the requisite funding for the unfolding Revolution.

According to data examined by the Second National Assembly at Astros (30 March–18 April 1823), the annual deficit of the revolutionary government was approximately 24 million [Ottoman] piastres, 'total expenditures of 38,616,000 piastres against revenues of 12,846,220 piastres'.[9] This deficit rendered the securing of a foreign loan critical to the continuation of the war.

The first loan was concluded in February 1824, and the second in February 1825, both with banks in London. These loans were especially precarious for the lenders (the name of the borrower appeared as the Greek Federation, and the intermediary, as the Greek Committee of London). Nevertheless, the financial conjuncture facilitated the securing of high-risk loans: the 'speculation fever' that pre-dominated at that time both in Britain and internationally allowed for their quick conclusion, with terms proportionate to corresponding loans in other countries during that time period, and relative to the proposals of the Greek provisional government towards the negotiators.

---

9   'The expenditures for one ship were estimated to be 10,800 piastres per month, after maintenance and repair expenses they amounted to 13,130. The threescore [60] ships of the national fleet required 780,000 piastres per month, in addition to 400,000 for munitions. A total naval budget of 1,180,000 piastres per month ... Army expenditures ... [F]or the 51,000 infantry men per month, 2,044,000 piastres, and their armament required another 40,000 piastres. So that the naval and army budget amounted to 3,624,000 piastres per month. The other administration assumed expenses of only 500,000 piastres. The total expenditures were thus 4,124,000 piastres per month, or 24,724,000 from May until November. During the winter months the expenses were estimated to be but half. *We thus have a total of 38,616,000 piastres in expenditures against revenues of 12,846,220 piastres*' (Andreades 1904, p. 8, emphasis added. See also Kofinas 1934).

England was then going through one of those speculative fevers, which when they would periodically appear would drive the people of the City of London into rather precarious enterprises. This period of speculation, which began to blossom in the middle of 1823 ... [A] particular characteristic is the unbridled tendency towards loans to foreign states, and in particular to states that had not been officially recognised, as were, e.g. Brazil, Chile, Colombia, etc. So a loan that had been concluded by a people, whose achievements made brilliant unrivalled ancestral splendour as well, could only find complete success.[10]

'Unrecognised' states, amongst them the Greek state of the Revolution, were evaluated by the money markets as viable, although they had not yet attained *de jure* international-political status; recognition was considered to be imminent. What was considered particularly precarious, and this precarity was reflected by a high interest rate and in the 'haircut' of the actual amount of the loan relative to the nominal debt that would have to be paid off, was the potential of the borrowing state to repay it; in other words, the risk of a default by the borrowing state was evaluated, as evidenced later, as especially high.

With the two loans of independence in 1824 and in 1825 Greece assumed an obligation of 2,800,000 pounds in nominal capital, against a real capital of 1,176,000 pounds ... Eventually, the revolutionary government found itself, on 6 April 1826, unable to pay the loans and announced the first bankruptcy of Greece, even before the country had achieved its independence.[11]

However, beyond the economic aspect of the loans, and irrespective of the reigning discourse as regards the effectiveness of their use, on a foreign policy level it concerned the *de facto* recognition of Greek authority as a government and as an independent state. German historian Georg Gottfried Gervinus (1805–71) writes:

It was also of course the conclusion of this loan that was a great victory, greater than any success on a battlefield. It was well known in Greece how often these monetary contracts served to protect English dominance and the policy of the English government; and in many a political circuit

10   Andreades 1904, pp. 15–16.
11   Psalidopoulos 2014, p. 76.

in England this financial approach was considered as being the *de facto* recognition of Greek independence.[12]

From this period of securing foreign loans and forward, the Great Powers also discounted, aside from the money markets, the final consolidation of some form of a Greek state entity; their interventions made a defining contribution to the eventual configuration of the independent Greek state.

2.3   *From the Protocol of St. Petersburg (1826) to the Battle of Navarino (1827) and the London Protocol (1830)*

With the military invasion and pre-dominance, to a great extent, of Ibrahim Pasha from 1825, the fate of the Greek state could be looked upon not by the strength of its military (which could not possibly hold up against the Ottoman advance), but by the intervention of the three Great Powers (Britain, France, Russia), all of which had in one way or another taken a stance in favour of a certain form of political existence for Greece.

At this juncture, the Russian proposal for partition of the Greek territory into three subject principalities under the suzerainty of the sultan created utmost disquiet in the Greek government, as did the fact that the training of Ibrahim's army had been assigned to the French colonel Joseph Anthelme Sève.[13] On 10 July 1825, the parliamentary and executive bodies, in a joint session, petitioned the British government for protection:

> That the Greeks have taken up arms in defence of mankind's natural and imprescriptible right to freedom of property, religion, and liberty, and have for four years resisted the colossal forces of Egypt, Asia, and Africa, thereby acquiring a title to political existence: That the agents of certain Continental and Christian powers have persisted in a line of conduct opposed to the principles which those powers profess, and that several of the said agents endeavour through their emissaries to draw the Greeks into improper engagements ... In virtue of the present act, the Greek nation places the sacred deposit of its liberty, independence, and political existence, under the absolute protection of Great Britain.[14]

---

12   Gervinos 1865, p. 18.
13   Clair 2008, p. 234. 'In France, where philhellenic sentiment reached a peak at this time, the government was secretly building warships for the Egyptian fleet and even sent French officers as advisers to accompany them when they went into service in 1827' (Beaton 2019, p. 101).
14   Cited by Gordon 1872, Vol. 2, p. 283.

Following the dismissal of the Greek petition by the British ambassador in Constantinople Stratford Canning, with his contention that Britain wished to remain neutral, the Greek government seemed disposed towards considering the proposal for a unified principality subject to the sultan.

The situation had irreparably deteriorated, as already mentioned, in the wake of the fall of Missolonghi in April 1826 and in the turn of the Ottoman forces towards the south, the Peloponnese and the islands in the Saronic Gulf. When news of the fall of Missolonghi reached Piada at Epidaurus, where the Third National Assembly (6–16 April 1826) was taking place, the body adjourned its work and assigned governance to an 11-member 'Administrative Committee'.[15]

All the factions of the Greek state now sought intervention by the Great Powers.[16] The situation would have a significant effect on the stance and strategy of those internal political forces, and thus on the moulding of the political scene. At the same time, the military retreat of the armed forces of the Revolution also meant that the territorial expanse of the dominion and the political form of the Greek state would depend definitively upon the agreements made between the Great Powers, something which clearly entailed the curtailment of the internal revolutionary dynamics and the complexion of the Greek state. Concurrently, needless to say, the Greek Revolution served as a catalyst in the transformation of the international relations of power, and tipped the scales on the political map of Europe, whilst the foreign policy of the Great Powers of the period were obliged (following the initial success of the Revolution) to take a stance with respect to the Greek question.

In April 1826, Britain and Russia signed the Protocol of St. Petersburg, according to which the two powers would intervene in the Greek-Ottoman war, even if by military means, in order to enforce negotiations in the war zones for the official formation of a Greek state entity. They thus invited the other Great Powers of the Holy Alliance, Austria, Prussia and France, to convene

---

15   Four members from the Peloponnese (amongst whom was Petrobey Mavromichalis) were elected to the Administrative Committee, along with three from the Mainland (Spyridon Trikoupis amongst them), three from the naval islands (Spetses, Hydra and Psara) (including Lazaros Kountouriotes) and one from the Aegean Islands. Kolokotrones refers to the news of the fall of Missolonghi as follows: 'The news came to us on Holy Wednesday ... that Missolonghi was lost; we were all plunged into great grief, for half an hour there was so complete a silence ... each was gauging in his mind our ruination' (Kolokotrones 2013, p. 220, corrected according to Greek original).

16   'Kolokotrones ... sought aid *as much* in England *as* in Russia and the USA' (Hering 2004, p. 166). 'The petition to G. Britain came from an initiative of Kolokotrones' (Dafnis 1961, p. 33).

for a summit in which final decisions would be taken; the invitation was accepted only by France.

In February 1827, the Third National Assembly of the Greeks convened, *de novo*, in Hermione, which subsequently continued in March 1827 at Troezen, where the 'Political Constitution of Hellas' (see below) was ratified and the new contracting of a loan from abroad was decided upon. On 17 February 1827 (the fourth session) the National Assembly decided that 'a letter should be written to the English ambassador Canning in Constantinople, assuring him of the gratitude of the Hellenic nation in favour of the mediation of Great Britain and the rest of the great Powers'.[17] In other words, the Greek government again appealed to Britain to intervene so as to secure once and for all (in collaboration with the other Great Powers) Greek independence. Britain took the decision to serve as intermediary between the warring parties with the aim of establishing a unified, semi-autonomous Greek principality under the suzerainty of the sultan, a solution which, with the military correlation of forces that were formed following the invasion of the Egyptian forces, it considered would be accepted by the Greek government.

One of the tasks of the National Assembly was the swearing in of the commander (*stolarchos*) of the Greek naval fleet, radical British officer Thomas Cochrane (1775–1860), who had served in the then recent past as admiral of a succession of naval fleets in Chile and Brazil in the struggles for independence of those countries.[18] Cochrane, who was personally acquainted with Alexandros Mavrokordatos, had exerted his influence, as a former member of the British Parliament and as Earl of Dundonald in Scotland, for the securing of the loans between the revolutionary Greek state and British banks. Radical British officer Richard Church, or 'Tsorts' as he became known in Greece (Sir Richard Church, 1784–1873), was appointed Commander of the Greek land forces ('Supreme Commander'), and was later Counsellor to the territory, plenipotentiary at the First National Assembly of Athens (1843) and Senator of the Kingdom of Greece.

In May 1827, after the fall of the Acropolis, the conditions of the Greek Revolution on the battlefield had become dramatic. The Treaty of London, a British initiative, was signed on 6 July 1827 by Britain, France and Russia, on the basis of which the three powers called for the immediate cessation of hostilities and the opening of negotiations on the Greek question. A 'secret article' of the treaty outlined that the Powers reserved the right to exact military force

---

17   Cited in Mamoukas 1839, Vol. 6, p. 84.
18   It could be argued that Cochrane, aside from being a 'Philhellene', was also a 'Philo-Chilean' and 'Philo-Brazilian'; or, simply, an internationalist-revolutionary of his time.

in order to enforce the terms of the treaty. On 4 August 1827 the Great Powers officially petitioned the Sublime Porte, by way of their ambassadors in Istanbul, for an end to hostilities in the Peloponnese, a petition that was rejected.

The following month, on 10 September 1827, the naval fleets of Britain, France and Russia put to shore at the Peloponnese and demanded of Ibrahim Pasha to cease all hostilities in compliance with the Treaty of London.

Ibrahim Pasha did not concede to the conditions of the three powers, and on 8 October 1827 the battle of Navarino ensued, during which the fleets of the three Powers, under the command of Englishman Edward Codrington (1770–1851), ravaged the Egyptian fleet. Ottoman casualties neared 6,000, 10 times those of the allied fleet, a fact that drove French admiral Henri De Rigny to declare that 'in all of history there has never been such great devastation of a fleet'.[19]

On 8 December 1827 diplomatic relations between the Powers and the Ottoman Empire were severed, and on 14 April 1828 the Russian-Ottoman war broke out. On 17 August 1828, French troops disembarked in the Peloponnese under Marshal Nicolas Joseph Maison (1771–1840) to purge the area of any remnants of the Ottoman and Egyptian army. On 27 September 1828 Ibrahim Pasha departed the Peloponnese, as the withdrawal of Egyptian forces had been concluded.

On 14 September 1829, the *Treaty of Adrianople* (also called the Treaty of Edirne) was signed between Russia and the Ottoman Empire, by which Russia's victory in the war between the two countries became official. The sultan was thence obliged to concede to the solution formulated by the Great Powers. On 3 February 1830, the *London Protocol* was signed by Britain, France and Russia, in which Greece was recognised as an independent kingdom and her borders defined. In 1832, with the Treaty of London, the three Powers appointed the 17-year-old prince Otto of Bavaria as the first king of Greece.

It becomes clear that the Greek Revolution broke out amidst a volatile and tumultuous international conjuncture. The Greek state created by the Revolution managed to capitalise on this volatility and turmoil in the international relations of power, though, under the pressure of military developments, it eventually ended up being subsumed into them. As shall be explained further below, any interpretation of the evolution of the Revolution based on the schema of Greece's 'dependence' on the three Great Powers would in no way grasp the essence of what was going on: the proclamation of the Revolution on the basis of the changing *social* relations in South and Central Greece, the

---

19   Katerina Sakellaropoulou, President of the Hellenic Republic, Speech at the anniversary of the Battle of Navarino, https://www.presidency.gr/simeia-omilias-kata-ton-eortasmo-tis -epeteioy-tis-naymachias-toy-nayarinoy/.

new political and social realities that were established, and further, the disparity of the foreign policy of the Powers concerning the Greek question and their diverging interests in south-eastern Europe.

3   Internal Conflicts, Dead-Ends, and the End of Constitutional Republicanism

3.1   *Affirmation of the Constitutional-Representational Framework before Its 'Provisional' Suspension*

The adverse course of the armed struggle beginning at the dawn of 1825 engendered ripples of disarray amongst the troops, as well as disruption in the apparatuses of the revolutionary Greek state.

> Amongst all factions one encounters the heavy dependence of the fighters on provisions of food and artillery and the requisition for a salary. When the administrators, due to frequent cessations of payment from the government, were not in a position to supply foodstuffs, to ensure spoils and pay an advance, the men would desert them.[20]

At this juncture, there was a proliferation of ceasefire agreements (*kapakia*) between certain warlords and Ottoman authorities,[21] a phenomenon that was condemned by the revolutionary Greek government; yet the official national historiography persists in presenting these agreements collectively as 'strategic manoeuvring' for the salvation of the populations and the restructuring of Greek forces – without, of course, attempting to explain why this 'manoeuvring' did not take place as long as the government was paying out salaries. In fact, sources indicate that in the majority of cases, these warlords 'before a salary [and lack thereof, J.M.] would forget national interests'.[22]

---

20   Hering 2004, p. 100. After the slump of the Revolution since 1826, one of the more principal
      sources of funds for the state was the trade of agricultural products. Kolokotrones, referring to the fighters from Missolonghi who survived the exodus (April 1826) and managed
      to reach the Peloponnese, notes: 'The soldiers who had come from Missolonghi hoped
      to receive their pay from grapes, because we had no other source of funds' (Kolokotrones
      2013, p. 225, corrected according to Greek original). A customary practice of Ibrahim's army
      in the Peloponnese was to destroy crops.
21   Kotarides 1993, pp. 171–240.
22   Hering 2004, p. 101; see also Papageorgiou 2004, pp. 59–60. 'One of the great warlords
      of Roumeli in 1821, Odysseas Androutsos, sealed the first period of the revolution by his
      action ... he deserted the Greek camp in order to negotiate with the Turks and to seek sup-

However, in spite of the disruptive phenomena, the revolutionary Greek state preserved its characteristics from the previous period until the very end of the hostilities, marked by the naval battle of Navarino: it survived as a constitutional-representational *republican state*,[23] a fact that was reflected in the *Third National Assembly of the Hellenes* in February–March 1827, and in the 'Political Constitution of Hellas' that was ratified on 1 May 1827, where in Chapter 3, under the title 'Public Law of the Hellenes', the most complete framework of human rights for the period in all of Europe is set forth.[24]

The constitution was supported by all the wings that participated in the Third National Assembly, a fact that demonstrates that constitutionalism comprised a common base, although it could be said that the ideological ascendancy of the liberal wing was thereby validated. The constitution of 1827 was the most democratic ever to exist in Greece, as well as being the most democratic constitution of its time in all of Europe.[25] Law Professor and former Prime Minister Alexandros Svolos writes: '... The Constitution of Troezen is noteworthy for its more complete articulation of individual rights (art. 7 et seq.) and because ... it highlights the increased formal validity of the Constitution'.[26] Concurring, Professor Dimitris Dimoulis observes:

> For the first time the source of constituent power and the boundaries of the Greek territory are being expressly defined: 'Provinces of Hellas are,

---

port from them in order to sustain the military force and his political influence' (Kotarides 1993, p. 91).

23   By the term 'republican state', I refer to a state regime not ruled by a king, in which governance is considered a *public affair* (*res publica*) and not a matter of some higher lord that personifies power. In the period of the Revolution, republican regimes existed on the American continent, in Switzerland and in a series of European 'free cities', most of which were German-speaking.

24   At the Third National Assembly the dissenting political wings of the Revolution revealed themselves as they were formed anew. The National Assembly initially convened in January 1827 on the island of Aegina, with the principal figures of Alexandros Mavrokordatos and Spyridon Trikoupis, leaders of the liberal wing, whence immediately thereafter there arose the so-called English Party (see the following section). Kolokotrones and his followers, however, convened another Assembly in Hermione, towards which Kolokotrones's former enemy from the second civil war, Georgios Kountouriotes, also turned. Of the parliamentarians who assembled at Hermione, the so-called Russian and French parties immediately formed; both of these trends sought the strengthening of the executive over the parliamentary. Eventually the two Assemblies united, when the one at Hermione reached a deadlock over the question of electing a governor, and on 19 March 1827, the joint National Assembly at Troezen commenced.

25   Petrides 1990, Svolos 1972, Stavropoulos 1979, Vol. 1, pp. 422–9.

26   Svolos 1972, p. 26.

those that have taken up and shall take up arms against the Ottoman dynasty' – in other words, potentially the entire territory of the Ottoman Empire. The territory is defined as 'one and indivisible' and 'Sovereignty is inherent in the Nation. Every power flows from it, and favours it'. In a Europe governed by absolutism, the Constitution of 1827 defines the source of state power (the nation) and its aim (national interest). This concerns a democratic 'lucidity', which has no precedent even in the Constitutions of the French Revolution. The fundamental conception of modern constitutionalism finds here its institutional validation: unity and the state-institutional organisation of a nation as an exclusive bearer of constitutional power, which is articulated in a text of supreme formal value. 'The present Constitutional laws take precedence over all others' ... As far as the foreign-born are concerned, the C 1827 abandons the criterion of language.[27]

Nonetheless, one month prior to the ratification of the constitution on 1 May 1827, on 27 March 1827, the National Assembly had decided to *provisionally suspend for seven years* the functioning of representational processes and to assign the governance of the country, with the title of Governor, to Ioannis Kapodistrias, who had been, until that time, Foreign Affairs minister for Russia, under the rationale that: '[T]he supreme science in the governance of the State ... demands much experience and high erudition, which the barbarian Ottomans never permitted of the Hellenes'.[28] Simultaneously, in the same resolution, the universal right to vote for men was recognised, something that did not exist in any other European country.

> This National Assembly had decided as early as 27 March 1827, that 'the legislative power shall be surrendered to one and only one', towards this it unanimously elected, by the resolution of 3 April 1827, Ioannis Kapodistrias as 'Governor of Hellas', determining the duration 'of [the] power entrusted to him by the Nation' to seven years.[29]

To conclude: at the Third National Assembly of 1827, on the one hand, a unique – by the European standards of the time – Constitution 'of an exclusively representative democracy was adopted',[30] and on the other hand, this

---

27   Dimoulis 2000, pp. 59–60.
28   Dimoulis 2000, p. 63.
29   Svolos 1972, pp. 26–7.
30   Dimoulis 2000, p. 60.

Constitution was 'provisionally' put on hold for seven years, ceding *carte blanche* the power of governance to the 'Governor' and those officers whom he would appoint.

It is reasonable to assume that the assignation of the government to Kapodistrias, which in essence meant the (supposed 'provisional') suspension of the validity of the constitution of 1827, was linked to the unfavourable course of the Revolution from 1825 onwards, something which rendered necessary a compromise of the Greek state with the international-political establishment articulated by the Great Powers, by whose intervention complete and utter military devastation of the Revolution was averted.

In spite of this, as Hering demonstrates in a cogent and analytical manner,[31] discussions and recommendations regarding the transfer of governance to a centralised structure, as in the form of a president of a republic or a king, *without, however, the suspension or adulteration of the constitutional nature of the state*, had been going on since the incipient stages of the Revolution, with particular intensity during the period of the civil wars (see Chapters 2 and 5). From the period of the first civil war forward, it became evident that the centralisation of state power would also necessitate the institution of a head of state, above and beyond the parliamentary, executive and judiciary, as a unifying element for the opposing fractions, while remaining true to the framework of the ratified constitutional-representational order.[32]

To understand the developments that led to the swift supersession of republican constitutionalism by a Bonapartist-type dictatorship (1828–31), to be subsequently replaced by an absolute monarchy (1833–43), what must be pointed out is the fragile political balance that had crystallised via the escalation and transformation of internal antagonisms within the Greek state, which continually rekindled the trend towards civil war.

What should also be mentioned at this point, albeit succinctly, is the disparagement of radical constitutions by the majority of 'official' (belonging to the establishment) approaches in 1821, of 'progressives' and 'conservatives' alike, of old and more contemporary alike.

---

31   Hering 2004, pp. 144–56.

32   'When in the autumn of 1823 the lords of the province of Vostitsa (Aegio) ... asked for a monarchy, they all agreed once again on the explicit pledge of the king to the constitution ... The proponents of a change in the structure of the executive power did not exclusively choose monarchy, yet even during the period of the first civil war they also considered the establishment of a presidential system based on the prototype of the USA ... One such proposal was prepared in 1826 by Alexandros Mavrokordatos' (Hering 2004, pp. 149, 151). 'The designation of a king or president embodied for the warlords an edge against the lords' (Hering 2004, p. 169).

According to 'the nationalist claim, which is repeatedly presented today under the guise of social criticism',[33] the institutions of the revolutionary republican Greek state during the period 1821–27 were 'imported', 'foreign', mere reproductions of the constitutions of the French Revolution, with no corresponding elements with the socioeconomic conditions of the Greek space and as such were incapable of being adapted.[34]

The previous analysis – in which the social, political and ideological antagonism amongst the factions that had formed within the Greek state, the disputes over the federal or centralist nature of the state, the intervention of the masses and troops for the establishment and preservation of representational institutions, the regional parliaments and national assemblies, the persistence in the constitutionality and in the ratification of three constitutional documents are all clearly outlined – illustrates the pervasiveness and dominance of the radical-Enlightenment (bourgeois) ideologies in the areas under revolt. Concomitantly, it also illustrates the definitive role of the nationally politicised masses in the prevailing of those ideas, that is, for the masses themselves to attain civil rights. In the words of Yannis Makriyannis: 'I wanted my country to be soon governed by laws, and not by the "because I say so"'.[35]

Practically speaking, it was entirely reasonable, on the one hand, for the Greek revolution to share certain aspects with the counterpart revolutions of the period (the American, the French ...):

Revolution means revolution, and thus revolutionary constitutions contain revolutionary designs – as much in Greece, as in America, Spain and Italy. It would be consistent for those who view the invasion of 'unfamiliar' and as such 'non-applicable' concepts to seek the root of evil in the revolution itself.[36]

Hering's observation is illustrative of what it is truly about: an attempt to discredit the revolution itself by 'progressives' and conservative publicists and historians, *fear of the masses, fear in the face of any potential revolution.*

---

33   Hering 2004, p. 130.
34   Hering insightfully and aptly critiques, and offers pivotal views on, exponents of such points of view, such as C. Paparrigopoulos, N.P. Diamantouros, Th. Veremis, G. Mavrogordatos, V. Mathiopoulos, M. Nikolinakos, P. Poulitsas, P.M. Kontogiannis, N. Svoronos, P. Karolidis, N. Mouzelis, J.A. Petropoulos, D.A. Petrakakos, V. Philias and others. See, for example, Hering 2004, pp. 25–9, 36, 40, 47, 54, 58, 130–40.
35   Makriyannis 2011, p. 134.
36   Hering 2004, p. 136.

On the other hand, and again factually speaking, the Revolution evolved to form its own particular characteristics, which in many ways have been silenced or denigrated by both successive and contemporary 'official' historians so as to specifically obfuscate the authentic nature of the Greek Revolution, whence the revolutionary dynamics and initiative of the masses and revolutionary leaders were brought to the forefront. This came about because the democratic-republican political systems of the period 1821–27 sprouted from the 'grounding' of revolutionary ideas into the requirements and conditions of the armed, liberating action and the specific social conditions within the territory of the new state:

> This very peculiarity in the intricate system of equilibration between the Parliamentary and Executive bodies, between the central and regional governments, between the guerrillas and the government politicians cannot be explained by the claim of an acceptance of measures coming from abroad, but with respect for the Greek reality: by the mistrust of the lords towards the dominance of certain members amongst them, by the tensions between lords and guerrilla fighters, by the local and mainly regional opposition against centralisation, as well as at the same time by the warlords' demand for effective organisation ... The Greeks experimented to a great extent, they made compromises and learned that they had yet to find the optimal and definitive solution. The concepts of natural law, the principles of popular sovereignty, equality and freedom ... [T]hey did not emulate any existing theoretical models. Far before the Revolution they had become accepted and had been developed by figures of the Enlightenment and revolutionaries such as Rigas Pheraios, they had been associated with local traditions and had been disseminated by the Philiki Etereia [Friendly Society].[37]

Contemporary 'official' historians and publicists who hope for a Greek nation without internal conflicts, without rivalling political passions and movements, obedient to the dictates of power,[38] 'unified' under state power and authority,

---

[37] Hering 2004, pp. 133–4. Concerning the espousal and internalisation of the ideas and dictates of the French Revolution by the Greek Enlightenment, see Kitromilides 1990.

[38] Constantinos Paparrigopoulos, *the* Greek 'national' historian, considers that the revolutionary constitutions had intentionally legislated an ineffective polyarchy: 'Yet in 1822 the polyarchy, the transiency of the principles, and amongst those, conflict, were legislated and as such the establishment of a government of consequence was rendered impossible'

in essence express the fear of the already deeply-entrenched capitalist order to the slightest movement of the masses, and all the more, to the potential and dynamics of a revolution.

3.2   Political Parties, Conflicts, Political Volatility: From Constitutionalism to Bonapartism

Following the close of the Third National Assembly, three parties emerged from political factions formed during the Revolution and civil wars, as well as from the political restructuring that took place during the final period of the armed struggle: the 'English', the 'Russian' and the 'French'. These parties proved to be long-lived; from them, the political stage of the Greek state was formed for over three decades, until the period of the movements that led to the expulsion of the first Greek king, Otto I, in 1862, and the constitutional change that ensued.

The names of the parties that prevailed, 'English', 'Russian' and 'French', had not been chosen by the parties themselves, but rather emerged through political debate. As Gunnar Hering notes: 'The names of the Greek political parties, as well as those of the British, initially designated by the rival politicians, quickly prevailed, as they were in a way apt and did not befool the group that they characterised'.[39]

The English Party was led by Alexandros Mavrokordatos, and its core members were Spyridon Trikoupis, Andreas Zaimis, Andreas Londos, Notis and Kostas Botsaris, Andreas Miaoulis and Emmanouil Tombazis. Its roots lay in the centralist-liberal current of the Revolution, which was delineated in Chapter 5. The party was founded by the conclusion of the Third National Assembly, when

---

(Paparrigopoulos 1899, p. 589). A similar perspective is adopted by Yanis Kordatos, a leftist historian, who subsequently integrates it into the schema of 'Greece, the dependent protectorate': 'Mavrokordatos ... with the adherents of Kountouriotes and other, like-minded kin, introduced the separation of governmental power into *legislative* and *executive*. Thus, there was no governmental consolidation and it paralysed every administrative action' (Kordatos 1972, p. 220). 'Greece must be a veiled protectorate of England and the Greek people must not exercise their sovereign rights. It must find itself in the condition of the semi-colonised' (Kordatos 1972, p. 273). How, however, would 'the Greek people' exercise 'their sovereign rights' were there not a 'separation of government power into the *legislative* and *executive*' (i.e. parliament and elections), but only 'governmental consolidation' (i.e. only Executive)? A query of merit. Unless the 'separation of governmental power into *legislative* and *executive*' itself is what distinguishes the 'condition of the semi-colonised'.

39   Hering 2004, pp. 141–2.

the followers of Mavrokordatos were infuriated at the decision of the assignation of an absolute, monarchical-type power to the Governor. Gunnar Hering
thus codifies:

> [A] restraint on state power, individual rights and freedom, a sovereign
> state without ecclesiastical ties with centres beyond borders, a written
> constitution and guarantees of a rule of law, parliamentary scrutiny of a
> responsible government as an intermediate goal – rallying cries whose
> exact opposites the Russian Party initially supported.[40]

The Russian (or 'Napist') Party encapsulated a continuation of centralist-
conservative trends of the Revolution (see Chapter 5) headed by Kolokotrones,
and amassed all those who sought a 'governo militare' and/or were engaged
to ensure the Greek Orthodox disposition of the state and people. They were
initially arrayed on the side of Ioannis Kapodistrias, and were named 'Govern-
mentals'. The head of the party was Andreas Metaxas, and amongst its influential officers, apart from Theodoros Kolokotrones and his son Gennaios, were
Kitsos Tzavelas, Nikitas Stamatelopoulos and Constantinos Economos.

  The French Party (whose official name was the National Party) was headed
by Ioannis Kolettis, and its origins can be found in the warlords of the mainland bands that formed during the civil wars, and perhaps also in the 'Philolaos
Society' that was founded in Napflion in 1825.[41] The leading officers of the
party belonged to those who had pulled out of the Assembly at Hermione in
1827, prior to the Third National Assembly in Troezen, in which they supported
the strengthening of the executive body over the parliamentary. Under Kapodistrias's rule they were integrated into the 'Constitutionalists', together with the
supporters of the English Party, but soon distinguished themselves and set out
to form their own party, the French Party, by recruiting from the masses, incor-
porating elements from the other two parties into their political and ideological
positions. Their emphasis lay, on the one hand, on the need for the state to
pay reparations to the revolutionary fighters, and on the other, on the need for
military preparedness for the imminent expansion of the borders.[42] The party
managed to achieve mass appeal throughout the Greek territory and brought

---

40   Hering 2004, p. 208.
41   See Chapter 5, note 55.
42   Kolettis appeared as being hostile towards the 'Western-minded', yet at the same time he
     was an adherent to Saint-Simonianism. In fact, in 1833 he appointed a disciple of Saint
     Simon, Gustave d'Eichthal, to the ministry of Finance (see Hering 2004, p. 209).

into its ranks influential personalities such as Georgios Kountouriotes, Yannis Makriyannis and Constantinos Kanaris.

When Ioannis Kapodistrias arrived in Greece on 6 January 1828, he promptly made clear his intention to abolish the constitutional framework that had been ratified by the Third National Assembly.[43]

> Kapodistrias … immediately proposed to the Parliament a *coup d'état* to suspend the functioning of the Constitution, which was approved via the resolution of 18 January 1828 … With the resolution … instead of the Parliament, which was dissolved, the 'Panhellenic' was introduced, a Body which '[together] with the Governor of Hellas should undertake the tasks and responsibility of Government'.[44]

With the electoral law of 4 March 1829, Kapodistrias extended electoral rights to the entire adult male population, while simultaneously offsetting that very measure via the indirect election of members of parliament. The Fourth National Assembly that resulted from the indirect electoral process ratified, on 11 July 1829, the decisions and further expanded the power of the Governor, 'e.g. instead of the "Panhellenic" body, the *Senate* was established, an advisory Body, consisting of 27 members elected by the Governor'.[45]

As Alexandros Svolos states, with the 'suspension of the Constitution of Troezen … in essence the period of absolutism in Greece begins, which endured until the Constitution of 1844'.[46] That notwithstanding, throughout the entire period of 'absolutism', the three political parties continued to exist and function, in spite of the fact that no form of electoral processes were carried out, as, e.g. 'since 1830 the government had been appointing the heads of communities'.[47] This issue, which at first glance may seem paradoxical, shall be discussed further in the present chapter. First, however, the ascent and drastic fall of Kapodistrias should be briefly addressed.

The reason why it was possible for Kapodistrias to be proclaimed Governor of Greece was the *catastrophic balance* between the rivalling factions that had formed within the Greek state towards the end of the armed conflict. The defeats of the Revolution from 1825 onwards, as well as the desperate economic

---

43 Kapodistrias denounced the Constitution of 1827 as 'containing every demagogic principle of the revolutionaries of 1793' (Dimoulis 2000, p. 64).

44 Svolos 1972, pp. 28–9.

45 Svolos 1972, p. 29.

46 Svolos 1972, p. 30.

47 Hering 2004, p. 114.

situation, determined to a great extent, as we have already seen, the political relations of power. *Catastrophic balance* means that not a single political force is strong enough to successfully lay claim to political leadership over the other political forces, while, in tandem, no single political force is weak enough so as to allow for the political domination of another faction.

The effect in this case, as with the majority of instances of catastrophic balance, was *Bonapartism*: a concentration of power in the hands of a head of state and dictatorial governance independent of the existing political forces.[48]

It is here that some care is needed concerning a particular point: Bonapartism arises as a result of catastrophic balance between active socio-political forces at a particular conjuncture, and not exclusively as a result of a catastrophic balance between the bourgeois class and the proletariat.[49] Political power relations constitute relatively autonomous concentrations of social-class relations, not direct reflections of relations of economic exploitation.

Bonapartism always draws its strength from an indigent (peasant) population where conditions have driven them to mere survival;[50] in the case of Greece, this particular population comprised all those who had lost nearly everything on account of the ravage and devastation of settlements and crops that Ibrahim Pasha had left in his wake. And, in fact, Kapodistrias initially garnered considerable support from the poor peasant population, as he enacted measures in support of the destitute, the heirless, widows, children

---

48   Regarding Bonapartism, see Marx 1972, Poulantzas 2018, p. 288 ff. Kapodistrias's regime is usually compared to absolutism, especially Russian Tsarism, which he served before assuming the government of Greece. 'All accounts agree that Kapodistrias tended politically towards the sort of autocracy that he had been used to in Russia. To that extent, his whole Governorship ran counter to the democratic and pluralist tenor that had been emerging throughout the Revolution. His politics could not have been more different from those of the Friendly Society, which had once tried to recruit him as its leader. Under Kapodistrias, Greece moved backwards politically' (Beaton 2013, p. 85).

49   As Poulantzas (1973) seems to believe.

50   Marx writes of the case of Louis Bonaparte, from whose dictatorship the term Bonapartism comes: 'And yet the state power is not suspended in the air. Bonaparte represented a class, and the most numerous class of French society at that, *the small-holding peasantry* ... A small holding, the peasant and his family; beside it another small holding, another peasant and another family. A few score of these constitute a village, and a few score villages constitute a department. Thus the great mass of the French nation is formed by the simple addition of homologous magnitudes, much as potatoes in a sack form a sack of potatoes ... But let us not misunderstand. The Bonaparte dynasty represents not the revolutionary, but the conservative peasant; not the peasant who strikes out beyond the condition of his social existence, the small holding, but rather one who wants to consolidate his holding' (Marx 1972, p. 62).

born out of wedlock: 'it had succeeded in making him likeable to the popular masses'.[51]

However, in order to survive, Bonapartism is forced to respect the very condition that arises from the situation of catastrophic balance from which it originated: to maintain even distances between the contending fractions, drawing strength from the inability of each party to impose itself onto another.

Kapodistrias, evidently carried away by his own ideological roots, made the fatal mistake of identifying with one of the three factions: the Russian Party, which in fact during that period bore the appellation Governmental, or Kapodistrian, Party.[52] The opposition that erupted against him was dealt with violently: police surveillance in schools, exiles, imprisonment, censorship of the press as well of written correspondence, the mandatory issuance of a passport for movement within the land, etc.[53]

Such measures only served to undermine the situation, while the opposition turned to open insurrection with all the hallmarks of a third civil war. The islands under the direction of the English Party, as well as the part of the mainland under the direction of the French Party, along with Mani, all broke away from the central authority.[54]

> The world was enthused by the revolution of July [1830, J.M.] in France: the French flag flew everywhere, in Sparta alongside the flags with Lykourgos and Leonidas. In December of 1830 the Maniates revolted and on 1 May 1831 the leader of the insurgents Tsamis Karatasos hit the area of Thebes. The demand of the guerrillas ... [was] the freely elected national assembly ... Fearing attack of the islands by the government by sea, the Hydriote combatant and admiral Miaoulis seized the fleet in the harbour on 14 July 1831 ... Miaoulis blew up the corvette 'Hydra' and the frigate 'Hellas'.[55]

---

51   Dafnis 1961, p. 38.
52   Papadakis 1934.
53   'So that he would have support he formed – in accordance with the prototypes of Corfu – a secret police. Strict measures were taken, Mavromichalis and many of his followers were arrested and imprisoned, and the most worthy of politicians, as Kolettis, Mavrokordatos and Trikoupis, were driven out' (Maurer 1976, p. 305).
54   Daskalakis 1934a.
55   Hering 2004, pp. 182–3. 'The intense growth of the opposition, notably in 1831, when the time came for it to vigorously claim power, signifies that Kapodistrias ... did not secure the consent of powerful social agents: The Kapodistrian party that formed (centred on the 'Russian' faction and devoted clerks) proved inadequate on its own to support him, while the passive acquiescence of the rural strata was a sort of footing without any meaningful weight' (Loukos 1988, p. 398).

On 27 September 1831 Kapodistrias was assassinated in Napflion by the brothers Constantinos and Georgios Mavromichalis from Mani. In the newspaper *Apollon* that was published on Hydra by Anastasios Polyzoides, the following text appeared in print on 30 September 1831:

> As human beings we could not but be sad and mourn for this tragic end of I. Kapodistrias. As citizens, however, friends of the salvation of the motherland, above all else, we are very far from condemning the act, while, in fact, we see divine retribution in this lofty decision, which was fulfilled as compensation of the unutterable and immoral evil deeds of which Hellas is over-satiated. As much as this act seems to us to be most valiant, as it was carried out by people bound not to external forces, nor to hirelings and those disgraced, but by people graced with spontaneity and solemnity.[56]

Commenting on the death of Kapodistrias, Adamantios Korais, the leading figure of the Greek Enlightenment, wrote:

> [T]he motherland, instead of conferring honour on the murderer as a tyrant-slayer, shall vilify him for not allowing her to judge him and punish him with a punishment incomparably worse than death. The befitting punishment for Kapodistrias would not be death, but expulsion from Hellas, accompanied by a great many wishes to live and live a long life, [and] to regard Hellas, whose future prosperity he hastened in every way to frustrate (cited in Daskalakis 1979, p. 575).[57]

Following the death of Kapodistrias, two governments were formed in the country. The first was initiated on 15 March 1832 from the 'Fifth National

---

56   Cited in Dafnis 1961, pp. 38–9. The publisher of *Apollon*, Anastasios Polyzoides (1802–73) was an eminent jurist, political-economist, politician and scholar, exponent of the liberal constitutional order (see, for example, Polyzoides 1971). In 1834, as president of the five-member tribunal of Napflion, he refused, together with Georgios Tertsetis, to sign the sentence condemning Theodoros Kolokotrones and Demetrios Plapoutas 'to death for high treason' and was incarcerated for four months, having been accused of 'refusing service and being in violation of confidentiality with self-serving intent to harm the state'. He later served as Minister of Education and of the Interior.

57   Roderick Beaton writes in this context: 'The assassins were hailed in some quarters as the heirs of Harmodios and Aristogeiton, the tyrant-slayers of classical Athens. The octogenarian Korais, he who had been the first to articulate the idea of Greece as a modern nation, unforgivingly complained in print that the murderers had saved "the transgressor against Hellenic laws from a punishment more just than death: expulsion in disgrace from Hellas"' (Beaton 2019, p. 109).

Assembly' at Argos, at which essentially only the Russian Party was represented and which elected the brother of Ioannis Kapodistrias, Augustinos, as provisional Governor, until the arrival of the king. The second government, that of the 'Constitutionalists' (the English and French Parties), originated in the 'Fourth ongoing National Assembly', and in charge of it was a committee consisting of Georgios Kountouriotes, Ioannis Kolettis and Andreas Zaimis. It is interesting to note that both National Assemblies were in favour of a polity of *constitutional monarchy*, with the conservatives of the Russian Party even enfeebling the incipience of popular sovereignty by introducing a Higher Parliament, members of which the monarch would appoint.

Nevertheless, this dyarchy survived for but a very short period of time, as 'Constitutionalist' troops entered the Peloponnese and Augustinos Kapodistrias was coerced to resign on 29 May 1832. A seven-member government was formed out of all of the parties, whose composition 'demonstrated complete dominance of the Constitutionalists'.[58] On 27 July 1832 the 'Fourth ongoing National Assembly' ratified the selection of Otto as *constitutional* king of Greece. However, 'the question of the constitution remained the principal object of friction amongst the parties'.[59]

Otto arrived in Greece in January of 1833. The choice of a foreign monarch was accepted by all the political parties, as it resonated with the general conviction that the supreme authority should remain equidistant from each faction so that the state could function as a unified apparatus.

Another common demand was that the political system would be a constitutional monarchy. The London Conference of the Great Powers in May 1832, together with the subsequent conference in London in August of that same year, both had spoken of the configuration of a 'definitive constitution' for the country. However, as in the case of Kapodistrias, 'the regency council also aimed for a socially levelling, patriarchically-governed state of smallholders'.[60] The throne made it patently clear that it did not desire a single deviation from the regime of absolute monarchy.

With the arrival of Otto, the highest posts of the Administration and of the military were occupied by Bavarians. Until his coming-of-age on 1 June 1835, his duties were carried out by a three-member regency council of Bavarian officers (Joseph Ludwig von Armansperg, Georg Ludwig von Maurer and Carl Wilhelm von Heideck, initially), which appointed the Greek ministers. Five thousand Bavarian soldiers constituted the core of the Greek army. Funding

---

58   Dafnis 1961, p. 40.
59   Hering 2004, p. 186.
60   Hering 2004, p. 122.

for the Administration was provided by the Bavarian regency council (and not by the Greek state), which secured a foreign loan of 64 million old drachmas in 1832, guaranteed by the Great Powers.[61]

The country was divided into prefectures and municipalities according to an administrative model that emulated that of the French. Such an administrative model did not allow for any preservation of power on a local level; on the contrary, it subsumed all local authority under the control of the central state administration.[62] This hyper-centralisation of the modern Greek bourgeois state apparatus fully precluded any form of resurgence of the local power enjoyed throughout the (pre-)revolutionary period. The pre-revolutionary bodies of primates, who were defeated and pushed aside during the years of the Revolution, ended up serving as something between municipal and prefectural authorities, in the modern sense of the terms.

In 1833, the Church of Greece was declared independent from the Patriarchate of Constantinople so as to preclude any possibility of the Ottoman Empire exerting influence upon the policies of the Greek Church.[63] Besides, as early as 1829, foundations of the public school system had been laid.[64] The University of Athens and the National Technical University of Athens were founded in 1837.

I shall not expand upon the developments that took place within the Greek state subsequent to 1833, as it is not in alignment with the objectives of this analysis. I shall only note that the short-lived regime of absolute monarchy (1833–43) was confronted with similar issues of political disobedience and insurgency as the Bonapartist dictatorship of Kapodistrias had been, and was hence forced to transform into a constitutional monarchy in 1843–44, before a new insurrection would take place, in 1862, which definitively expelled the first monarch of Greece.[65]

---

61 'In the aftermath of the 1st bankruptcy, in 1826, it was impossible for the state to find a loan without a guarantee from the Great Powers' (Andreades 1925, p. 50). Regarding the loan of 1832, see Kostis 2006, pp. 317 ff.

62 Daskalakis 1934a, p. 577, Tsoukalas 1981, pp. 264–5.

63 The Ecumenical Patriarchate of Constantinople recognised the independence (autocephaly) of the Church of Greece in 1850.

64 Andreou 1987, Maurer 1976, pp. 499–616.

65 'The uprisings against the second regency council obliged Armansperg to call to arms a contingent of the guerrilla fighters that had disbanded: 3,000 irregulars marched against the insurgents in 1834. 2,000 brave young men undertook to restore order in Aetolia and Acarnania. An agent of power was thus revived, which the political parties could now also capitalise on' (Hering 2004, p. 124). See also Vournas 1956.

3.3   Political Parties, the Social Dynamic and Fear of the Masses

One particular characteristic of the revolutionary constitutional Greek state (1821–27) was the early formation of parties in international comparison, to which we referred in the previous section. Moreover, the safeguarding of the substantive political role of the three parties throughout the periods succeeding the suspension of the representational institutions is seemingly paradoxical: the period of the Bonapartist dictatorship (1828–31), and that of the absolute monarchy (1833–43). In fact, throughout these periods, 'the parties survived and later increased their power and influence, and that bears absolutely no relation to their alleged ties of political patronage'.[66] It was the parties that backed, and to a great extent organised, the uprisings against the autocratic regimes of the early post-revolutionary periods, which soon thereafter led to their dissolution.

An interpretation of the early formation of the three political parties in Greece, as well as of the preservation of their leading political role for nearly four decades, can be found only in the social dynamics, in the movement of the masses in the context of the new bourgeois institutional-state framework created by the Revolution. It concerned mass-level 'national' parties, that is, bourgeois parties, institutions that mediated relations between the *nationally politicised masses* and the state, and that incorporated the activity of the masses into the (capitalist) state and into the strategic interests that it represented.

Articulated differently, the bourgeois political parties were not each direct expressions of a specific class, class coalition or class fraction, but were more expressions, as a constitutional-representational system, of bourgeois rule over the lower classes and of the shifts taking place in this rule. The national *bourgeois* political parties were thus made up of representatives of the dominant bourgeois class only in a metaphorical sense of the term. The true representative entity of the bourgeois class is the capitalist state as a whole. The bourgeois parties, or rather, the bourgeois parliamentary system – which Althusser calls a Political Ideological Apparatus of the State – comprises only a part of that state, it effects an individual function within its frameworks: the organisation of popular representation, the reproduction of consensus in bourgeois political (and social) sovereignty via the parliamentarisation of various social and political practices and demands and their integration into the framework of the bourgeois-state strategy.

Through the distinctive ideological positions and dictates that are put forth, i.e. through a particular nuance that it imparts to the 'national strategy', each

---

66   Hering 2004, p. 123.

party realises certain forms of 'coalitions' of strategic bourgeois interests with certain fragmentary and direct interests of the 'lower-class', that is, it subsumes the lower classes via the institutional (parliamentary) representations into the bourgeois political and social order.

The bourgeois parliamentary relations of representation hence indirectly inscribe the lower classes, or masses, and their dynamics, deep within the bourgeois political institutions: as the dominated pole of a political correlation of power. Articulated differently, in 1824, Georgios Psyllas (1794–1878), publisher of the *Newspaper of Athens* 1824–26, writes:

> We are, nevertheless, always in the opinion of those, who want the Administration built upon the representational system, as, after all, we all concede, that the villagers and most citizens of Hellas are virtuous, and this seems to us a characteristic of a nation worthy of freedom.[67]

The (indirect) presence of the masses within the centre of bourgeois political parties always registers the potentiality for a future political crisis, and especially (primarily in the phase of early parliamentarianism, when social and syndicalist apparatuses of representation-subsumption of the masses into the bourgeois state are absent or have not been developed) of a crisis of catastrophic balance amongst the active (bourgeois) political forces.

It is in this context that the period of governance under Kapodistrias, as well as the period of absolute monarchy, might be understood. This was not a result of compromise between the bourgeois class and the (non-existent, in any event) 'feudal lords', nor of the volition of the Great Powers, but of the 'catastrophic balance' (and crisis) as was earlier defined; that is, that gap in political rule which was sought to be urgently filled by a non-representational state form of 'emergency'. While this 'absolutist' political form, as has been shown, may initially secure the support of a portion of the indigent or impoverished peasants, it does not succeed in stabilising in the medium term the consent of the politicised masses, nor is it able to impose absolutism onto them, principally by repressive means; put differently, it does not succeed in subsuming the lower strata under the capitalist social and political order, which it concomitantly promotes (dictates) as being of national interest.

The limited potentiality of integrating the masses into absolutist forms of bourgeois governance led to a crisis in legitimation of the regime, and to seditious activity, through which the road to establishing bourgeois constitutionalism and parliamentarianism eventually opened up again.

---

67   Cited in Hering 2004, p. 145.

At the same time, the previous analysis constitutes a critique of those dominant interpretations of the early appearance of political parties in the Greek social formation, interpretations that consider the parties either 'political patronage networks', or 'conveyor belts' for foreign interests, or apparatuses to promote individual interests. This largely concerns the very same authors who have dispraised the constitutions of the period 1821–27[68] as 'foreign' and disproportionate to the Greek reality. Gunnar Hering believes that such widespread 'underestimation of the ideological elements in the programme and policy of the parties sprouts in part from an ignorance of related sources, and in part from the absence of any methodology'.[69]

According to the problematic developed in the present chapter, there is one additional, perhaps even more significant, parameter concerning 'the underestimation of ideological elements in the programme and policy of the parties', well beyond ignorance and a lack of methodology: the *fear of the masses* and the ideological repercussions associated with that fear, as has been already mentioned.

In the period when nationalism, mass national politicisation, first made its appearance, the majority of regimes, even the constitutional-parliamentary ones, would discredit or attempt to eradicate political parties: 'Rousseau denounced the parties, the Jacobins later disparaged parties as criminal coalitions',[70] and George Washington wrote in 1796 concerning parties:

> [T]o put, in the place of the delegated will of the nation the will of a party, often a small but artful and enterprising minority of the community ... to make the public administration the mirror of the ill-concerted and incongruous projects of faction ... It serves always to distract the public councils and enfeeble the public administration. It agitates the community with

---

68 See Chapter 6, note 34.

69 Hering 2004, p. 54. The following observations by the same author are of interest: 'No one can found a political party on a national level resting upon the solidarity of friends and relatives' (Hering 2004, p. 128). 'Yet customs duties, tax rates, organic laws of the municipalities and smaller communities and the market regulations codes, road construction and the railway, the school system and the structure of public administration, the role of the Church in society and the organisation of civil liberties, the dilemmas of kingship or republic, war or peace, to mention but a few examples, none of these are questions that can be judged in the context of dyadic relations of political patronage. Contrarily, there should be general objectives and values that will appeal to at least certain social groups and ensure the cohesiveness of active members and affiliates who are not in direct communication with each other' (Hering 2004, pp. 44–5).

70 Hering 2004, p. 17.

ill-founded jealousies and false alarms, kindles the animosity of one part
against another, foments occasionally riot and insurrection. It opens the
door to foreign influence and corruption, which finds a facilitated access
to the government itself through the channels of party passions. Thus the
policy and the will of one country are subjected to the policy and will of
another.[71]

Yet in Greece as well, the views that political parties constituted political patronage, bonds of self-serving interests and foreign influence, were propounded
for the first time by officials of the Bavarian regency during the period of 1833–
35.
    A most characteristic example of this concerns a member of the regency
council, Georg Ludwig von Maurer,[72] who drew parallels between the National
Assemblies and parties, and the divide and 'unrest', as he also considered the
parties as agents of the foreign Powers.

> When the chieftains ... and the primates [kotsambasides] stood together,
> the place enjoyed tranquillity. As soon as they would fall into discord,
> Hellas would enter a state of disarray, the national assemblies would get
> underway either to justify the unrest, or for the strongest party to take
> the reins of the government ... Everything had been turned into political
> parties, which were protected and directed by foreign diplomats, each on
> behalf of one of the interests of the three Great Powers.[73]

---

71   https://www.ourdocuments.gov/doc.php?flash=false&doc=15&page=transcript.
72   Georg Ludwig von Maurer (1790–1872) was an eminent jurist and legal historian, professor
      at the University of Munich and later minister and prime minister of Bavaria. He stayed in
      Greece from January 1831 until July 1834 as a member of the three-member Regency. His
      studies on the communal legal forms in German-speaking European regions had a pro-
      found influence on the thought of Karl Marx. In a letter to Friedrich Engels, on 4 March
      1868, Marx writes: 'At the Museum I studied, amongst other things, the latest writings ...
      by OLD Maurer ... The view I put forward that the Asiatic or Indian property forms every-
      where mark the beginning in Europe receives new proof here' (Marx 1973, p. 547). See also
      Tairako 2016.
73   Maurer 1976, pp. 302, 305. Along similar lines, Gustav Geib (1808–64), royal government
      advisor to the Greek ministry of Justice during the same period (January 1833–July 1834),
      theorises that the law inaugurated by the Revolution articulated an 'anti-nationalist trend'
      ('antinationale Richtung', Geib 1835, p. 108), as it had been influenced by French law. Gun-
      nar Hering points out that similar perspectives concerning the parties as agents of the
      Great Powers were adopted by authors of the Left, 'who, precisely as their right-wing peers,
      when assessing events and situations in a negative light, readily lay blame on the foreign
      factor, on foreign governments, on some international host' (Hering 2004, p. 40). Views
      according to which the political systems of the Revolution were 'polyarchical' and as such

And yet parties do not divide, nor do they fracture, a nation, despite all appearances. Parties, rather, serve to *unify* a society fractured by conflicting interests: they mediate and inscribe into the centre of the state, into 'national interest' – which achieves corporeality within the broader institutional state system and hence crystallises on the political scene – the class practices of the exploiters and those subject to exploitation, of those dominating and those being dominated, of the governing and those being governed. In Greece, this 'national interest', the 'national strategy' into which all parties ultimately converged, was nothing but the expansion of the borders of the state, the *Grand Idea* as it was later called, the ever-present locus and desire quintessential to the nation and its agents.

---

would incite conflict are common to this day. See, for example, Katerina Sakellaropoulou, now President of the Hellenic Republic, who wrote in 2017: 'On account of the polyarchical nature of the first two Constitutions, frictions developed between the legislative and executive powers. Political life was characterised by a gradual increase in distrust between politicians and the military' (Sakellaropoulou 2017).

CHAPTER 7

The Formation of a Capitalist State and Social Formation

1 The Revolution and Its State as a Point of No Return in the Process of Consolidating Capitalist Social Relations

The Greek Revolution was the final political condensation of the process of dissolution of pre-capitalist ('Asiatic') production and social relations, and the consolidation of capitalist relations and forms of power. At the same time, it was also the result of new forms of social cohesion emerging alongside the dissemination of nationalism – the national politicisation of the masses, which is linked to the demand for political representation and social rights. The incorporation-subsumption of this new nationalist mobility of the population into capitalist power relations moved through the processes of state formation and irredentism.

The process of this transformation had begun prior to the outbreak of the Revolution, but accelerated with its eruption. With the institutional crystallisation of the new relations in the modern Greek state, the process of transformation reached, at all social levels, a point of no return. In the following, I shall attempt to summarise a few conclusions that emerge from my analysis up to this point.

At the economic level, the transition to capitalist power relations took place in concert with the development and expansion of the field of domination of commercial, ship-owning and manufacturing capital, with the parallel dissolution of collective-communal possession of land and the moulding of relations of individual possession in the countryside.

At the political level, the political function of the communal structures had already been transformed prior to the Revolution, with the transformation of the primates into mediators of the interests of commercial capital, and into political protectors of the new social relations against the interventions of the central Ottoman state apparatus. A similar role was reserved, in the context of the social transformations taking place, for the military archons (lords), whether they were a part of the apparatuses of communities (as was the case in the Peloponnese and on the islands), or were autonomous structures of warlords (*armatoloi-martolos*) and *klephts* ('thieves') (as in Central Greece). The Revolution subsumed these military rulers into the new structures, which gave rise to new military protagonists and hierarchies.

In addition, before the Revolution, a Greek bourgeois political body of employees had been formed in Constantinople, as well as in other large cities of the empire and abroad, which provided the Revolution and the new state with important cadres.

At the ideological level, the process of disintegration of Asiatic (economic, institutional, political) communal relations and forms introduced, even in the countryside, the new ideology of nationalism, alongside the ideologies of liberalism, of the 'civilised' economic and social order, etc.

The Revolution marked the rapid progression of this process of transition at all levels of society.

At the political level, it dismantled the forms of local power, laid the foundations for the formation of a formally bourgeois state apparatus, raised and established bourgeois parties and hence a formally bourgeois political scene, and imposed capitalist forms of law – bourgeois law.

At the ideological level, dominance of bourgeois ideological subsets was secured: nationalism and bourgeois political ideology now dominated on a consistent and permanent basis over religious and communitarian ideologies. Christian Orthodox ideology thus underwent a process of transformation under the hegemony of the dominant bourgeois ideological subsets. Only in the autonomous (from the new state power) regions, in the areas that for a time continued to feed the armed bandit collectives, would Christianity and communitarianism continue as the dominant ideological forms (see below).

Finally, at the economic level, the conditions for the stable and permanent domination of capital were bolstered by the Revolution, with commercial and maritime capital constituting its prevailing fractions, but also constituting the basis for the expansion and diffusion of capitalist relations in the field of manufacturing production. Moreover, the process of universalising the private property relations of peasants to the land was set in motion and ensured the anchoring of the peasant family economy to capitalist relations of production and the bourgeois state; hence, a basic precondition for the expanded reproduction of capital, i.e. for capitalist growth, was ensured.

As Gelina Harlaftis notes:

> In his renowned memorandum of 1803, Adamantios Korais wrote that the Greek area was in a process of unification, through dense networks, which were economic (commerce, navigation), social (prosperity, western way of life and interaction) and educational (press, schools, libraries, publications). He believed that these networks, maintained by a fledgling bourgeoisie and supported and staffed by the intelligentsia, unified Greek societies. This inspiring man outlined the model and creative apparatuses

of the Greek state and was not far off the mark. It would not be an exaggeration to argue that during the first forty years of its existence, one of the
main driving forces of economic development of the small Greek state
was trade and shipping.[1]

However, to the conditions of capitalist integration and growth just briefly
presented (the economic, political and ideological domination of capital, an
absence of pre-capitalist ruling classes), two limiting factors seemed to be jux-
taposed: the economic devastation and human losses caused by the seven-year
war, and the resistance of parts of the population to the new social and political
order – which manifested in the form of banditry.

2   Capital as a Relationship: Manufacture, Shipping, Trade and
         Financial Activities

The War of Independence (1821–27) resulted in the destruction of much of
the country's manufacture business. According to historian Kostis Moskov, the
value of pre-revolutionary manufacture establishments in Greece was almost
completely destroyed during the Revolution. Other authors present a similar
picture.[2] Even if this assessment seems to be unverifiable, the war obviously
had disastrous consequences on the first Greek state.[3]

A more accurate picture is provided by Professor Stergios Babanasis, who
considers that the Greek national income in 1830 was 75 percent of the income
of the corresponding regions in 1820.[4] In that same year (1830), seven industrial
enterprises and many manufactures are mentioned, which accounted for 13.87

---

1   Harlaftis 2006, p. 421.
2   'Manufactured capital had reached the peak of its development ... there around 1815, at a
    level of 200,000,000 gold francs ... almost nothing was preserved amidst the disasters of the
    Struggle' (Moskov 1979, p. 136). Katsoulis, Nikolinakos and Filias (1985, p. 470) argue that at
    the moment of the handover of power to Kapodistrias (January 1828): 'The country was in
    complete military, administrative, economic and moral decline'.
3   'It has been estimated that by 1828 the civilian population of the regions that would make up
    the Greek state had been reduced by 20 per cent since the outbreak of hostilities. Destruction
    of crops, flocks, mills and houses – the means of livelihood for an agricultural population –
    was on an even greater scale, up to 90 per cent in the case of livestock. By the time it was
    over, no Muslims remained in most of those regions. Minarets were demolished, mosques
    turned into warehouses, town halls or (much later) cinemas. Often, today, only their orienta-
    tion towards Mecca, at variance with the surrounding buildings, gives a clue to their original
    purpose' (Beaton 2019, p. 75).
4   Babanasis 1985, p. 57.

percent of the country's total employment.[5] In other words, it seems that after the cessation of hostilities, economic activity began to recover rather rapidly. This picture is consistent with the available data on public finances:[6]

> The revenues of the state soared, so that from 8,530,000 piastres in February of 1828, in April of 1829 12,378,000 piastres were collected, hence an increase of 51% [45% – J.M.] should be noted.[7]

Coastal and naval-commercial towns that were not destroyed during the war, or that were quickly rebuilt following the end of hostilities, such as Hydra, Spetses, Koroni, Skiathos, Skopelos, Santorini, Andros, Galaxidi, Aegina and Mykonos, were centres of manufacture, shipping and international commercial activity. At the end of the war, these centres became hubs for many of the business networks of Greek and Greek-speaking entrepreneurs that had developed in the Ottoman Empire, the Danubian Principalities and Russia (see Chapter 4). The case of Syros is typical in this respect:

> During the Struggle, Syros was the haven for the remaining Greek refugees from the coasts of Asia Minor, Chios and Psara ... After Independence, Syros became the leader in commerce, industry and shipping, accumulating the necessary funds ... Hermoupolis, the capital of Syros, was bestrewn with shipyards, so that 8/10 of the Greek ships were built there, and even a special type of Syriot ship was launched. The shipyards of Hermoupolis were constantly working as hives of activity, providing income to shipbuilders, carpenters, blacksmiths, coppersmiths, rope merchants and traders of all kinds connected with shipping. These incomes were received by thousands of workers, specialised in all kinds of trade, and were adequate for their families to live, but also for saving and investing in homes, land, etc. ... During the mayoral period of George Petritzis (1835–1837), companies were also established for the sake of more effi-

---

5 Babanasis 1985, p. 55.
6 'Of the domestic crafts of the countryside, silk processing took on the dimensions of a proto-industrial activity, especially concentrated in Laconia and Messenia, but also on the islands of Andros and Tinos, in the 1830s and 1840s, due to the great demand from the French silk industry. Cottage industries of a commercial nature also existed in the region of Livadia-Arachova (wool processing), in Argolis and elsewhere' (Agriantoni 2006, p. 223; see also Agriantoni 1986, pp. 33–40). For the rapid development of industrial production from 1860, which was centred in Piraeus, the 'Greek Manchester', see Tsokopoulos 1984 and Kambouroglou 1985.
7 Houmanides 1990, p. 200.

cient transport, such as that of the sailing ships of Feraldis, while in 1837 the Lloyd's Steamship Agency was established as an initiative aiming at further promoting the already flourishing trade of the island. These were followed by the agencies of the French 'Maritime Transports', the 'Dutch', and the Egyptian company 'Khedivie'.[8]

Maritime trade did not cease to be a key sector of the economy of the Greek state, not even during the second phase of the Revolution (1825–27), despite the advance of Ibrahim Pasha and the destruction he wrought. In 1830, 285 seagoing vessels (sailing ships) of over 60 tonnes, with a total capacity of 43,448 net tonnage, were recorded,[9] constituting the shipping capital of Greek shipowners.[10]

Capital, however, is not primarily a 'thing', the means of production (in this case, the sum total of all the merchant ships), but a social relation of value and surplus value production; in other words, it is a process of social reproduction on an ever-expanding scale of a specific form of exploitation of labour[11] which includes, on the one hand, the owners and managers of the means of production and the production process, and on the other hand, the direct labourers who are subject to exploitation. Therefore, in the context of this relationship, an ongoing, expanding scale of the reproduction of owners-managers and direct labourers alike is required. Such conditions of the expanding reproduction of capitalism existed from the very first moment of the foundation of the Greek state and formed the basis for further capitalist growth: within forty years, in 1870, the Greek merchant fleet numbered 2,360 ships (sailing and steamships) of 361,807 net tonnes. By the end of the Revolution, Greek merchants and shipowners had already secured a central hegemonic position in the export trade of grain from southern Russia and Romania (the Principalities) in the ports of the Black Sea and the Danube.[12]

The dynamics of shipowner capital thus aligned with the corresponding dynamics of commercial and financial capital: merchants and shipowners were bankers on the side, who expanded their turnover through their financial activ-

---

8   Houmanides 1990, pp. 252, 254; see also Kardasis 1987.

9   Harlaftis 2006, p. 456; see also Andreou 1934.

10   See also Leontaritis 1996; Papathanasopoulos 1983.

11   See Milios 2018, Chapters 1–3.

12   'The 2,500 Greek-owned seagoing ships of 1870 had been built almost exclusively on the islands and in the ports of the Ionian and Aegean seas, sailed exclusively by Greek seamen and were owned by Greek shipowners. All of this income from the international activities of Greek shipping was channelled into the economic ... development of Greece' (Harlaftis 2006, p. 432; see also Kardasis 1993).

ities and were associated with (or established) businesses beyond state borders (Ottoman Empire – Principalities and Asia Minor, Russia, Western Europe), or were affiliated with foreign businesses.

> The strong and closed caste of Syros's Chiote merchant-bankers also constitutes a tangible example of this cooperation of the outside with the inside. In the same period, among the first to invest in an initial industry in the country are those international businessmen.[13]

The Revolution had abolished all the economic and institutional-political forms of the 'ancien régime', namely, it had eliminated any pre-capitalist forms of surplus extraction and political organisation still in existence (timars and hierarchical 'Asiatic' communities, based on the absence of private ownership of land, tributes, etc.). It had thus eliminated class power relations related to the Ottoman regime, and capital remained the only form of exploitation and the only ruling class in the Greek social formation. And this, despite the fact that the majority population in the country were subsistence farmers (the peasantry). This ruling class, moreover, had the support of the state almost from the very first moment of its existence.[14]

The issue at stake here, of early (pre-industrial) capitalism and the preconditions of capitalist development, was the subject of Lenin's dispute with the Narodniks during the period 1893–97.[15] According to Lenin's analysis, to which I mostly subscribe, a social formation is capitalist not when the majority of the population consists of wage-earners, or even of workers informally subsumed under commercial capital (putting-out relations, see Chapter 4), but when the ruling class is capitalist, when the dominant form of surplus labour takes the form of surplus-value and capitalist exploitation is the main form of exploitation (the direct subsumption under capital – wage-employment – and the informal subsumption under commercial capital of the 'façon' type: domestic toll manufacturing). In other words, the relationship between the capital owner and the direct labourer was one from which the (main) form of surplus was derived and on the basis of which the whole social structure (type of state, ideological representations, etc.) was built.

As the British Marxist historian Ste. Croix points out:

---

13   Harlaftis 2006, p. 453. Regarding the productive character (production of value and surplus value) of commercial capital, see Milios 2018, pp. 69–73.

14   In January 1837, the first law promoting national industry was passed.

15   See Milios 2018, Ch. 3, pp. 31–44.

A class relation, involving class *conflict*, the essence of which is exploitation ... [entails] *the appropriation of a surplus from the primary producer ...*
The nature of a given mode of production is decided not according to *who
does most of the work of production* but according to the specific *method
of surplus appropriation*, the way in which the dominant classes extract
their surplus from the producers.[16]

Through the institutional framework established by the new state, but also
through the market mechanisms (in which the relations of the buying-up of
the product of small- and medium-sized farmers played a significant role), the
non-capitalist sectors of the economy, and first and foremost family subsistence agriculture, were indirectly subsumed under the expanded reproduction
of capital.

3   **Agricultural Production, Rural Property Relations and 'National
     Lands'**

As has already been mentioned, in areas where the territory of the first Greek
state expanded, large, landed property was but a marginal form, which in total
did not exceed five percent of the arable land. Some confusion concerning
conditions of property ownership in the countryside arose from the fact that
more than half of the arable land in the new Greek state had been defined, as
early as 1822 (at the First National Assembly), as being property of the state
(*national lands*). It had been granted to small farmers, who were considered to
be mere tenants of the state property. In 1833, national lands comprised approximately 12.9 million *stremmata* (1 *stremma* = 0.1 hectares) out of a total of 18.6
million *stremmata* of land used for agriculture and animal husbandry.[17] The
market value of land and crops ('land and plant capital') was estimated to be
approximately 364 million drachmas around 1840, and constituted 76 percent
of the value it reached in 1860.[18] Again, this portrays an agricultural economy
which, in spite of the devastation from the war, possessed the preconditions for
recovery-and-growth in the medium term.[19]

---

16   Ste. Croix 1984, pp. 101, 107.
17   Karouzou 2006, p. 182.
18   Petmezas 2006, p. 121.
19   In 1887, the market value of land and crops was estimated at 127 percent of its price in
      1860.

Farmers who cultivated national lands were obliged to pay the state a series of taxes (including the tithe), which ranged between 25 and 40 percent of the value or volume of their gross product.[20]

These conditions only appeared to simulate the regime of land ownership that prevailed in the Ottoman Empire. In reality, the Greek state, with its regulation of national lands, did not inherit the Asiatic ownership of the past, but established completely different, bourgeois-type, property relations regarding land: the state, as owner of the land in the bourgeois (capitalist) sense of the term (full ownership of an asset), acquired the right to sell it, to mortgage it, etc., rights that were unthinkable under the regime of Asiatic-Ottoman relations of production. And, in fact, the Revolutionary government of 1822 did establish land as national property only to then put it up as collateral for its international creditors: that is, were the Greek government unable to repay the national loans it had received from abroad (which were eventually granted, as previously discussed, in 1824 and 1825), it would undertake to sell off the national lands, or part of them, in order to repay its creditors.

In this way, the new power simultaneously proclaimed the *radical transformation of land ownership relations*: the Asiatic-Ottoman, collective, God-given property (which excluded any possibility of sale or mortgage) gave way to 'full' property, adhering exclusively to the social (and legal) relations of capitalism.

Moreover, the tithe is a form of rent that, conditionally, can be incorporated into the capitalist system as an equivalent, in this case, to a tax on a product, as has occurred in most capitalist countries. Karl Marx highlighted the character of 'church tithes' in Britain and the Tithe Commutation Acts, Parliamentary resolutions in 1836 and 1838, which provided for the replacement of the tithe in kind with monetary payment:

> An incorrect conception of the nature of rent has been handed down to modern times, a conception based on the fact that rent in kind still survives from the Middle Ages, in complete contradiction to the conditions of the capitalist mode of production, partly in the tithes paid to the Church and partly as a curiosity in old contracts ... where it continued to exist on the basis of the capitalist mode of production, it was nothing more, and could be nothing more, than an expression of money rent in medieval guise.[21]

---

20   Xifaras 1992, p. 121.
21   Marx 1991, pp. 923–4.

In fact, the Greek state, by appropriating a part of the peasants' tithes in kind, made them available on the market, accelerating the incorporation of that part of the agricultural economy that had remained partly self-sustaining into monetary market relations.

However, the Greek state, although it acquired legal ownership of the national lands by law, did not in fact manage to acquire actual *full* economic ownership of them. The peasants who tilled the national lands, as possessors (tenants) of state property, paid the state only a portion of the taxes that corresponded to what was due,[22] as they regarded the land as belonging to them, or at least that it could not be taken away from them, though, needless to say, most public revenues were reaped from this taxation of the peasants.[23] Soon the cultivators even secured the right to bequeath the piece of land they cultivated to their descendants, or to cede it, while at the same time only they would decide what to produce and how to cultivate their tracts, therefore also assuming the risk of any potential disaster that might occur.[24]

The national lands thus belonged to the state in the legal sense of ownership. This legal ownership also bore an economic dimension to the extent that it allowed the state to cover a part of its budget with the revenues it collected from the tenants, or to take out international loans by mortgaging the national lands as collateral for its creditors. State legal ownership of the national lands, nevertheless, was a far cry from achieving a complete form of state *economic* ownership of the land. With the (economic) rights that were secured in their favour from the outset, the smallholder peasants who were in possession of the national land were able to transform themselves within a short period of time into the real owners of the land they were cultivating: owners who were subject to a kind of 'property tax', and whom the state was in no way willing, or even able to, evict from the land they were cultivating. In this respect, as Vassilis Panagiotopoulos points out:

> The fact that between the state and the cultivators of the national lands, there was no swath of large landowners to intervene, who through the

22   Tsoukalas 1977, pp. 75–8.

23   In the first period of the Greek state, '65 % of tax revenues were represented by direct taxes and mainly taxes on land production' (Kostis 2006, p. 309). As Dimitris Xifaras observes: 'It was a budget that absorbed income primarily from the peasants, while at the same time essentially not taxing the economically dominant class at all ... The social class, which included the representatives of trade and shipping, strengthened its position within the Greek social formation as well as through favourable tax treatment ... The preferential fiscal treatment is, amongst other things, further proof of the true nature of the state. It is a bourgeois state' (Xifaras 1992, p. 167).

24   Stavropoulos 1979, Vol. B, pp. 57 ff.

mechanism of land rent, would reorganise the agricultural economy according to their own interests, allowed the peasants to feel like independent producers and to be active in the direction of intensive cultivation. On this point, the bourgeois state managed to play its role perfectly: By preventing the formation of a class of big landowners and by organising the new commercial cultivation based on the small, traditional unit, it developed agricultural production in a spectacular way and left the field open to the activity of commerce and all the class interests that flow from it.[25]

The negligible significance of large landed property in the areas that were incorporated into the Greek state with the Revolution, coupled with the ability of peasants to claim actual economic ownership of the fields they cultivated from the state, were both the direct result of the social correlations of forces within class struggle: the non-existence of feudal relations of production, or their 'commercialised-entrepreneurial' forms (plantation-like agricultural exploitation: *çifliks*), the specific process of dismantling the Asiatic mode of production and, above all, *the particular social and political weight acquired by the peasant masses through the revolutionary process*, explained their capability to defend their interests on the land. In an entirely different social balance of forces, the modern Greek state would have perhaps (as is known to have happened in Thessaly and Macedonia during the period 1881–1917) favoured large, landed property. The legal and tax regime that was formed after the Revolution with the regulation of national lands (payment in money and in kind – withholding in the form of a tax rent of part of the production –, the right to mortgage the land, etc.) could well have been based not on the small farmer-tenants, but on big landowners.

To sum up, it can be stated that the social and political correlations that were consolidated within the newly established Greek state resulted in the universalisation of small estate ownership, in spite of the fact that the state appears as the legal owner of the largest part of arable land. The social and political weight of large estate ownership therefore remained of little consequence. This dominant form of ownership in the countryside (small landed property) can theoretically correspond either to a marginalised-subsistence rural economy, or to the economic form of simple commodity production (when rural households sell their product on the market or potentially to several traders), or, finally, to the system of putting-out – buying-up, i.e. the exclusive affiliation

---

25   Panagiotopoulos 1980, p. 228.

to a wholesaler – buyer-up, who provides (and partly advances) the producer a form of 'piece-wage'. The period inaugurated by the Revolution can be
mostly characterised by a sustained and rapid expansion of the social space of
simple commodity production and buying-up relations in the countryside, to
the detriment of self-sustaining farms. The commercialisation of agricultural
economy and the subsumption of independent small farmers under commercial capital are evident from the continual diversification of crops as products
aimed for export in the decades to follow.[26]

The diversification of crops for the benefit of having tradable and export-
able products had already begun before the Revolution of 1821 (see Chapter 4).
It should therefore be of no surprise that in the resolutions of the first revolutionary National Assembly (1822), we read: 'The administration shall take active
measures to achieve any potential encouragement of trade and agriculture in
Greece, taking care, amongst other things, to establish agricultural and commercial companies'.[27]

The Revolution therefore marked a phase in the rapid integration of agriculture (of independent farmers) into the dominant bourgeois relations through
the subsumption of agricultural production (and farmers) into market mechanisms and under commercial capital. Production tended therefore to spe-
cialise in one or two products per region, to be sold (largely through the
putting-out – buying-up system) to traders based in the major ports or urban
centres. Commercial capital, by concentrating the entire production of individual small farmers through buying-up relationships, in effect appropriated
their surplus labour, leaving them (through price fixing) only what was necessary for the reproduction of their labour power and their means of production
(see Chapter 4). It placed them, as previously mentioned, in a domestic toll
production system (an early form of the 'façon' system), or 'piece-wage labour',
extending the domination of capital to the peasantry.[28]

---

26 In 1830, the cultivation of raisins covered 3,800 hectares, in 1845 7,300, in 1851 17,250, in
     1860 22,000, in 1871 34,630 and in 1878 43,500 hectares. The production is, respectively,
     as follows: in 1830 11.7 million Venetian pounds in weight, in 1845 39, in 1851 86.3, in 1860
     101, in 1871 173.2, and in 1878 435 million Venetian pounds. By 1870, nearly all production
     was exported (Kribas 1934, p. 94). In 1856, tobacco cultivation covered 1,750 hectares (pro-
     duction: 1 tonne), in 1875 4,200 hectares (production: 2.7 tonnes) (Argyroudis 1934, p. 87).
     Finally, olive groves covered 25,000 hectares in 1830, 37,000 in 1861 and 182,900 hectares
     in 1881 (Tsoukalas 1977, p. 91).
27 Cited in Evelpides 1934, p. 73.
28 In order to stabilise these relations, the state sought the 'sale' of national lands to their
     tenants, through which it also hoped to expand and intensify agricultural production.
     However, in the context of the given balance of social forces, the sale of land to the small-

To conclude this section, a further remark ought to be made concerning the role that the prevalence of small family production in agriculture may have played in the prospects and dynamics of capitalist growth.

The absence of pre-capitalist ruling classes and systems of exploitation is naturally one of the preconditions for capitalist growth, yet its dynamics are likely to be found in class struggle. For, generally speaking, the political and social potency of peasant smallholders in the early phases of capitalist development produced contradictory effects: on the one hand, it entailed the depression of agricultural prices,[29] and therefore also the reproduction cost of labour power, something which favoured profitability and capital accumulation;[30] on the other hand, however, it signified an increased resistance of peasants to the tendency of their being transformed into wage labourers, which would hamper industrial development.[31]

That notwithstanding, the fact that, with the exception of Britain, in most European countries the 'model' of small- and medium-sized family units, rather than large-scale, capitalist agriculture, has dominated the agrarian sector seems to attest to the fact that it is rather erroneous to consider the historical

---

holder tenants was not practicable (and was postponed for several decades following independence), *inter alia* because it was considered that the farmers' inability to buy the land they cultivated would also make it difficult for tax revenues secured through the tenant status to be collected: 'As regards the national lands, their redistribution was rather urgent. Two great benefits were hoped for: a) To cultivate vast areas of land and thus increase the national wealth and public revenues. b) To create a class of small farmers, thus not only solving the social question but also reducing the costs of finding work not only for refugees, but also for many thousands of destitute former fighters ... But the scarcity of private and public money made the redistribution of land impossible, as farmers could not buy land even in small instalments, and the state could not advance the costs of settlement to the needy' (Andreades 1925, p. 30; see also Chapter 5).

29   See Milios 2018, Ch. 4: 'Capitalism and the agrarian sector'.

30   Marx writes: 'In order for the peasant smallholder to cultivate his land or to buy land to cultivate, therefore, it is not necessary, as in the normal capitalist mode of production, for the market price of the agricultural product to rise high enough to yield him the average profit, and still less an excess over and above this average profit that is fixed in the form of rent. Thus it is not necessary for the market price to rise either to the value of his product or to its price of production. This is one of the reasons why the price of corn in countries where small-scale ownership predominates is lower than in countries of the capitalist mode of production ... This lower price of corn in countries of small-scale ownership is a result of the poverty of the producers and in no way of the productivity of their labour' (Marx 1991, p. 942).

31   This view is supported in the case of Greece by Panagiotopoulos 1980, p. 229, and Sakellaropoulos 1991, p. 177.

developments in Greece as a 'peculiarity', and especially a 'peculiarity' which supposedly undermined the prospects of capitalist growth.[32]

4   Remnants and Resistance of the 'ancien régime'

Commodity production did not occupy the entire agrarian production in the territory of the new Greek state. At the same time, there were agrarian zones in which, although small-scale individual cultivation relationships prevailed, they were not connected with the production of marketable products, neither for foreign trade nor for the domestic consumer and production market. These primarily mountainous, self-sustaining areas constituted the 'other Greece', in which the practices and values of the 'ancien régime' survived, and which provided the ground for the development of forms of 'resistance' to the state and the dominant economic and social order, such as brigandage as a way of collective existence, the taking of hostages for ransom, etc.

Bandits were both a remnant of the old (transformed Asiatic) social relations (the milieu of *klephts* and *armatoloi*), and a spontaneous resistance to the new, bourgeois order. They formed armed bands based on hierarchical, community-type relationships under the direction of a leader who was occasionally called a king, and the groups used the symbols of Orthodoxy as their flag.[33] Marx writes of the mass that, outside of the market and labour market, emerges from the dissolution of pre-capitalist modes of production:

> [A] mass of living labour powers was thereby thrown onto the labour mar-
> ket ... *free of all property*; dependent on the sale of its labour capacity or
> on begging, vagabondage and robbery as its only source of income. It is a
> matter of historical record that they tried the latter first but were driven

---

32   As Marx states: 'The moral of the tale, which can also be extracted from other discus-
      sions of agriculture, is that the capitalist system runs counter to a rational agriculture,
      or that *a rational agriculture is incompatible with the capitalist system* (even if the latter
      promotes technical development in agriculture) and *needs either small farmers work-
      ing for themselves or the control of the associated producers*' (Marx 1991, p. 216, emphasis
      added).

33   Edmond About's book, *Le Roi des Montagnes*, was published in 1857 and refers in fictional
      form to a gang of Greek bandits who engaged in kidnapping for ransom. About writes:
      'They had not yet noticed that the ladies wore earrings and did not order them to remove
      their gloves. So we are not faced with the bandits of Spain and Italy, who cut off the fin-
      ger to take the ring and tear off the ear for a pearl or a diamond. All the misfortunes that
      threatened us were ransom' (About 1968, p. 53).

off this road by gallows, stocks and whippings, onto the narrow path to the labour market.[34]

Eric Hobsbawm points out that banditry was a universal phenomenon endemic to rural societies,[35] and that in times of revolution banditry resurfaces:

> Bandits ... share the values and aspirations of the peasant world, and as outlaws and rebels are usually sensitive to its revolutionary surges. As men who have already won their freedom they may normally be contemptuous of the inert and passive mass, but in epochs of revolution this passivity disappears. Large numbers of peasants *become bandits*.[36]

In the case of the first period of the Greek bourgeois state, the tendency of this disengaged mass to move towards banditry could not be eliminated by the state armed forces, all the more so as the organisational forms of the 'ancien régime', the thieving bands – or *klephts* – provided them with considerable experience and armed strength.

> Where the tradition of communities and traditional social ties remain strong, we find the warlord/bandit of the first decades of the Greek state occupying (or behaving as if he occupied) the position of rival to the state representative ... For, in the process/period of transition to the modern world, the 'law' and the state take the place of the 'foreigner' and of 'other' and are perceived as an external threat.[37]

In June 1835, large gangs of bandits occupied villages in the area of Missolonghi, taking hostages, while in April 1839 bandits plundered Gytheion.[38] On occasion

---

34   Marx 1993, p. 507. '... [T]hese men, suddenly dragged from their accustomed mode of life, could not immediately adapt themselves to the discipline of their new condition. They were turned in massive quantities into beggars, robbers and vagabonds, partly from inclination, in most cases under the force of circumstances' (Marx 1990, p. 896).

35   'All rural societies of the past were accustomed to periodic dearth ... and to occasional catastrophes, unpredictable in themselves ... All such catastrophes were likely to multiply banditry of one kind or another ... An efficient modern state like France after the Revolution could liquidate the huge epidemic of (non-social) brigandage that swept the Rhineland during the 1790s' (Hobsbawm 1991, p. 22).

36   Hobsbawm 1991, p. 99.

37   Kotarides 1993, p. 297.

38   'On 8 April 1839 two hundred bandits ... attacked the town of Gytheion, broke into houses, forced the merchants to hand over their money on threat of death, looted two ships carrying loads of wheat and oil and caused so much indignation among the inhabitants that

they would attempt to play a political role, both by kidnapping foreign person-
ages, as well as through their connections with political figures.[39] As Yannis
Koliopoulos observes, for the first years of the 1830s:

> In the winter of 1834 and spring of 1835, banditry dangerously spiked and
> took on threatening dimensions, in the form of large bands of robbers that
> perambulated the border provinces in a highly provocative manner. The
> robberies of this period ... were not usually seizures and kidnappings, but
> took the form of illegal taxation or systematic looting ... Thus 93 adju-
> dicated cases of robbery were reported in 1835, of which 45 had been
> committed in the two prefectures bordering Turkey, in Aetolia-Acarnania
> and Fthiotida-Fokida.[40]

Banditry as a way of collective existence in the mountainous, self-sustaining
rural areas of the country, i.e. as a form of survival of the communitarian-
Ottoman structures of the pre-revolutionary period, was soon to disappear,
giving way to modern forms of individual or 'entrepreneurial' robbery that were
closer to the capitalist order, those that continue to characterise contemporary Western societies. The development of capitalist relations of domination
would gradually integrate the entire rural space into market mechanisms and
lead to the gradual subsumption of each rural area into state institutions and
the laws of capital circulation.

It is not within the aims of the present book to track the evolution of Greek
social formation following the end of the Revolution.[41] What we have mentioned here of the 1830s, as well as what shall be presented in the next part
of this book concerning the functioning and efficacy of the Grand Idea – the
expansionist vision of the Greeks – is intended solely to demonstrate the effectiveness of the trends and processes that were formed and set in motion in

---

they, aided by the surrounding villages, attacked the gang and destroyed it long before
the military forces from Athens arrived' (Bouropoulos 1931, p. 75). However, Bouropoulos
confuses the bandits with the 'constitutional' rebels following the dissolution of the irregulars by the regency council, such as Demos Tselios and Nikos Zervas, whom he classifies
amongst the bandits, and more generally he refers to the armed movements that demanded of King Otto the adoption of a Constitution. As Koliopoulos (1988, p. 21) rightfully
points out, 'the official terminology and scale, "bandits", "bandit-renegades" and "reneg-
ades" used by the representatives of state power, is far from helpful in estimating the
number of the former'.

39   Bouropoulos 1931, pp. 74–5.
40   Koliopoulos 1988, p. 8.
41   For a concise approach along these lines, see Milios 1988, pp. 142–285.

society and state alike by way of the Revolution. With this in mind, I shall close this chapter with an excerpt from Athanasios N. Vernardakis's book, *On Trade in Greece*, which was written in 1879 and published in 1885, and which outlines – like several other books of its time[42] – the dynamics of the Greek capitalist social formation created by the Revolution during the first four decades of its existence:

> In the span of forty years ... the expanse of cultivated land has quadrupled, products have proliferated, and some of them have also increased to an incredible extent; the livestock industry is not inferior to that of many nations (when small animals are estimated accordingly and included in the calculations). Maritime travel, though it has not increased in parallel with other advances, is, at least in proportion to the population, among the foremost in the world ... Commerce has always occupied its enviable position, industry has begun to transform slowly but steadily, and special-ised work holds a prominent position, cities have been built as if by magic on ruins and rocks; landed property reached great dimensions, its value increasing day by day, and the Hellene is living and prospering, rather like the more developed nations, saving more than most countries ... A nation ... having acquired property worth 7,300 million drachmas and being able to produce annually 689 million drachmas, of which 480 million drach-mas shall be spent and 208,800,000 drachmas shall be saved, this nation has secured its future.[43]

42   Indicatively, 'When Otto was elected first king of the Hellenic nation, Athens was a miser-able town ... Half a century has passed away, and the changes which it has brought about in the condition of Athens are such, that the first king of the Hellenes, could he revisit it, would fail to recognise his capital, were it not that the imposing rock of the Acropolis, with the ruins of the glorious Temple of the Athene, till towers over the city' (Cheston 1887, p. 82).

43   Vernardakis 1990, pp. 315–16.

PART 3

The Revolution as the 'Grand Idea' and as the 'Present'

∵

CHAPTER 8

'Hellenisation of the East': The Vision and the Reality

1   A Partial Review: A Genuine Bourgeois Revolution

Arriving at the last part of our analysis, we need to reflect upon the answers to the questions posed in this book, beginning with Chapter 1. It was seen that the designations Hellene-Greek, Bulgarian, Serbian, Albanian, etc. all retained their pre-national content when the Revolution broke out: the content referred to the (native) tongue and region of origin (see, e.g. in Chapter 1, the self-identification of revolutionaries in Wallachia and Moldavia who had fled to Russia and were registered by the authorities there). It has also been seen that the Revolution was an unprecedented historical breakthrough which differentiated it from all previous local insurrectionary movements (of *klephts* and military archons [*martolos*], Pashas, etc.) or religious uprisings (crusade-type anti-Muslim campaigns under the auspices of foreign Christian states: Venice, Russia – for example, the Orlov revolt; see Chapter 4). However, the Revolution also incorporated certain 'old' practices of armed bodies or local military archons (warlords) for as long as the benefits of victorious plundering and a salary (as in the cases of Savvas Kaminaris Phokianos and certain military archons of Central Greece; see Chapters 1 and 6) could be guaranteed.

The economic, ideological and political processes of the unification of populations and regions brought about by the development of capitalist relations and its related commercial networks constituted the background for the broad national politicisation of the masses – the development of nationalism – in regions of southern Greece. This was an unprecedented social development of enormous importance which lay at the very core of the Revolution. In other words, the Revolution was primarily the result of the dominance of nationalism, and thus also of the demand of a large segment of the population for a representative-constitutional state, for political rights for the nationally mobilised masses. It was for this reason that the formation of a bourgeois republican representative state became initially possible during the period 1821–27 (see Chapters 5 and 6). Even if, in the course of events, the representative-constitutional form of state subsequently and temporarily gave way to Bonapartism and absolute monarchy, the dynamics of the politicisation of the masses soon (in 1843–44) imposed a *constitutional* monarchy. Factors such as the economic recession and unemployment after 1815 in the geographical area where the Revolution broke out,[1] or the competition between Greek commercial centres (Hydra, Spetses, Psara) and corresponding Muslim Albanian-speaking commercial centres such as Durrës,[2] were merely secondary components that facilitated the mobilisation of the masses. And, as discussed in Chapters 5 and 6, this mass mobilisation included the class and political antagonisms that manifested in a variety of ways and outlets: in the National Assemblies, in the confrontations between different centres of power and in the civil wars.[3]

In short, the Greek Revolution of 1821 was a genuine bourgeois revolution. Having said that, I will reflect on its main features, stressing on the one hand what it had in common with bourgeois revolutions in general and more specifically the French, and on the other, what distinguishes it from them.

First of all, '1821' was *a revolution stricto sensu*. In other words, an armed struggle of the politicised masses, the 'direct interference of the masses in historical events ... the forcible entrance of the masses into the realm of rulership over their own destiny'.[4] If one, in the tradition of Antonio Gramsci, were to utilise the term 'revolution' to describe any form of political or social change, which (according to her or his opinion) would pave the way for the further development of capitalism, then one would be adopting a stance of absolute relativism in an effort to prove something that cannot be proved: that all social change (and especially the prevalence and further rise of capitalism) always presupposes a revolution. Of course, 'there is nothing that may not be proved

---

1 Kremmydas 1980, 2016a, pp. 49–53.

2 Stoianovich 1994, p. 105.

3 As Vassilis Kremmydas notes: 'The demand advanced by the Society of Friends is the establishment of a free, independent, modern, i.e. bourgeois, state with a parliamentary representative government. In other words, constitution, parliament, government, opposition. A very progressive position, by the standards of the time, but such was the demand that ran throughout the whole revolution and from which no one backed down. In the political climate of Europe at that time, the mere formulation of such a demand was tantamount to a revolution – a revolution that transcended the most advanced demands of European modernity. The Greek Revolution was, from beginning to end, and in all its details, an ongoing struggle between the traditional and the modern. It was in the civil war that this became most evident. Both factions knew that they were not fighting to eliminate the other, they were fighting to defeat the other, and would force it to integrate into its own ideology. It was the modern that won, the contemporary, the modernist. This process hit a wall in only one case: in the case of Kapodistrias' (Kremmydas 2016b; see also Kremmydas 2016a, pp. 204, 210).

4 Trotsky 1930. 'The most indubitable feature of a revolution is the direct interference of the masses in historical events ... The history of a revolution is for us first of all a history of the forcible entrance of the masses into the realm of rulership over their own destiny' (Trotsky 1930).

by a new definition. A composition of flour, milk, suet, and stones is a plum-pudding; if by stones be meant plums'.[5] To put the same argument differently, I consider formulas like 'passive revolution',[6] 'revolution from above',[7] 'revolution without revolution'[8] of little, if any, theoretical potential. A revolution cannot be 'passive', in the same way that a war cannot be 'peaceful'! And there cannot be any revolution in the absence of 'the forcible entrance of the masses into the realm of rulership'.[9]

Besides, as with all bourgeois revolutions, the Greek Revolution took place in a territory where capitalism had already established itself as the dominant mode of production. Marx or Lenin never understood bourgeois revolutions as processes of transition from one mode of production (e.g. the feudal) to another (the capitalist). Marx writes on pre-revolutionary France:

> The centralized state power, with its ubiquitous organs of standing army, police, bureaucracy, clergy, and judicature organs wrought after the plan of a systematic and hierarchic division of labour originates from the days of absolute monarchy, serving nascent bourgeois society [Bourgeois-gesellschaft] as a mighty weapon in its struggles against feudalism. Still, its development remained clogged by all manner of mediaeval rubbish, seignorial rights, local privileges, municipal and guild monopolies and provincial constitutions.[10]

And as regards the French Revolution, he explains:

---

5   Thomas Malthus, *Definitions in Political Economy*, cited in Rubin 1979, p. 311.

6   'If liberalism was the form of "passive revolution" specific to the 19th century, wouldn't fascism be, precisely, the form of "passive revolution" specific to the 20th century' (Gramsci 2007, p. 378).

7   '[T]he Italian and German principalities were eliminated by bourgeois revolutions from above' (Anderson 1974, p. 431).

8   '[T]he Risorgimento [was made] possible in the forms and within the limits in which it was accomplished as a revolution without revolution' (Gramsci 2011, p. 137).

9   Trotsky 1930.

10   Marx 1986, pp. 328–9, corrected according to original, Marx 1976, p. 336. As it can be inferred from Marx's analysis, and as I have extensively argued in the past in criticism to contesting approaches (Milios 2018, pp. 57–62), the absolutist state, although transitional, constituted *a state with manifestly capitalist characteristics*, an institutional form already corresponding to the capitalist political power in the historical period of formal subsumption of labour under capital. Along with the patrician-led Republics extending from the Italian peninsula to the Aegean – Venice, Genoa etc. – the absolutist states constituted an early form of *bourgeois states*. They comprised the type of political power necessary to safeguard the consolidation of capitalism, subsequently stabilising the social power of capital.

The gigantic broom of the French Revolution of the eighteenth century swept away all these *relics of bygone times*, thus clearing simultaneously the social soil of its *last hindrances to the superstructure* of the modern state edifice.[11]

In a similar vein, Lenin argued in 1899 in his famous *The Development of Capitalism in Russia*[12] that Russia was already a capitalist social formation, without having emerged from any 'bourgeois revolution'.[13]

The view that capitalism pre-existed bourgeois revolutions is widely accepted amongst Marxists.[14] However, the prevailing interpretation is an 'economistic' one: that bourgeois revolutions erupted *in order* to serve the more or less predestined cause of 'sweeping away the relics of bygone times', *so as to* accelerate capital accumulation.

> [A] bourgeois revolution is a political transformation – a change in state power, which is the precondition for large-scale capital accumulation and the establishment of the bourgeoisie as the dominant class. This definition requires then, a political change with certain effects. It says nothing about the social forces which carry through the transformation.[15]

> The absolutist state had either preserved the feudal and guild legal forms or had not fully eliminated them, and was thereby impeding the development of capitalism; the small size of the economic regions had become an impediment to the development of the forces of production ... As a consequence, the bourgeoisie aimed everywhere to overthrow the prevailing legal order, to destroy the existing state.[16]

What is missing from the afore-cited analyses, is, above all, the role of the masses in the process of transformation of the capitalist state and society from the ancien régime of capitalist rule to a modern capitalist state based on constitutionalism and parliamentarism. These masses were, of course, being hegemonised by capitalist power: as extensively argued in this book, consti-

---

11   Marx 1986, pp. 328–9, corrected according to original, Marx 1976, p. 336, emphasis added.
12   Lenin 1972, Vol. 3.
13   See Milios 2018, pp. 31–44.
14   See Davidson 2014 for a detailed presentation.
15   Alex Callinicos, 'Bourgeois Revolutions and Historical Materialism', cited in Davidson 2014, p. 477.
16   Bauer 2000, p. 154; also cited in Davidson 2014, p. 185.

tutionalism and bourgeois representational democracy was the new, modern form of subsuming the masses into capitalist power relations.[17]

However, their 'forcible entrance into the realm of rulership over their own destiny', their national politicisation as analysed in the previous chapters of this book, always bears the sperm of subversion, the tendency towards direct democracy and communism.[18] That is why Marx describes bourgeois revolutions not merely as processes of 'clearing the social soil of its last hindrances to the superstructure of the modern state edifice',[19] but also stresses the political and institutional reshuffling caused by the 'forcible entrance of the masses into the realm of rulership over their own destiny' and its taming through the formation of 'the political system of the new European society':

> The revolutions of 1648 and 1789 were not English and French revolutions, they were revolutions in the European fashion. They did not represent the victory of a particular social class over the old political system; they proclaimed the political system of the new European society. The bourgeoisie was victorious in these revolutions, but the victory of the bourgeoisie was at that time the victory of a new social order.[20]

Economism neglects the role of the state, reducing at the same time the dynamics of class struggle to some pre-destined vehicle of the economic development of capitalism ('the development of the productive forces'). Yet historical evolution is contingent upon a variety of factors, which also means that the development of capitalism is contingent upon the class correlation of forces that are shaped by those very same factors. Marx stressed the unpredictability of the course of the French revolution at the moment of its commencement:

> M. Guizot forgets entirely that the French Revolution began just as conservatively as the English, indeed much more so. *Absolutism*, particularly as it manifested itself finally in France, *was here, too, an innovation*, and it was against this innovation that the parliaments [French higher courts before 1789] rose and defended the old laws, the *us et coutumes* of the old mon-

---

17   See also Chapter 5, esp. section 5.4.
18   'Communism is for us not a *state of affairs* which is to be established, an *ideal* to which reality [will] have to adjust itself. We call communism the *real* movement which abolishes the present state of things. The conditions of this movement result from the premises now in existence' (Marx and Engels 1998, p. 57).
19   Marx and Engels 1998, p. 57.
20   Marx 1977, p. 161.

archy based on estates. Whereas the first step of the French Revolution was the resurrection of the Estates General [body representing the clergy (First Estate), the nobility (Second Estate), and the commoners (Third Estate)], which had been dormant since Henry IV [1553 (1589)–1610] and Louis XIII [1601 (1610)–1643], no fact of equal classical conservatism can be found in the English Revolution.[21]

In the following sections of this chapter, I will show that a main outcome of the 1821 Revolution was not only the creation of the new (modern-national) Greek state, but also that this state became a point of reference for Greek capitalists and Greek communities in the main centres of the Ottoman Empire, thus providing an economic 'argument' to the imperial vision of the 'Grand Idea' created by the Revolution itself. These capitalist enterprises owned by Greeks, as well as the Greek communities surrounding them, continued to rapidly 'grow' in the Ottoman Empire, i.e. outside the Greek state and national territory, exactly as those within Greece did; yet they were overwhelmed by the 'desire' to become part of the new state, which conceived them, in turn, as part of a 'second (wannabe) Greece'.

Capitalism is not simply 'capital accumulation'; it is a system of economic, political and ideological domination of the ruling class over the social majority. However, the social majority of the working class and the intermediate strata is, in 'normal times' (and under 'normal' conditions), 'recruited' by way of the workings of the state apparatuses, as well as by nationalism and other subsets of the ruling ideology, into the 'visions' and expansionist-imperialist strategies of the rulers.

In closing this analysis on the bourgeois character of the Greek Revolution, it is worth mentioning two elements which differentiate it from the 'prototype' of the French Revolution: (a) the Greek Revolution was organised by a secret society (the influence of which, naturally, very soon vaporised when the first state power structures and representational institutions were formed); (b) it was also oriented against not an absolutist, but an Asiatic, state, which did not necessarily hinder capitalist entrepreneurship, as has already been mentioned herein, but which certainly, after some historical moment, began to be perceived as a 'national yoke'.

Surprisingly enough, and despite these two characteristics of the Greek Revolution, especially in light of the fact that it was part of a conspiratorial plan of a secret organisation inspired by bourgeois 'Enlightenment' ideologies

---

21   Marx 1978, p. 253, emphasis added.

and the deliberately aiming at the formation of a constitutional-parliamentary state (which met the desires of the popular masses that participated in the insurrection), English-language Marxist historiography has effectively ignored the Greek Revolution – with the exception of the works of Eric Hobsbawm and some sporadic references in works by other authors. Indicative of this is the following statement by Neil Davidson, who extensively reviewed vast literature on the concept and characteristics of bourgeois revolutions:

> In Europe, those who sought to emulate the French Revolution were either defeated, as in Ireland or, more commonly, a minority within their own societies who relied on the external support of the French in order to achieve power and who consequently could not retain it.[22]

On the contrary, Greek Marxists, from the beginning of the twentieth century, considered that the interpretation of the 'social character' of the 1821 Revolution ought to be the starting point for the documentation of the revolutionary socialist or communist strategy that would change society. Their views thus conflicted with the official 'national' historiography in its various versions and were grounded as regards the character and contradictions of modern Greek society in their theoretical conclusions with respect to the outcome of the 1821 Revolution. These issues will be the subjects of the next and final chapter of this book, in which it will be shown that the Revolution was in fact a matrix of ideologies (and as a consequence, also of political practices and strategies) that remained active in the Greek social formation throughout the two centuries of its existence.

I shall presently be referring to the Grand Idea, or *Megali Idea*, the expansionist policy of the Greek state whose initial strategic aim was to occupy Constantinople and expand the territory of Greece into the Balkans, to the Black Sea coast and into Asia Minor.

My analysis in the sections to follow shall necessarily make selective reference to eras posterior to the historical period that has been addressed so far in order to illustrate the effectiveness of the ideological framework inaugurated by the Revolution.

---

22   Davidson 2014, p. 597.

2   The Grand Idea of the Revolution

From the very first moment, the Revolution set the framework for the subsequent expansionist strategy of the Greek state, later labelled the 'Grand Idea'.

The term 'Grand Idea' is usually attributed to Ioannis Kolettis, from his
speech at the *National Assembly of the Third of September* (3 November 1843–
18 March 1844).[23] Kolettis, after noting 'how far we have diverged from that
grand idea of the motherland, which we first saw expressed in the song of Rigas',
states: '[W]e, who, carrying the banner of religion in one hand, and that of
freedom in the other, *have for many years worked hard for the liberation of all
Orthodox Christians in general*'.[24] However, this formulation by Kolettis (apart
from the term 'Grand Idea' as such) did not convey anything new for the period,
nor for the National Assembly. Indicative of this is an earlier speech of a delegate at the 29th Session of the National Assembly (11 January 1844), in which we
read:

> When the trumpet of freedom sounded, it was not the voice of a province,
> of a group of people, but of the entire Greek race, whose purpose was to
> liberate the Ottoman Empire in its entirety.[25]

---

23   See Skopetea 1988, p. 257 ff.
24   Kolettis 1843–44, emphasis added. At the 31st Session (14 January 1844), Kolettis began his
     speech as follows: 'I shudder, remembering that day when we took the oath for the liber-
     ation of the motherland, when we swore to offer everything, even our life, on the altar of
     the motherland. How much of the weight of this oath must we feel on this occasion, now
     that we have come together to draw up the constitution, this gospel of our political exist-
     ence'. And he continues: 'Through her geographical position Hellas is the centre of Europe;
     standing with the East to her right, and to her left the West, she is destined to enlighten,
     through her decline and fall, the West, but through her regeneration the East. The first of
     these missions was accomplished by our forefathers, the second is now assigned to us ...
     in the spirit of this oath and of this grand idea, I have been observing the plenipotentiaries
     of the nation come together to decide no longer just the fate of Hellas but of the Hellenic
     race ... [H]ow far we have diverged from that grand idea of the fatherland, which we saw
     first expressed in the song of Rigas' (cited in Beaton 2019, pp. 127–8). And the speech con-
     tinues as follows: 'United then by one spirit, those of us who had the surname of Hellenes
     achieved only a part of the whole cause; we are now engaged in vain distinctions between
     Hellenes and Hellenes, Christians and Christians; we, who, carrying the banner of reli-
     gion in one hand, and that of freedom in the other, have for many years worked hard for
     the liberation of all Orthodox Christians in general ... What hopes does Hellas offer today,
     reborn and united into one State, under one cause, and one power, under one religion,
     and under, finally, one Constitution, which we are now bringing to completion?' (*Praktika*
     ..., pp. 190–1).
25   *Praktika ...* [*Proceedings* s.a. ...], pp. 165–6.

Besides, as Kolettis himself noted, this 'idea' was 'first expressed in the song of Rigas'. It is that very 'idea' that Alexandros Ypsilantis attempted to put into practice when on 24 February 1821 he proclaimed in Iaşi, Moldavia, that 'Morea, Epirus, Thessaly, *Serbia, Bulgaria*, the Islands of the Archipelago, *in a few words the whole of Hellas* took up arms' (see Chapters 1 and 2).

In 1843–44, little had changed in comparison with 1821–27 in terms of the ethnic geography of the Balkans. As Spyridon Ploumides states: 'The spirit of 1821 was the soul of the Grand Idea'.[26] The Grand Idea rested on four beliefs, which constituted common ground amongst the leading strata of the Greek population:

a) That all Christians in the Ottoman Empire were Greeks, or at least quasi-Greeks. As a delegate to the 'National Assembly of the Third of September' pointed out, the Constitution of Troezen (1827) included 'the whole of the Greek race, as well as those Slavic and Albanian ones'.[27]

b) That these Christian-Greek populations would move to demand the 'union' of the regions they inhabit (more or less as with what happened in 1821) with 'free Hellas'.

c) That it was incumbent upon Greece not only to prepare itself militarily to liberate the unredeemed part of the nation from the Turkish yoke, but also to civilise the East ('it is destined to enlighten the East through its regeneration', according to Kolettis), in order to accelerate the movement of the enslaved part of the nation towards liberation.[28]

d) That the West and the Great Powers would assist in the expansionist Greek vision, as the 'barbarian' Ottoman Empire has no place in 'civilised Europe'.

It is clear that the conception of the 'barbarian East' that was destined to be civilised by the Greek 'Model Kingdom' does not simply refer to the pre-national or pre-capitalist character of the Ottoman state, but also bears elements of racist denigration of the populations classified as belonging to the 'East', i.e. of the

---

26 Ploumides 2018, p. 556.

27 *Praktika*, p. 178.

28 The 'enlightenment of the East' should not, however, be interpreted as the 'European-isation' of the Ottomans, but rather as their expulsion, with a parallel 'awakening' of the national (Greek) consciousness of the Christian populations. As Vassilis Kremmydas observes in his analysis of the proclamation of A. Ypsilantis in Moldavia, entitled 'Fight for faith and motherland' (24 February 1821): '[T]he Turkish national enemy is ... an Asian tyrant, unable to follow Europe, and civilisation, an approach which, of course, reflects bourgeois ideology' (Kremmydas 1992, p. 29). On the role of the University of Athens in 'civilising the East', see Dimaras 1994, pp. 349–50; Filiopoulou 2019.

Muslims and possibly of the Christian populations of the Ottoman Empire who lacked a 'national consciousness'.[29]

Illustrative of the above is the following extract from the eulogy delivered by the poet Panagiotis Soutsos at Ioannis Kolettis's funeral on 1 September 1847:

> What glory to us, if, at a time when the aping Muslim spells out the alphabet of civilisation, we render Greece a breeding ground for distinguished men in every branch of government, and turn our state into a model of harmonious and enviable state in the East; and thus we shall instil in the expatriates who live in the vicinity of this autonomous state a heartfelt yearning to unite with us, and in the European nations we shall restore so much enthusiasm for us that their kings shall engage in the expulsion of the barbarian Asian from the European family! ... Behold, O Greeks, the road to Byzantium![30]

The 'vision' of the Grand Idea was not generally the reconstitution of the Byzantine Empire as such, as is often claimed, but the extension of the borders of a modern constitutional (bourgeois) state, an 'enviable state' or a 'model kingdom' within the *geographical boundaries* of the Byzantine Empire. 'The nation assembled will elect its elders, and to this highest parliament all our acts will yield', proclaimed Alexandros Ypsilantis on 24 February 1821 (see Chapter 1); and this constitutional-representational bourgeois order was served by the Revolution and the National Assembly of the Third of September.

The 'vision' was therefore a modern expansionism of the era of colonial capitalism: the 'enlightened' ideal of the 'civilisation of the East'[31] through the

---

29   On this issue V. Kremmydas comments by referring to the aforementioned proclamation of A. Ypsilantis: 'And yet something else, equally important, as equally class-oriented: those who will not comply will be punished by the "motherland", "which shall denounce them as illegitimate and as Asian seeds and will hand over their names, as other traitors, to the anathema and curse of posterity"' (Kremmydas 1992, pp. 29–30). As Naoki Sakai aptly notes, 'We should call a person Asian whenever we find some effect of social adversity or a trait of barbarism from the alleged ideal image of a Westerner in that person, regardless of his or her physiognomy, linguistic heritage, claimed ethnicity, or habitual characteristics ... It is in order to break through the putative exclusive-ness of our cultural, civilizational, and racial identity that we must address ourselves to others by saying you Asians. As long as you are barbaric in one measure or another, you are fully qualified to be an Asian' (Sakai 2006, pp. 188–9).

30   Cited in Ploumides 2018, p. 561.

31   As Gunnar Hering notes: 'liberal nationalism ... which covered a broad ideological spectrum, did not contain a clearly defined programme. The many variants of the Grand Idea that were discussed from 1844 onwards had only one point in common: to bring freedom

unification of all Christians into a modern bourgeois state that had emerged from the Revolution in what was considered an empire in disintegration. The Greek state,

> with Constantinople as its centre, would include ... all the former Byzantine and Turkish provinces inhabited by Orthodox Christians, from the Danube to the Libyan Sea and from the Ionian and the Adriatic to the coasts of Syria and the Black Sea.[32]

The 'enlightened' constitutional-representational ideological framework that united the political elites, and to a large extent the majority of the population of the Greek state until at least the middle of the nineteenth century – as can be deduced from the mass mobilisations in support of 'national issues' as early as the first decade following the advent of King Otto,[33] but also from the participation in the electoral processes – essentially precluded any substantial identification of the Grand Idea with the Byzantine regime:

> What had essentially been contested by the representatives of the Enlightenment was the Greekness of the ethos and the nature of the moral and political heritage of the Byzantine (and Macedonian) emperors (as well as of the senior Byzantine clergy ...) – that is, the possibility of something that had been despotic and obscurantist to be considered Greek.[34]

The vision of the Grand Idea did not seem unattainable *at first*, because in the first half of the nineteenth century it did not encounter any 'national resistance' of note from the Christian populations of the Balkans, Asia Minor and the Black Sea area. As professor of constitutional law and later minister Stephanos Streit (1835–1920) pointed out in 1893,

> Revolutionary Greece had extended her arms to all those who wanted to settle in it ... While Greece fought against the Turkish dynasty, the dis-

---

and progress in the sense of Europeanisation to those under the yoke. The parties agreed that Greece, the "Model Kingdom", could not deny its mission: to one day re-draw the borders laid out by the diplomacy of the Great Powers and to unite all those of the same nationality in the realm' (Hering 2004, p. 275).

32   Daskalakis 1934b, p. 758.
33   For example, see Vogli 2007, pp. 289–93; Hering 2004, pp. 274–5; Skopetea 1988, p. 273.
34   Koumbourlis 2018, p. 623.

tinguishing mark against the despots was religion. At that time the rival peoples inhabiting the Balkan peninsula, each of whom possesses today its own nationality, then considered it an honour to belong to the Greek nationality ... and they reaped this consciousness from the common religion in conflict with the dynasts, and joined us with a clear consciousness that they were Greeks, because they were Orthodox Christians.[35]

Streit's belief that all Orthodox Christian populations 'considered it an honour to belong to the Greek nationality' reflected the wishes of the Greek state more than the reality.

3   Greek and the Greek-Speaking Populations of the Ottoman Empire

In section 4.5.2. of Chapter 4, the spread of the Greek language amongst the influential economic and administrative strata of Christians throughout the Balkans in the late eighteenth and early nineteenth centuries was discussed. This trend persisted following the formation of the Greek state into the middle of the nineteenth century.[36]

The non-ecclesiastical education of Christians in the Ottoman Empire remained Greek until the mid-nineteenth century, when the first secular Bulgarian school was founded in 1850 by Nayden Gerov (Найден Геров, 1823–1900), who functioned as a pioneer of Bulgarian nationalism. As Raymond Detrez observes regarding Philippopolis (Plovdiv),

> Characteristic of the linguistic situation in Philippopolis, as in most other Balkan cities during the first half of the 19th c., is the mass Hellenisation of the Bulgarian Orthodox population that settled in the city. It is the result of the presence in the city of a patriarchal clergy and a Greek-speaking middle class of merchants and professionals, into which have been incor-

---

35   S. Streit, *Constitutional Law*, Part A, Athens 1893, pp. 108–9, cited in Dimoulis 2000, p. 61.
36   'For a full century after 1750 ... Greek was the primary language of commerce in the Balkans, and Balkan merchants, regardless of ethnic origin, generally spoke Greek and often assumed Greek names. Often of Greek nationality, "Greeks" were sometimes "Greeks" only in the sense that they were not "Latins". In Hungary, Croatia and the villages of Srem and Backa, the term "Greek" did not contain a narrow ethnic significance, for Greeks, Macedo-Vlachs, Macedo-Slavs, Wallachians, Bulgarians, Serbs, and Orthodox Albanians were all "Greeks", that is, of the "Greek" faith. The religious connotation yielded even to the economic: a "Greek" was above all a peddler or merchant, and in this sense even a Jew could be a "Greek"' (Stoianovich 1992, p. 50).

porated a sizeable number of Hellenised Bulgarians, who exert social pressure on the rest of the Bulgarian Orthodox population to become Hellenised. The Hellenised Bulgarians, or 'Graecomanes', in Philippopolis are called 'Gundiloi' ... By the term 'Greek language' we mean at least two variants. The first is the archaic Katharevousa which ... is taught at school as a literary language. From the language of the guild codes it appears that during the first half of the 19th c. it was also used as a written language in Philippopolis. The second variant of Greek is popular Greek, called demotic, which is spoken as an everyday language. In Philippopolis there is also the Northern Greek dialect, which is spoken in the northern part of the Greek language zone, in Thrace.[37]

Although the 'linguistic Hellenisation' of populations whose mother tongue was not Greek in the *cities* of the northern Balkans meant in many cases the formation of a Greek national consciousness, this was not always the case. In order to hasten the process of 'national Hellenisation', the Greek state, from the initial period following the Revolution, established Greek schools and (sub)consulates in cities where there was a Greek (or, in many cases, Graecophone) population of note.

Andreas Lyberatos studied the case of the Greek-speaking community of Stenimachos, a city called Assenovgrad in today's Bulgaria, and concluded that the *national politicisation* (accession to Greek nationalism) of the Greek-speaking populations there began decades after their linguistic Hellenisation; in fact, it took place in the mid-1850s, on the eve of the Crimean War, concurrent with the emergence of Bulgarian nationalism.[38]

Even if the example of Stenimachos is not generalisable, it shows that the process of linguistic Hellenisation of the Balkan educated strata did not necessarily constitute proof of their *national* Hellenisation. Put otherwise, linguistic

---

37   Detrez 2014, p. 400.
38   'Vlasios Skordelis, a prominent intellectual from Stenimachos ... in a confidential letter to the Greek vice-consul in Philippopolis [in 1862, J.M.], describes his experience in Stenimachos in the 1840s, when he himself was a student: "Twenty years ago in Stenimachos (and for the most part in the small villages) there was a most faint concept of the nation, not to say none. Hellene back then denoted IDOLATER. The Greek school, which was founded in 1843, gave a vague and confused interpretation of Hellenism ... That rare Hellenism was a spirit without substance. Hellas began to be admired, but in the way that an artistic statue is admired, a beautiful picture. *No conviction up to that point could yet support it*. Besides, I dare say, that *the idea of some type of a close relationship between the people there and free Greece, of true kinship, of intimacy, was either completely absent or obscure and confused*"' (Lyberatos 2018, p. 418, emphasis added).

Hellenisation was one of the preconditions for their national Hellenisation, but it did not pre-determine the final outcome of the process.

Once again, with the example of Stenimachos and its counterparts, the position I argued in Chapters 3 and 4 of this book becomes evident: nationalism, national consciousness, has a political content; it is neither predominantly a 'common language', nor a 'common education' (nor a 'common culture'). It is *the national politicisation of the masses*: it is a demand of the masses to the state (or *for* a state, when one does not exist), a demand related to the interior of a state territory (for political rights, and yet for national 'clarity' and 'purity' as well), and a demand related to its exterior (for the expansion of state influence and a 'correction' of its borders). And this national mobilisation of the masses expresses the historically fresh, 'modern' form of their subsumption (of the ruled, dominated classes) under capital, as its permanent function is to integrate class antagonisms into 'national unity', while in tandem immersing the state in popular support and strengthening its expansionist-imperialist strategies.

It has been seen, however, that the Greek-speaking community of Stenimachos in the 1840s did not share the national politicisation of other Orthodox populations within the Ottoman Empire, as the 'idea of some type of a close relationship between them and free Greece, of true kinship, of affinity, was either completely absent or obscure and confused'.[39]

In fact, given that the majority of the populations (both rural and non-rural) in the central and northern Balkans remained cut off from the educational apparatuses and spoke only their mother tongue, it can be concluded that until the middle of the nineteenth century, the majority of these Orthodox populations in the empire had not formed any national consciousness; in other words, until the middle of the nineteenth century (and later), these populations possessed no trace of nationalism.

Yet if the Graecophone of Stenimachos remained Romans (Greek-speaking Orthodox Christians) in a somewhat friendly climate towards Greece, there were categories of Greek-speaking Romans – clerics, diplomats of the Ottoman Empire[40] and others – who not only adhered to the pre-national ideological schemes of the Ottoman regime, but continued to adopt the 'paternal teachings' of the Ecumenical Patriarchate (see Chapter 3). The sultan's authority was 'theopneustic' for the Roman genus; the latter therefore owed allegiance to the

---

39   See note 38.
40   Constantinos Mousouros, the Ottoman ambassador in Athens, whose confrontation with King Otto led to a temporary break in Greek-Ottoman diplomatic relations in 1846, is a classic case in point.

Ottoman authorities, which, moreover, ensured the free exercise of religious duties of the Orthodox and in parallel ensured 'all that is necessary for present life'.[41] An example typical of this is a text published in 1836 by the hieromonk Gerasimos Papadopoulos, entitled 'Proof that God granted authorities to the human race, and for this reason not only should subjects not wage revolutions against the authorities, but also submit to every authority'.[42] In this text, brought to the fore by Professor Nikos Kotarides, Gerasimos, after explaining that the *so-called Hellenes* 'were motivated and inspired by the Devil to such a terrible and most senseless great revolution',[43] describes, amongst other things, his stance during the first months of the Revolution:

> Wherefore let us write letters of agreement, that all evils done by the Turks to the Romans and by the Romans to the Turks be forgiven ... and that any Turk or Roman who harms a Turk or Roman, the rest of all Turks and Romans shall pursue him ... and so shall Mavromichalis call the fighters from Mani to return to their homes, likewise the rest of the Romans ... so that peace may be concluded.[44]

Despite such marked instances of a clear distinction between Graecophones and Greeks, even after the end of the Revolution, the official 'national' discourse of the Greek state from the moment of its foundation considered all Christians in the Balkans, Asia Minor and the Black Sea to be Greeks, one of the reasons being that the Greek language was spoken amongst the educated elite in those areas. In contrast, Bulgarian nationalism, which emerged in the mid-nineteenth century, argued from the outset that speaking Greek did not signify national integration. Andreas Lyberatos refers to the views of Nayden Gerov, according to which the educated elite who spoke Greek were nothing but 'Romans', i.e. Christians of the Ottoman Empire, without the language defining any national affiliation:

> Our common people do not distinguish the difference between Roman and Greek, but when they hear someone speaking Greek, they call him a Greek, even those belonging to their own Genus; when they speak Greek and call themselves Romans, they call them Greeks.[45]

---

41   See Chapter 3, note 22.
42   Kotarides 2017, p. 295.
43   Ibid.
44   Cited in Kotarides 2017, p. 304.
45   Cited in Lyberatos 2018, p. 420.

The process of linguistic and national Hellenisation in the Balkans, from the middle of the nineteenth century, was hindered by three factors:

a) Rural migration to the cities, which displaced the use of the Greek language in favour of the mother tongues of the populations entering the cities (Bulgarian, Serbian, Romanian, etc.).[46]

b) The penetration of Russian political and ideological influence in the context of the politics of 'Pan-Slavism'. 'Pan-Slavism' forged clear objectives of cultural and national 'awakening' (in the development of Slavic nationalism) of the Slavic-speaking peoples of the Balkans following the Crimean War, although, according to some sources, its roots can be traced back to the Russo-Ottoman war of 1828.[47]

c) The reforms introduced by the Ottoman government, first in 1839 when the Tanzimat was decreed, and thereafter when the Hatt-ı Hümayun was decreed in 1856, both of which recognised equal rights for all subjects of the Ottoman Empire (with the abolition of the distinction between 'the faithful and the faithless'). The purpose of these reforms was to integrate the Christian communities into the empire's social, political and economic system, the former of which included almost exclusively not only capitalists, but all kinds of elites (scientists, technicians, merchants of all categories) – and even the majority of workers. These reforms raised hopes, to a certain extent, in certain educated sections of the Christian populations, of attaining a more influential role in the life of the empire, 'though much of what was associated with the *Tanzimat* reforms was hypothetical, implemented only at limited scales, in later years, or not at all'.[48]

---

46   'Due to the Greek cultural and social dominance in the cities, particularly in the 18th and 19th centuries, a large part of the Bulgarian urban population was Hellenized. By the end of the 18th century, massive immigration of Bulgarian peasants to urban areas ("rustification of the cities") started a process of re-Bulgarization of the cities, which involved a struggle for cultural autonomy – the so-called church struggle – during which the Bulgarian national consciousness crystallized' (Detrez 1997, p. 100).

47   'The campaign against Turkey in 1828 yielded an abundant harvest of valuable chorographical and ethnological information for the great Russian Cabinet, the most important of which was the topography of the Balkans and its mountain passes, and the revelation that on the Balkan hillsides there is a people that can be called Slavic, as a result of the affinity that has been shown to exist between the dialect of this people and the Russian language. Thence the plan was hatched and resolved in the Russian cabinet for these people to be used in order to solve a twofold problem, free passage through the Balkans and the claim of Slavic rights over Thrace and Macedonia. The people were the Bulgarian people, and the mastermind behind the plan was Dievic, who was awarded the title of Knyaz-Savlansky (prince conqueror of the Balkans) by the Tsar' (Aspreas 1930, pp. 56–7).

48   Evered 2012, p. 13.

Despite these contradictory and largely countervailing trends, the only nationalism that had developed amongst the Christian populations in the Ottoman Empire in the first decades of the nineteenth century was Greek nationalism (a Greek national consciousness). This development rested on the ideas of the Enlightenment and the Graecophone educational, ecclesiastical and administrative apparatuses of the Christians in the Ottoman Empire, yet also stemmed from the policies of the Greek state and the presence of flourishing Greek enterprises – as well as migratory flows from Greece into the empire that were connected to the activities of these enterprises.

4   The Economic Dimension of the Grand Idea

With the foundation of the new Greek state, the expansion of Greek business networks into the broader Balkan area, Asia Minor, the Mediterranean and Western Europe did not cease, but actually intensified (see sections 4.6. and 7.2.). In fact, this extensive entrepreneurial activity was linked to the Greek state and its services, and drew its workforce in part from the population of the kingdom. As a consequence, the strong economic presence of Greek businesses and communities suffused the Grand Idea with the appearance of viable future development.

In the middle of the nineteenth century, Greek shipping controlled more than half of sea transport to and from the ports of the Ottoman Empire (Thessalonica, Constantinople, Smyrna, etc.). On the Danube, the Greek flag was second only to the British flag. In the Crimea and in the ports of the Sea of Azov the Greek merchant fleet was foremost.

The economically hegemonic presence of Greek capital in the region was followed by a stream of migration from Greece to the major cities of the Balkans, Asia Minor, Southern Russia and Egypt, and was intertwined with the further expansion of capitalist (commercial and industrial) enterprises owned by Greeks in these regions. The majority of the immigrants were employed in businesses of Greeks abroad. The rest simply availed themselves of the opportunities created by the strong presence of Greek capital in these regions. It was thus a migration that followed, and was fully entangled with, the expansion of Greek capital in south-eastern Europe.[49] The migratory stream from Greece into the Ottoman Empire had a particularly unique colonial nature from its outset.[50]

---

49   Kardasis 1998; Tsoukalas 1977 pp. 97–155 and pp. 269–371; see also Paraskevopoulos 1896.
50   Indicative of this was that the Greek population of Asia Minor went from 7.9 percent of

What was thus of great significance was not the number of Greeks abroad (who constituted a minority in nearly all of the aforementioned regions), but the economic (and by extension, international-political) role played by the Greek minority communities outside the Greek kingdom.

By the mid-nineteenth century, the Greeks controlled about 50 percent of industrial production in the entire Ottoman Empire (as a whole, not only in the regions with a pronounced Greek element), and more than 50 percent of Ottoman foreign trade. It is worth noting that in the nineteenth century, only 15 percent of the empire's industrial production was in Ottoman hands, while the rest was controlled, apart from the Greeks, by Armenians (more than fifteen percent of industrial production), Jews (5 percent) and other non-Muslim minorities.

In Russia and Romania (the Principalities), Greek merchants held the majority of cereal exports, which, in the case of Russia, in the mid-1830s constituted 15 percent, and in 1870, 31 percent, of the country's total exports.[51]

Gelina Harlaftis summarises the dominant position of Greek capitalists in the greater Mediterranean region in the nineteenth century as follows:

> From the end of the Napoleonic Wars until the First World War, the trade of the Eastern Mediterranean and the Black Sea, and especially that of bulk cargo, was organised and developed thanks to an entrepreneurial network of Greek trading communities scattered in the main ports of the Mediterranean and the Black Sea. This merchant shipping network, which started in the region of the Ottoman Empire at the end of the 18th century, had taken on its full 'pan-Mediterranean' shape by 1830 and during the 19th century its members outstripped other European competitors … Its prosperity lasted for two generations, from the 1830s to the beginning of the twentieth century.[52]

---

the total population of the region in the eighteenth century, to 21 percent of the total population of Asia Minor in 1880. The increase in the Greek minority populations in Romania, Southern Russia and Egypt was similar, although in those regions it appertains to much lower percentages of Greeks relative to the total population. Throughout the nineteenth century, Greeks abroad clearly outnumbered the inhabitants of the kingdom.

51 Kardasis 1998; Tsoukalas 1977 pp. 320 ff. 'Having a direct connection with the rural hinterland and expanding commercial networks with branches in the major European markets, they ensured strong access to both production sites in the hinterland and to western markets, wherever agricultural products were pushed' (Patronis 2015, p. 31).

52 Harlaftis 1993, p. 69.

Greek capitalists abroad should not be considered merely a part of the bourgeois entrepreneurial activity in the country where their capital was invested. For reasons that can be traced to the economic as well as political and ideological level, being agents of nationalism in an originally pre-national empire, Greek capitalists abroad constituted a distinct type of expansionism of the Greek capitalist social formation: the close relationship between Greek shipowner capital and Greek capitalists abroad has already been mentioned, as well as the relations between the latter and the Greek population (the migration stream). To this can be added the import of capital or transfer payments (donations and remittances) by Greek emigrants abroad and Greek capitalist 'benefactors' to Greece.[53]

Needless to say, what constituted the most decisive factor in the entanglement of Greek capital and Greek populations abroad with the Greek state was the prospect of the geographical expansion of Greek territory into nearly every area of the Ottoman Empire where the Greek element maintained a hegemonic economic and social position. This political perspective harboured an adjunct counterpart indispensable to the ideology of expansionism (the Grand Idea), while synchronously maintaining a link to a series of economic functions that attached, or at least closely linked, Greek capital and Greek communities abroad to the process of expanded reproduction of social relations within the Greek social formation. The Greek capitalists and the Greek communities in other lands functioned as 'harbingers' or 'ambassadors' of the expansionism of the Greek state. The expansion of the borders of the Greek state was, after all, the precondition for the stabilisation and 'elevation' of their (economic) domination into real (political) power.

Greek capitalists outside of Greece were therefore not simply a part of the ruling classes of the country where they had settled; they formed relatively autonomous and self-reproducing communities with their own educational, religious, cultural and to some extent political apparatuses in close connection, and in mutually determining relationships, with the processes of economic and social evolution of the Greek social formation. Greeks from abroad studied in

---

53 One of the most prominent Greeks of Russia in the nineteenth century was Grigorios Maraslis (1831–1907), who served as mayor of Odessa from 1878 to 1894, founded the Marasleio Commercial School (today, the Athens University of Economics and Business), the Marasleio Elementary School of Athens, the Marasleio Orphanage of Corfu, the Patriarchal Marasli Urban School in Phanari, Istanbul, the Marasleion Commercial Orphanage of Thessaloniki, the Marasleion School in Philippopolis (Plovdiv), the library in Gano, Eastern Thrace, and supported the construction of the building of the Hippocratic General Hospital of Athens (Papoulides 1989).

the Greek educational system,[54] while concomitantly functioning as important financiers of Greek education.[55] To a certain extent, they based their economic and social ascent on the existence of the Greek state (and on its diplomacy), while investing in projects involving local infrastructure, as well as in Greek politics.[56]

As Friedrich Thiersch (1784–1860) observed as early as 1833:

> Examining Greek trade outside the borders of the kingdom, we find first the Greek trading houses in Turkey ... This trade, although being carried out in the Ottoman Empire, nevertheless belongs to Greece, since ... the Greek nation was almost exclusively entrusted with this trade before the Revolution. Almost nothing has changed in this respect. For *the separation of Greece is nothing but a political separation.*[57]

The presence of Greek communities in the Ottoman Empire thus constituted a factor that reinforced expansionism of the Greek social formation: the prospect of geographical expansion of the Greek state into regions of the Ottoman Empire where the Greek element maintained a hegemonic economic and social position was thence rendered far more viable.

Through their close connection with Greek society and on the basis of their leading economic position in the Balkan, Asia Minor and Mediterranean areas, Greek capitalists and the Greek communities of the diaspora constituted a material precondition of the expansionist policy and ideology of the Greek state.

The Grand Idea did not therefore constitute an ideological cover to conceal a 'pathogenesis' of Greek society. In an era of rapid territorial reshuffling and national expansion, or 'awakening', the Grand Idea could claim for Greece those areas in which Greek capital and Greek communities were or could be the economically – but also socially and culturally – dominant element.

---

54   In the 1890s 'the government wanted to impose tuition fees at the University ... they were accused of callous class politics and a violation of national obligations, because the fees worked against the young people coming from unredeemed Hellenism' (Hering 2004, p. 580).

55   Andreou 1987.

56   Exemplary here is the case of large estates in Thessaly, the *çifliks* (*tsifliks*), belonging to Ottoman landlords until the annexation of the territory to Greece in 1881: at the urging of the Greek government, Greek capitalists from abroad bought a large number of these *çifliks*, thus facilitating the peaceful annexation of Thessaly to Greece.

57   Thiersch 1972, Vol. B, pp. 71–2, emphasis added.

The power of persuasion of this nationalist vision can thus be characterised:

> [W]hen, under Otto, the seat of the kingdom was transferred from Nafplion to Athens, many people seriously considered whether they should build houses in the new capital, since the day was so near when Constantinople would once again become the centre of Hellenism.[58]

The unrealistic aspect of this expansionist strategy lies not least in the fact that the political and military power of the newly established Greek state would not, under any circumstances, be able to carry out such an expansion of Greek territory. However, as historical development has demonstrated, the material preconditions for the expansion of the borders of the Greek state had existed from the outset, and were fanned by the Grand Idea for an entire century, until the crushing defeat of the Greek army at the Sangarius (Sakarya) River in Anatolia.

The Greek population was thus convinced throughout the first century of the existence of the Greek state, that beyond state borders there existed a second 'homeland', the Greater Greece, which was destined to be integrated at some point in the future into its national borders. According to an article in the newspaper *Athena* in 1861,

> And the capital of Greece, Athens, is the focus and centre of enlightenment and culture of two, so to speak, concentric states, the state of free Greece and the great state of enslaved compatriots.[59]

The internal cohesion of the Grand Idea should therefore not be underestimated: Greek capital held a strong presence and often dominated in nearly all areas that were staked out, and was supported by flourishing Greek minorities there. National intellectuals and historians 'proved' historical 'continuity' and 'Greekness' (through the centuries) of these territories. All that remained was for the Greek flag to follow. In fact, until about 1860, Athens was the centre of financing and 'executive planning' not only for many movements or attempts against the Ottoman Empire, but also for similar movements within the Italian national movement of the Risorgimento ('Rising Again').[60]

---

58   Daskalakis 1934a, p. 758.
59   *Athena*, 11 November 1861, cited in Skopetea 1988, p. 291.
60   'In 1859, volunteers joined the "Greek Legion" which intended to fight in Italy. In 1861–1862 the Greek Garibaldists headed the committees preparing for revolt in the areas of Hellenism still under yoke. On 25 March 1861, the portraits of the royal couple were no longer

In the era of nationalisms, of the national politicisation of the masses, capital, nation and state are different aspects of one and the same class domination: capitalism. At the same time, expansionism emerges as a tendency intrinsic to capitalist domination.

5   Contraction and the 'Stability' of the Grand Idea Following the Development of Balkan Nationalisms

The Crimean War (1853–56), between Russia on the one hand, and the Ottoman Empire, Britain and France on the other, and the rapid development of Balkan nationalisms that ensued, was a turning point in the history of the Grand Idea.

With the outbreak of the war between Russia and the Ottoman Empire, the majority of the political world and population of Greece, and above all King Otto, believed that the moment for the realisation of the Grand Idea had arrived. Despite official Greek neutrality, at the encouragement of Otto, Greek armed paramilitary units, led by Demetrios Karaiskakis (son of Georgios) and Demetrios Grivas, invaded Thessaly and Epirus, and within a short time occupied the entire region but for a few castles. High-ranking officers in the Greek army such as Kitsos Tzavelas, Giannakis Ragos, Andreas Iskos and Georgios Varnakiotis also hastened to assist in the operations, though they had previously resigned from the army. The clashes extended to Western Macedonia under the leadership of warlord Tsamis Karatasos. In February 1854, however, Britain and France joined forces with the Ottoman Empire against Russia, and in May 1854 French troops landed and occupied Piraeus to put a halt to Greek involvement in the war. Greek troops retreated from the territories of the Ottoman Empire, but the occupation of Piraeus lasted until 1857.[61]

The failure of the Greek invasion of Thessaly and Epirus shattered the prestige of the king, who was considered by a large segment of politicians and the population to be responsible for the failure. All the more so when, at the end of the Crimean War, it became evident that Russia, in whose foreign policy the king seemed to have pinned his hopes, was not promoting Greek interests, but in fact had been supporting and promoting the national endeavours of other

---

displayed, yet a portrait of Garibaldi and the flag of Sardinia were placed in a house opposite the Metropolitan Cathedral of Athens' (Hering 2004, p. 346). See also Liakos 1986.

61   Kambouroglou 1985.

Balkan peoples, something which came to the fore after the war: first, with the systematic activity of Bulgarian intellectuals and clergymen in favour of the independence of the Bulgarian Church from the Ecumenical Patriarchate of Constantinople (efforts that were accomplished in 1870), and thereafter with the initiatives for the establishment of independent states, with the *de facto* independence of Serbia in 1867 and Bulgaria in 1878, a period when the separatist Albanian nationalist movement began.

The Crimean War can therefore be viewed, schematically, as the starting point of the formation of Balkan nationalisms,[62] aside from, naturally, the Greek one.[63] Following the end of the Crimean War, any prospect of Greek expansion throughout the Balkans could no longer be sustained. The Grand Idea did not retreat; its goals and tactics were merely reshaped.

To conclude, during a time of transformation of the European political map,[64] the Grand Idea was not dissonant with reigning ideologies: on the contrary, it expressed the reality of the unique form of expansionism of Greek capital in the Balkans, Asia Minor and the Black Sea, while also being the result of the historical formation process of the Greek state and Greek nationalism (modern Greek national consciousness).

Expressing the dominant views of the Greek state after the Crimean War, Nikolaos I. Saripolos (1817–87), professor of 'Forensic Science' (and later of Constitutional Law) at the University of Athens, published in Trieste in 1866 his 186-page treatise entitled *Le passé, le présent et l'avenir de la Grèce (The Past, Present and Future of Greece)*. In this work, which was clearly addressed to the educated European public and European authorities, he reiterated the basic principles behind the Greek 'national strategy' and the establishment of the Greek state since the Revolution. 'Greece was commissioned by God to wage

---

62   In an article in the *New York Daily Tribune* in October 1858, Karl Marx noted: 'The Crimean war offered to the oppressed peoples an opportunity, which they ought to have seized upon with the rapidity of lightning; for want of organization they have allowed it to faint away' (Marx 1984, p. 38).

63   'We may mark the year 1856 as a typical date for the conspicuous emergence of the "Bulgarian Question". As early as July 1856 a "supplication in the name of the Bulgarians" was presented to the sultan, making an appeal for the same privileges as those shared by the Greeks and Armenians' (Matalas 2002, pp. 163–4).

64   '... [H]opes for a great alliance of the "new peoples", for a common uprising of the Hungarians, the Italians, the Balkan Slavs and the Greeks were growing stronger and stronger. Since the Turks in 1858 had been defeated by the tiny Montenegro, why should the united forces of these peoples not be victorious? ... [A] forbidden prayer for the victory of Sardinia was sung in a chapel on Lycabettus' (Hering 2004, p. 346).

"war against Asian barbarism" and to create a "new civilisation", which it would transmit to the peoples of the East'.[65] The new element relative to the original conception of the Grand Idea was the assertion that other states aside from Greece would emerge from the dismemberment of the Ottoman Empire, namely the kingdoms of Romania, Serbia and Bulgaria, while Jerusalem would be declared an autonomous hegemony or republic (as the question of the ownership of the 'Holy Sepulchre' had been an ongoing point of friction between Catholic France and Orthodox Russia and one of the disputes of the Crimean War).

What is important for the analysis of the present chapter, however, is whither Greek territory would extend according to Saripolos's analysis-proposal. In the Balkans, Greece would include Thessaly, Epirus, Macedonia 'up to the Šar Mountains [Шар планина]' (i.e. entire present-day North Macedonia) and Thrace (Western and Eastern). Greece would also include:

> the islands of the Archipelago, as well as all the coasts of Asia Minor as far as the straits of Cilicia and Syria ... where the Taurus ends and Lebanon begins. The boundaries of the Greek state would also include the northern coast of Asia Minor up to Trebizond 'where the last boundaries of the Greek nation ended', as well as the islands of Cyprus, Rhodes and Crete.[66]

From Saripolos's treatise, which presents the official Greek irredentist claims to the European public, it becomes clear that, despite the then obvious presence of other Balkan nationalisms, Greek expansionism continued to envision a 'Greater Greece' of the Balkans, the Black Sea and Asia Minor.

The act of independence of the Bulgarian Church (Bulgarian Exarchate) from the Patriarchate of Constantinople in 1870 made it clear to the Greeks that their hopes of expanding into Balkan regions even further to the south, first and foremost into Macedonia, were in danger.

> The first blow to Greek aspirations in Macedonia was the sultan's firman of March 11, 1870, establishing the Bulgarian exarchate church ... Article X of this act stated that new dioceses could be added to the exarchate upon the vote of two thirds of the inhabitants. This opened the way to the indefinite expansion of the exarchate in Macedonia. The Greeks reacted

---

65   Ploumides 2018, p. 563.
66   Ploumides 2018, p. 564.

sharply to the setback. An anti-Slav society was organized in Athens, while Greek crowds shouted in the streets of Constantinople, 'We won't be absorbed by the Slavs; we won't let our children be bulgarized'.[67]

Although events such as the incorporation of the Ionian Islands in 1864, the Cretan Revolt of 1866 and the annexation of Thessaly and Arta in 1881 continually raised the irredentist expectations stemming from the Grand Idea, even if on a less ambitious scale, nevertheless, from the latter half of the century, Greek nationalism and the corresponding expansionist ideology and political strategy that accompanied it were in a perpetual state of readjustment: they would constantly oscillate between 'anti-Turkism' and 'anti-Slavism'. In the words of Charilaos Trikoupis[68] in 1875 and 1876:

> The national idea of Hellenism is the liberation of the Greek land and the establishment of a unified Greek state including the entire Greek nation ... Eirenic or pro-war policy, action or inaction, friendship or distrust towards the [Sublime] Porte, alliance or neutrality towards the other Christian peoples of the Ottoman state, all these are not principles of their own accord, but are the results of the influence of circumstances on the uniform national idea of Hellenism. It is towards the realisation of this idea that Greece is steadily treading, sometimes through this policy and sometimes through that.[69]

A further repercussion of the developing Balkan nationalisms following the Crimean War, but also of the reforms introduced by the Ottoman Empire

---

67 Stavrianos 1958, p. 468. 'The declaration of the Bulgarian schism did not only identify the new "external" enemies of the nation but also defined the internal boundaries of *Hellenism* ... The Bulgarians – and by extension Slavism – would evolve from being "brothers", into the worst enemy of Hellenism' (Matalas 2002, p. 343). In an initial version, according to Greek elite circles, the Bulgarians were not a distinct nation, but had simply been misled by Russian pan-Slavist policy. The prominent Greek banker and industrialist Andreas Syngros (1830–99), operating both in the Ottoman Empire and in Greece, wrote in his diary in 1877: 'Did Bulgarians 15 years ago ... divide the races into Bulgarian and Greek? Who, then, of the civilised did not study and did not speak Greek? ... Knowing the nature of this conflict between the two races, it is readily understandable that, as soon as the causes of the rupture have disappeared, little by little the gap will be closed and unification will come about' (Syngros 1908, p. 279).

68 Charilaos Trikoupis was a leading Greek politician who repeatedly served as elected prime minister of Greece in 1875, 1878, 1880, 1882–85, 1886–90, 1892–93 and 1893–95.

69 Cited in Skopetea 1988, p. 270.

and Russia, and alongside the rapid development of Russian capitalism in the second half of the nineteenth century,[70] was the shrinking role of Greek businesses abroad in the final decades of the nineteenth century.[71]

The precarity of the international political situation, however, would constantly recalibrate visions of Greek expansionism, in spite of the limited political and military scope of the Greek state.

The Greek Grand Idea was a 'logical possibility' or an anticipated contingency for a significant fraction of 'public opinion' in 'civilised' (i.e. capitalist) countries of the time. The words of the German historian Ferdinand Gregorovius (1821–91), writing in 1889, are illustrative of this:

> The star of Athens, which is rising again on the horizon of history, may be darkened again by Constantinople if, following the withdrawal of the Ottomans from the Bosphorus, the Greek army reappears in Aghia-Sophia and a civilised modern Greek state with Byzantium as its centre is re-established, which would attract like a magnet the vital spirits of Greece.[72]

The Grand Idea reached its limits in the twentieth century, in the wake of Greece's gains in the Balkan Wars and the First World War, which was followed by the Asia Minor campaign and 'catastrophe'. Despite radical changes in borders, politics and ideologies at the global level, the Grand Idea harboured the pretence of being a 'great and sacred task of civilising the East' until its expiration in 1922:

> [T]he Greek nation is once again entrusted by humanity with the great and sacred task of civilising the East.[73]

---

70   See Milios 2018, p. 31 ff.

71   'The commercial reforms ... which took place in Russia, according to which foreign merchants could enjoy the same privileges as local merchants, reversed the advantageous position of Greek merchants who had acquired Russian citizenship. The port of Odessa ceased to be a "free port" in 1857 and thus lost its advantages for importers in the region ... Competition from other grain-producing countries, such as Romania, America and India, further reduced the profits of the old export trading houses ... Thus, the large Odessa trading houses were gradually replaced by a large number of Jewish brokers, speculators, agents and suppliers who were prepared to accept smaller profit margins' (Harlaftis 1993, p. 116).

72   Gregorovius 1994, p. 470.

73   Ministry of Foreign Affairs, Press Office (1921), *Greece in Asia Minor*, Vol. 1, p. 33; 'Greece entered Asia Minor as the guardian of European civilisation.' Ministry of Foreign Affairs, Press Office (1922), *Greece in Asia Minor*, Vol. 2, p. 3; citations in Ploumides

The crumbling of the Grand Idea greatly undermined the strategy of 'civilising the East'; it did not, however, eradicate either the intensity of Greek nationalism or the irredentist elements within it.

6   After the Grand Idea: 'A Rupture within Continuity'

The Grand Idea reined in the popular masses to the dominant bourgeois political strategies for an entire century. Even the 'national schism' of 1915–18[74] constituted a rupture *within the national ideology*, just before the apogee (and the demise) of the Grand Idea, with the invasion of Asia Minor by the Greek army.

2018, pp. 565–6. Arnold J. Toynbee (1889–1975), Professor of Byzantine and Modern Greek Studies at the University of London and holder of the Koraes Chair at King's College 1919–24, and to whom I referred in Chapter 3, was an eyewitness to the 'civilisation of the East' in 1921, and wrote the following year:

> My wife and I are also witnesses for the Greek atrocities in the Yalova, Gemlik, and Ismid areas, with which the reports of these latter investigators are largely concerned. We not only obtained abundant material evidence in the shape of burnt and plundered houses, recent corpses, and terror-stricken survivors; we witnessed robbery by Greek civilians and arson by Greek soldiers in uniform in the act of perpetration; we also obtained convincing evidence that atrocities similar to those which had come under our observation in the neighbourhood of the Marmara during May and June 1921, had been started since the same date in wide areas all over the remainder of the Greek occupied territories (Toynbee 1922, p. 502).

74   The period 1909–22 was one of the most eventful phases of Greek history. A military coup in August 1909 organised by young officers who demanded the remodelling of the Greek army was the point of departure for mass demonstrations in Athens and Piraeus the following month, which resulted in a reshuffling of the country's political scene under the leadership of the liberal-reformist Cretan politician Eleftherios Venizelos (1864–1936), who in 1910 was elected Prime Minister of Greece. With the Balkan Wars (1912–13) and World War I, Greece had tripled its territory by 1920; but its military defeat in 1922 by the Turkish nationalist forces of Kemal Atatürk cut back its territorial gains to double of what the national land had been before the wars. After the victorious but highly sanguinary Balkan Wars (1912–13) against the Ottoman Empire and Bulgaria, a large part of the Greek population rejected the strategy of prime minister Eleftherios Venizelos for the country's involvement in the First World War in 1914 on the side of the Entente Powers. The king also favoured the neutrality of Greece, basing his decision on reports by the General Staff. After a period of Greece's neutrality, the threat to the country's territorial integrity from the initially victorious Central Powers (Germany, Austria, Bulgaria) in the Balkans led to a split of the polity into two governments, before the final victory of Venizelos – with Greece joining the Entente forces in June 1917. See Milios 1988, pp. 173–91.

The Grand Idea being spent, Greek nationalism was remodelled through the quest for a new 'national vision'. As Dimitris Xifaras observes, the new vision was based on two pillars, between which tensions often developed; however, they were not incompatible with one another, as they originated from the same historical-ideological matrix.[75]

The one pillar had to do with a project of 'modernisation', which logically succeeded the 'enviable state' or 'model kingdom in the East'. In the words of Prime Minister Eleftherios Venizelos, it was a project of the 'contemporary state ... which, if not a pioneer, will nevertheless follow in the vanguard of other nations that are at the forefront of civilisation'.[76]

The second pillar concerned a search for 'national self-awareness' and 'national identity', of which Orthodoxy, as the 'cradle of the nation', was a component.[77] Amongst liberal intellectuals, this approach, which to this day has had a 'brilliant career', was shaped by the periodical *Idea*, whose founders and members of the editorial committee were Spyros Melas (1882–1966), George Theotokas (1906–66) and Yannis Economides.[78] It was Melas who conjoined Greek nationalism with the Christian tradition in a systematic fashion. He and the *Idea* circle would introduce the notion of the necessity of distancing the nation from 'irredentist nationalism' in the name of 'spiritual Hellenism', a supposed superiority of the Greek nation over all other nations that emerged from the Hellenic-Christian heritage. In the very first issue of *Idea*, Melas writes:

---

75   Xifaras 1995, 1996.

76   'We are now a nation that has passed through the age of childhood, is completing its youthful years and is beginning to enter manhood. Whoever bears this in mind, how is it possible to doubt that the career-path of the nation in the second century of its free life will be better than the first? I am certain that in the second hundred years we shall achieve great results, most certainly in another direction, not in the direction of substantial territorial expansion or the liberation of enslaved brothers and sisters, who, I do not want to consider how, assembled within the borders of the free homeland, but towards the creation of a contemporary state, which, if not a pioneer, will nevertheless follow in the vanguard of the other nations that are at the forefront of civilisation' (El. Venizelos, speech to the inhabitants of Kalavryta, 28 May 1930, cited in Xifaras 1995, p. 76).

77   Xifaras 1996, p. 78.

78   The first issue of the periodical states its objectives, which include, amongst others, that these objectives shall 'be realised without breaking the continuity of civilisation, without sacrificing the spiritual and moral heritage of centuries, without social and national disasters, without barbaric tyrannies. To this end we shall strike down the preachings of class hatred and blind fanaticism, from whomever it may come. *Idea* is an instrument of the free spirit high above parties and social classes and against all demagogy' (cited in Xifaras 1996, p. 61).

In the place of the old idea of nationalist Hellenism with its irredentist and imperialist aspirations, we raise today, in the name of their great sacrifice, the flag of a new spiritual Hellenism. This cannot be understood as a denial of national values and of national heritage, the priceless treasure that Hellenic-Christian civilisation has accumulated. It can only be their realisation and fertilisation, a new interpretation, a new adaptation.[79]

As Georgia Ladogianni notes:

Melas's arguments, on which he bases his view of the nation as a spiritual and moral category, are that Christian morality and cultural values, which are created and protected only within the framework of the nation, contributed to its creation. According to this definition, the Greek nation, with the greatest cultural tradition, rightfully claims the leadership over the other nations of humanity.[80]

On the ruins of the vision of a 'Greater Greece' promised by the aggressive nationalism of the Revolution and the Grand Idea, the new nationalism simply attempted to put into theory the defensive-bewailing nationalism that spontaneously developed within the popular masses: the Greek nation perpetually 'betrayed' by foreigners, the Greeks who are 'the best' (and that is why they are highly successful abroad) – while the country remains trapped in mediocrity due to internal divisions and discord, entanglement in a quagmire of personal ambitions, etc.

Yet it is worth mentioning that the ideological scheme of the 'Hellenic-Christian' identity as 'the soul of the Greek nation' has its roots in decades preceding the year 1922 and the collapse of the Grand Idea. As Paraskevas Matalas argues,[81] it essentially goes back to the period of the Bulgarian 'schism' from the Ecumenical Patriarchate, when the 'identification' of Orthodoxy with Hellenism was promoted as an argument against the 'schismatic Bulgarians'.

---

79 Spyros Melas, 'Nation and Humanity', cited in Xifaras 1996, p. 62.
80 Ladogianni 1989, p. 141. Additionally, as the main ideological foe of the journal was Marxism, some of its writers, such as Constantinos Tsatsos in 1933, later President of the Hellenic Republic (1975–80), on occasion felt themselves obliged to present themselves as 'progressive' and denounce 'the social injustice of capital', stating that 'pure ideocrats would never endorse the capitalist regime ... Nothing goes more against modern capitalist society than the ideocratic idea "on polity"' (cited in Xifaras 1995, p. 87).
81 Matalas 2002.

Since then, from the 'Hellas of Hellene Christians' of the junta of the Colonels (1967–74), to the more recent 'movements' of 'neo-Orthodox' ecclesiastical circles and intellectuals, this attempt to identify 'Orthodoxy with Hellenism' persists as a point of contention within the most reactionary Greek bourgeois ideologies.[82]

Further, it should be emphasised that the views on the superiority and 'uniqueness' of modern Hellenism, whose 'idiosyncracy' has been forged by the 'Orthodox tradition', have been anything but distanced from 'irredentist and imperialist aspirations'.[83] Allow me to present just one example of Greek irredentism after 1922:

After the German occupation of Greece (April 1941–October 1944) and the December 1944 armed conflict between EAM (the leftist 'National Liberation Front' in which the Communist Party of Greece was the leading political power) and the Greek government supported by the British army (what is referred to as the 'December events'), and despite conditions of an imminent civil war, a strong nationalist climate formed in the country which demanded the intervention of the Greek army in Albania in order to re-annex so-called 'Northern Epirus'.[84] This demand was shared for the most part by the EAM and 'nationalist' camps alike. Opposed to this prospect was Evangelos Averoff, a conservative politician and later minister of National Defence, then a member of the Informal Inter-Allied Committee in Rome, who, in a confidential report to the Greek Foreign Ministry, advocated that any aspirations concerning Albania should be abandoned, contending that first, 'the Greek-speaking population of Albania' constituted 'a small proportion, confuting the ethnological basis of our claims', and further, that a significant part of that minority population actu-

---

82 See also Milios and Mikroutsikos 2018. 'Systemic Hellenic-Christianity of the 20th century was rooted in the Slavophobic Greek Orthodoxy of the 19th century. Schismatic *Bulgarians* as internal/external enemies of the nation would eventually be replaced by all advocates of Slavism, and later by EAM-*Bulgarians* [i.e. the Left of the National Liberation Front, EAM (1941–46), J.M.] (who were then supposedly still controlled by Moscow); that is, those who betray Greek Orthodox ideals place themselves outside the "nation", becoming "Bulgarians". More recently, however, the collapse of bipolarity and traditional anti-communism has facilitated the rise of a "neo-Orthodox" trend suspicious of the West, which often borrows contradictory elements from a left-wing nationalism while rediscovering Orthodox "ecumenism"' (Matalas 2002, pp. 351–2).

83 Melas, cited in Xifaras 1996, p. 62.

84 In 1940–41, the Greek army, after pushing back the Italians invading the Greek territory, invaded Albania and occupied the southern part of the country, so-called 'Northern Epirus', according to Greek nationalist jargon. The Greek army evacuated Albania following the German invasion of Greece in April 1941.

ally looked forward to their assimilation into the new Albanian regime.[85] The nationalist climate in the country was of such intensity, however, that the Communist Party of Greece (KKE), which participated in EAM, was forced to declare on 1 June, 1945 that although it opposed military intervention in Albania, if the Central Committee of EAM took a different decision, 'KKE was ready to accept and implement the opinion … on the Northern Epirus issue that would be expressed by the majority'![86]

---

85   See *Anti*, 105, 12 August 1978, pp. 12–14.

86   'KKE [the Communist Party] rejects [the prospect of] a direct occupation of Northern Epirus by the Greek army, as this would involve us in adventurism and because it is contrary to the decisions of our three great allies, who have declared that any territorial change will be resolved peacefully at the Peace Conference. KKE has always proclaimed that there is an unresolved Northern Epirus question. The issue is a rightful one and should be resolved by the Northern Epirus population as a whole. It is they who will articulate where they will go and what they will do. The KKE delegation to the Central Committee of EAM further states: In order to ensure democratic unity, KKE is prepared to accept and realise that opinion of the democratic people concerning the Northern Epirus question, which will be expressed by its majority. If this majority decides on a direct military occupation of Northern Epirus by the Greek army, KKE will express its objections, but it will toe the line' (cited in Karagiannis 2016).

CHAPTER 9

1821 'in the Present': On the Ideological Uses of the Revolution

1   Introduction: On the Ideological Uses of History

In this last chapter of the book, I shall refer to some of the 'ideological uses' of the Revolution of 1821 that have shown – and continue to demonstrate – resilience over time. I have borrowed the term 'ideological use of history' from historian Philippos Iliou (1931–2004) to describe the 'metamorphosis' and selective use of aspects of the Revolution and specific (real or not) events belonging to it, with the aim of 'substantiating' a particular ideological (and political) stance towards history that becomes effective the moment that the 'historical analysis' is stated.

The 'ideological use of history' should be understood as a function or practice of 'producing regimes of truth', something which has influenced the evolution of the Greek state (and the policies advanced within it) for 200 years. Therefore, the 'ideological use of history' is not only a tool of deception, but generates manifold effects, both in terms of the construction of the scientific discourse/discipline of historiography itself (and also of philology and folklore), as well as in terms of the organisation/assembly/arrangement of political practices (in their content and expression).

The 'ideological use of history' necessarily sacrifices scientific methodology and the analysis-evaluation of events on the altar of a pre-selected ideological-political objective which concerns contentious issues at certain junctures. Naturally, every historical analysis (and thus the present study) bears the theoretical and ideological imprint of the person who formulates it. Yet this theoretical-ideological imprint relative to a scientific approach is subject to a trial of the intrinsic coherence of the argument, to the criterion of the logical consistency of the interpretation, as regards historical data and evidence. In contrast, ideological uses of history are consciously indifferent, as we shall see below, to any substantiation, theoretical or factual.[1]

---

1   The 'ideological use of history' goes far beyond what may be described as an ideologically prejudiced evaluation of historical events, as, e.g. the disparagement of the radically democratic constitutions of the period 1821–27, or of political parties, issues that we have dealt with in Chapter 6.

As Philippos Iliou observed in 1976:

> Throughout modern Greek history, and especially since the formation of the free Greek state, Greek historical science has shown a steady divergence towards the pronounced ideological use of history, which is unwaveringly called upon to serve some purposes other than its own: 'what should be valid is the national criterion. For what is national is also true' ... this is precisely the tendency that, in the last 150 years, with some exceptions, has dominated Greek life, falsifying national history for 'national' purposes.[2]

The 'falsification of national history' for ideological and political (generally 'national') purposes that has invariably characterised official historiography has left neither historians nor intellectuals on the Left immune to its influence, as shall be seen below.

2   The Tradition of the 'Continuity of Hellenism' and Its Transformations in the Nineteenth Century

As we have seen in the previous chapters, from the heyday of the Greek Enlightenment in the eighteenth century, and in a more universal way throughout the Revolution, the conception of the continuity of the Greek nation was promoted with certainty by all those involved in the Revolution (the 'Philhellenic' movement included): the ancient Greeks, and particularly the Athenians, were stereotypically considered 'the ancestors' whom the Greeks of 1821 (and of subsequent periods) ought to imitate.

This conception has yet to be challenged by official 'national historiography'. What changed during the nineteenth century were beliefs about the conditions of existence and 'slavery' of Hellenism throughout the centuries of its existence.

The pre-revolutionary 'enlightened' perception, as with similar perceptions during the first decades of the existence of the Greek state, considered that the Greek nation had lived in 'slavery' for *two thousand years*: Hellenism had been free and had flourished in antiquity (ancient Athenian democracy, etc.), only to be subjugated first to the Macedonians, and then to the Romans, subsequently

---

2 Iliou 2014, p. 16. Iliou paraphrases here words attributed to Dionysios Solomos (1798–1857), the 'national poet' of Greece (his *Hymn to Liberty* has been the Greek national anthem since 1865): '[T]he nation must learn to regard as national what is true'.

to the Byzantines and finally to the Ottoman barbarians. In other words, any-thing that did not assume a democratic form, from which the nationally politi-cised populations drew their model, was tyrannical rule (over the Greeks and over Greece). The state that emerged from '1821' was considered to be the 'resur-rection' of a nation, while the entire historical period that intervened was one of national slavery. For, and this is of particular importance, the Enlightenment insisted on the concept of the 'free citizen' (and the corresponding [capitalist] legal order) as the foundation of the state, something that ceased to exist in the constructs of polity that prevailed in 'Greek territories' after classical antiquity.[3]

The American 'Philhellene' Samuel G. Howe, in his book *An Historical Sketch of the Greek Revolution*, first published in New York in 1828, reproduces the the-oretical schema of the enslavement of the Greeks since the Macedonian, and even Roman, conquests, which was dominant during the period of the Revolu-tion:

> The glories of Greece were not extinguished by the Macedonian conquest, but the spirit of liberty was gone ... and before the Romans had triumphed in the East, we find the Greeks divided into three parties ... but the most important change which happened to the Greeks, was their national con-version to Christianity .... Religion has ever since been to the nation like a band of iron, uniting particles which would have otherwise fallen to pieces ... From the fifth to the thirteenth century, the history of Greece is little known, and probably of but little importance; it was merely a province of the Eastern Empire, which was feebly governed by a race of monarchs, at last known by the name of the Greek Emperors ... The suf-ferings of the country had been such, that the population had materially decreased, and no spirit of improvement was visible. But still Greeks pre-served in a strange degree many of their national characteristics ... the modern Greeks have preserved in a wonderful degree the characteristics of their ancestors ... Were there wanting any more convincing proof of the genuineness of the descent of the Modern Greeks from their illustri-ous ancestors than that they speak the same language ... and a century ago, we find that Greek vessels of considerable size were cruising in every part of the Archipelago, and beginning to compete with the Europeans, for the carrying trade ... an extensive and enterprising marine popula-

---

3 As argued in Chapter 2, it was Rigas Pheraios (1797), the text *Hellenic Nomarchy* (1806) and Adamantios Korais that introduced these narratives.

tion made Hydra, Spetzia, Ipsara, Miconi, Cranidhi, Galaxhidi, and other places, until lately unknown, important posts.[4]

The assertion 'that truly the modern Greeks are descended from their illustrious ancestors' as 'they speak the same language', an argument stereotypically repeated by 'national historiography', obviously constitutes an ideological use (and falsification) of history, firstly due to the fact that language is not an adequate enough criterion for determining national identity (see Chapter 3), and secondly, because the revolutionary Greeks, although they wrote in the official language of the Christian apparatuses of the Ottoman Empire – the Atticised *Katharevousa* oratorical Greek – spoke various languages, including 'Albanian, a heroic language which was spoken by the Admiral Miaoulis, Botsaris and all of Souli' (see Chapter 2).

The perception that Greece had been continuously subjugated since the time of the Macedonians and Romans prevailed in the Greek state throughout the first half of the nineteenth century. Even when we encounter statements such as 'the Turks have learned and been taught nothing since they *conquered Greece*',[5] it is not presumed that Greece is identified with Byzantium, that is, that Byzantium is considered a Greek state. The same applies to all formulations of the period that refer to 'four centuries of (Ottoman) slavery'; they do not necessarily suggest that the centuries preceding the Ottoman conquest were characterised by 'freedom', or by the existence of an independent Greek state (see Chapter 2). Even those who believed that the newly established Greece ought initially to have been governed in an autocratic manner (as the supporters of Kapodistrias and absolute monarchy believed) did not recognise Byzantium as a Greek state. A case in point is Professor Dimitrios Vernardakis,[6] in his book *Kapodistrias and Otto*, first published in 1875, where he argues:

> The day after the one when this nation tried to crush the servile chains, which it carried *not for four hundred years* ... but as far back as the centuries before Christ, if, to be certain, we do not want to wipe the slate

---

4 Howe 1828, pp. xi–xxviii.
5 Trikoupis 1993, p. 29.
6 Vernardakis contends that it was a mistake to approve a constitution immediately following the outbreak of the Revolution, arguing that it was premature: 'This contriving of Mavrokordatos was miraculous. The Constitution was a magical word, which electrified the most lettered, those who read in the books and newspapers of Europe of so many miracles regarding this political panacea' (Vernardakis 1962, pp. 50–1).

clean of the pre-Turkish history of the Greek nation, but to impassively and silently acknowledge, that during the Macedonian period, as well as under the Romans and the Byzantines and even under the Franks, the Greek nation not only had no 'constitutional freedom' whatsoever, but also, to be precise, no national independence, and it was in bondage.[7]

And even in 1885, the historian Constantinos Sathas, in the introduction to his essay *Greek Soldiers in the West*, wrote:

> [T]his small corner of the infinite Macedonian, Roman and Ottoman state, so-called Greece, *forgotten for two whole millennia and almost erased from the bible of life*, managed to recover from the great cataclysm that had struck so many historical nations.[8]

In the first decades of the existence of the Greek state, 'the possibility of something that had been *despotic* and obscurantist to be considered *Greek*' was questioned.[9]

Yet this dominant schema ceased to be effective when Bulgarian, Serbian and other Balkan nationalisms began to take shape from the mid-nineteenth century onwards: *on the one hand*, a Greek could no longer be identified as only an Orthodox Christian; *on the other hand*, to the extent that the territories claimed by the Greek state were no longer inhabited only (or primarily) by Greek-speaking populations, much less by populations with a Greek national consciousness, what was now sought was the abiding *Greekness of the territory*, which could only be ensured by the idea of the Greekness of the Byzantine Empire.

Since there were different nation states claiming the territories of the Ottoman Empire, it was necessary to demonstrate that prior to the invasion of the Ottomans, a *Greek state*, Byzantium, had existed in the disputed territories. In this way, the New Greek state was documented as being the 'legitimate' claimant to the Ottoman territories. The new, historical 'school' of Spyridon Zambelios and Constantinos Paparrigopoulos, whose focus was the 'Greekness' of Byzantium, could thus easily prevail, with the support of the central admin-

---

7   Vernardakis 1962, p. 50.
8   Sathas 1986, p. 9, emphasis added.
9   Koumbourlis 2018, p. 623; see also Chapter 8.

istration and the educational apparatus of the Greek state.[10] Again, it was the *ideological and political use of history* to serve '*national purposes*' in the new phase of the international-political antagonisms in which the Greek state was entwined.

In concluding this section, it is worth noting that, in spite of their differences, both versions of the (in each instance, dominant) 'national' Greek history are sustained by the same ideological core: the 'historical continuity of Hellenism' from antiquity to the present day as the unity of a 'people' in a 'territory'; or, in the words of Nikos Poulantzas, as the 'historicity of a territory and territorialization of a history'.[11]

3   The Ideology of 'National Continuity' as a Devaluation of the Revolution and as a Self-Contradiction

In concluding Chapter 4, I pointed out that the reigning nationalist narrative regarding the continuity of the Greek nation, which has supposedly existed from the time of antiquity, negates itself in a paradoxical way; that is, it downplays and largely silences the political and administrative rupture with which the prevalence of national(ist) ideology is associated and which it expresses – the historically unprecedented institutional and constitutional changes related to the national politicisation of the masses and (through the Revolution) their demand for institutions of representation (and thus for a bourgeois national-constitutional state of 'citizens'), which formulate new ways of integrating populations into the state. In other words, new ways of subsuming populations under capitalist relations of domination have formed.

According to the ideological use of history by the Greek official national(ist) historiography, the Revolution of 1821 was but the final, decisive moment of an ongoing *resistance* and enduring *rebellion* of 'the Greeks' against the 'Turkish yoke', something which persisted throughout the entire period of the 'four centuries of slavery'. As the historian Apostolos E. Vakalopoulos writes:

> The atmosphere of rebellion was a permanent phenomenon in the Greek peninsula before Constantinople had even fallen. Therefore, the revolution of 1821 was but the last great phase of the Greek people's incessant and unremitting resistance against the Turks, a merciless and undeclared

---

10   See Koumbourlis 2018, Xifaras 1993a, 1993b, Platis 2008.
11   Poulantzas 1980, p. 114; see also Chapter 5.

war that began from the very first years of slavery. Therefore, Philemon rightly characterises the Revolution as 'active' even in the years of
slavery.[12]

If the dominant constitutive element of the 'Greek people' is 'resistance', and
in fact 'before Constantinople had even fallen', then the social transformations
that took place from the fifteenth to the nineteenth century are of little or even
infinitesimal importance: the nation (the 'Greek people') constitutes a transhistorical unity, independent of such transformations, essentially independent of
social relations.

Moreover, if the dominant element is this 'incessant and unremitting resistance', then the political and constitutional breakthroughs brought about by
the national politicisation of the masses (nationalism) and the Revolution –
namely the construction of the republican constitutional state of 1821–27, the
civil conflict for its restoration in 1830–32, the challenge and final overthrow
of the absolute monarchy in 1833–43, etc. – are all of trifling importance, and
indeed can even be dismissed as 'divisions' and 'discord' amongst the 'Greek
people'.[13]

Nationalism refutes itself, its historical specificity, the break it introduces
in the historical timeline; it proclaims that what matters is what preceded the
break, the supposed 'unity' of the 'Greek people' through 'resistance'.

The ideological use of history is apparent here, too. In Chapter 4 it was seen
that, even at the beginning of the eighteenth century, the hypothesis of the
'incessant and unremitting resistance of the Greek people against the Turks'
cannot be substantiated. The local Christian populations, the 'Romans', who

---

12   Vakalopoulos 1980, pp. 27–8. In George Finlay's *History of the Greek Revolution*, the following is mentioned in the same spirit of the supposed 'incessant resistance' of the 'Greeks':
'The Greeks, during their subjection to the yoke of a foreign nation and a hostile religion,
never forgot that the land which they inhabited was the land of their fathers, and their
antagonism to their alien and infidel masters, in the hour of their most abject servitude,
presaged that their opposition must end in their destruction or deliverance' (Finlay 1861,
p. 2). A related example is the subtitle of Constantinos Sathas's book *Greece under the
Turkish Yoke* (1869): *An Historical Essay on the Revolutions of the Greek Nation Aiming at
Throwing off the Turkish yoke (1453–1821)*.

13   As regards the ideological constructs that attribute a supposed 'Greek malady' to the
lack of 'national unanimity' and self-serving divisions, the following comment by Vassilis
Kremmydas is apt: 'the Greeks ought to be the chosen people; with the civil war they
showed that they are a useless people, they do not love their country and in the end foreigners must come to save us. Conclusion: civil war is a bad, very bad thing' (Kremmydas
2016a, p. 192).

slipped from Byzantine into Ottoman rule (exemplary of this is the case of the Galaxidians; see Chapter 4, section 4.4. regarding the Galaxidians) were for the most part integrated into the administrative system, specifically that of exacting tributary 'taxes', etc., without any particular change in their social status and degree of autonomy from the central authority. Indeed, with regard to coastal commercial settlements and cities, and given the dominance of the Venetians and Genoese in the Byzantine monetary merchant economy after 1204,[14] Ottoman rule was an 'opportunity' for the 'Romans' to promote economic recovery and expansion. The Ottoman Empire protected trade and all other money-begetting activities of its subjects in order to collect tribute from them. In other words, 'absorption into the Ottoman Empire did not ring desolation, as many Western Christian writers have implied'.[15] As Traian Stoianovich notes:

> The victory of the Ottoman Empire symbolized, in the sphere of economics, a victory of Greeks, Turks, renegade Christians, Armenians, Ragusans, and Jews over the two-century-old commercial hegemony of Venice and Genoa.[16]

However, when historical analysis becomes more specific, it can be noted that the very historians who, from the time of George Finlay (1836), Ioannis Philemon (1834, 1859) and Constantinos Sathas (1869) to the present, have traditionally 'defended' the existence of a 'Greek people' and a 'Greek nation' that have endured throughout the centuries on account of their 'resistance', have been forced to silently modify or 'revise' their approach and the narrative of 'national continuity'. Only the case of historian Apostolos E. Vakalopoulos (1909–2000), professor at the Aristotle University of Thessaloniki from 1951 to 1974, shall be herein presented as one of the representatives most characteristic of the official 'national' history of Greece.

Seeing that prior to the end of the eighteenth century, essentially before Rigas Pheraios's time, to document demands, much less movements, for *national* liberation and attempts to establish a *Greek state* (see Chapter 4) proves to be of utmost difficulty, Vakalopoulos espouses an approach involving the 'devitalisation' and then 'awakening' of the eternal national consciousness of the 'Greek people':

---

14   See Milios 2018.
15   Lane 1973, p. 299.
16   Cited by Lane 1973, p. 300.

The national consciousness of the enslaved Christian inhabitants of the Ottoman Empire was weakened and eventually devitalised. In its place, the consciousness of the Christian emerges, develops and dominates, rising up against the consciousness of the Muslim.[17]

And yet, according to the ideology of 'national continuity', there must also be a mediaeval history of Hellenism, before the 'devitalisation', or sapping, of the consciousness of the 'enslaved people':

> The back-to-back defeats of the Slavs in Greek lands in 688 ... and in 783 ... as well as the crushing of a mutiny in the years of Irini (797–802), contributed greatly to their *swift assimilation and Hellenisation*.[18]

Yet again, in order *to describe a different context*, that of the occupation of Constantinople by the Crusaders in 1204, the Hellenisation of the Byzantine populations and the 'national awakening' of the *Greeks* ought to be placed a few centuries subsequent to the 'Hellenisation of the Slavs':

> The Fourth Crusade (1204) and the national awakening of the Greeks ... Out of the ruins and chaos left by the storm of the Fourth Crusade, the new Hellenism vigorously springs forth.[19]

However, this approach is deficient when it comes to describing the 'Greek nation' at the time of the fall of Constantinople to the Ottomans: the historical moment of the 'national awakening' must be redefined once again:

> Constantine XI Palaeologos as 'King of the Greeks' and the national consciousness of the inhabitants of the Greek lands ... It is not possible today to determine with precision, what the spread of the national consciousness of the new Hellenism by regions was at that time, since this concept was still fluid and *the assimilation of the foreign races* (mainly the Albanians) *had not taken place*.[20]

The ideological use of history is therefore obliged to constantly vary the narrative of 'national continuity' through the window of the 'incessant and unremit-

---

17   Vakalopoulos 1966, p. 70.
18   Vakalopoulos 1974, p. 19, emphasis added.
19   Vakalopoulos 1998, p. 12.
20   Vakalopoulos 1974, p. 303, emphasis added.

ting resistance' of the 'Greek people'. Articulated differently, it will endlessly refute its previous conclusions and put forward new ones, as it attempts to underscore the existence (and 'awakening') of 'Hellenism' throughout different historical periods.

4   'National Continuity' and Racism

In Chapter 3 it was argued that 'nationalism is inherently characterised by a tendency towards racism'. Interestingly, the approach of the 'historical continuity of the Greek people' as 'resistance' to conquerors has been widely used as a supposed rejection of racism: the Greek national character, which has existed without interruption throughout the centuries irrespective of and beyond social regimes and relations, is not a race, but a 'people' created and bound together by the practice of 'resistance'.

Historian Nikos Svoronos (1911–89) is a typical representative of the 'school' that attempts to base the scheme of 'national continuity of Hellenism' on the supposed 'rebellious character' of the Greek people. He writes:

> The Greek nation was born at the end of the Byzantine Empire, and was established through opposition and resistance against foreign occupation, which was Western for some areas and Ottoman for most of the country ... I believe that Hellenism ... is one of the few peoples that acquired national consciousness precisely within and in opposition to larger sets. Primarily as a conquered people. And the fact that it retained its language, its national consciousness, is for me a phenomenon of resistance ... The problem is *to remain what you are*, and this is of course combined with the *cultural continuity* of Hellenism. With the fact that, *when the Greek people were conquered*, either initially *by the Romans* or later by the Turks, *they had national unity* and *consciousness* of this unity. There was a unity of the people, in language, customs and traditions, and the people were *conscious of this identity, which made it possible for them to resist*, to resist the absorption by other peoples, who were their conquerors.[21]

In the afore-cited passage, which essentially reiterates the perception of Apostolos Vakalopoulos and other traditional 'national historians' of the 'in-

---

21   Svoronos 1995, pp. 159–60, 161, emphasis added.

cessant and unremitting resistance of the Greek people', the cyclicality of the argument, that is, the identification of cause with effect, is patently clear: *resistance creates national consciousness; national consciousness creates resistance.*

Svoronos also presents this conception as a means of distancing himself from the racial conception of the continuity of Hellenism:

> I do not, of course, believe in racial continuity ... That there has existed, from long ago, from very long ago, a Greek nation cognisant of its unity and of its being different from other peoples, and aware of its distinctiveness and *its cultural continuity*, I have no doubt.[22]

Yet the main form of racism following World War II and the quashing of Nazism is not racial racism, but *cultural* racism. As Étienne Balibar observes:

> Many researchers insist on the fact that contemporary developments are based on a shift in targets, intentions, and discourses – even though they are contained within the general limits of a social and symbolic paradigm of *exclusion of the Other* ... This observation has led some authors to develop the themes of 'cultural racism', 'differential (or differentialist) racism', or even, to highlight the paradox, 'racism without races.' ... [They] have drawn attention to the negative effects of 'anti-racist' policies and discourses that overlook or euphemize the 'non-biological' or 'non-hierarchical' forms of racial discourse, which are based on essentializing cultural difference.[23]

The Greek people's conception of their 'cultural difference' through their ongoing resistance to conquerors is far from being exempt from such cultural racism, which Balibar, in other writings, has also defined as 'differentiating racism'.[24]

Svoronos writes:

> The local populations were therefore already constituted into a single people, a nationality with strong material and spiritual ties, with a *superior intellectual culture without any substantial interruption*, embedded within a large centralised state and enveloped by a wonderfully organised administrative and ecclesiastical hierarchy, they would naturally absorb,

---

22   Svoronos 1995, p. 104, emphasis added.
23   Balibar 2005.
24   Balibar, in Balibar and Wallerstein 1992.

in their vast majority, *the semi-barbaric and politically unorganised foreign elements*, which would occasionally flow into the Greek lands.[25]

One might wonder who these 'semi-barbaric and politically unorganised foreign elements' at the time of the 1821 Revolution might be. Recall that, according to the leaders of the Revolution, 'the Rights of the free Hellene citizen, it is equally just for their brothers to enjoy the same ... The Serb, the Bulgarian, the Thracian, the Epirote, the Thessalian ... the Athenian, the Euboean, the Peloponnesian, the Rhodian, the Cretan ...'.[26] For those involved in the Revolution, Greeks were all Christians who would take up arms to stake a claim for 'freedom', that is, 'all the provinces of Hellas ... that have taken and shall take up arms against the Ottoman dynasty', according to the Constitution of Troezen (see Chapter 6). These provinces, which, pursuant to Alexandros Ypsilantis's Proclamation on 24 February 1821, included Serbia and Bulgaria (see Chapter 1), were not divided into those of 'superior intellectual culture' and other cultures, where 'the semi-barbarous and politically unorganised foreign elements' prevailed, as Svoronos claims.

I would therefore agree with Akis Gavriilides, who has pointed out, with regard to Nikos Svoronos's approach, that

> in this glorification of cultural difference and the preservation of a people's cultural specificity, we should have the courage to recognise what it really is, namely a paradigmatic expression of differential racism.[27]

Considering that Nikos Svoronos was a historian and intellectual affiliated with the communist and broader Left,[28] at this point there arises the following

---

25 Svoronos 2004, p. 46, emphasis added.

26 Negris 1824, see Chapter 1.

27 Gavriilides 2005, p. 19. A milder but substantial critique of the view of the 'rebellious character of Hellenism', which simultaneously acknowledges Svoronos's contribution to modern historiography, was set forth by Panagiotis Stathis: '[I]n the period 1953–1956, the appearance of Nikos Svoronos with his *Review of Modern Greek History* (*Episkopisi tis neoellinikis istorias*) and his articles in the *Art Review* (*Epitheorisi Technis*) constituted a much more solid and contemporary Marxist historiographical narrative ... Svoronos's approach, an outgrowth of its era, has been partially overrun by the current historiography, mainly because essentialist interpretations lay dormant in the concept of the "rebellious character of the history of modern Hellenism", while Svoronos's perception of the concept of the nation is also subject to traditional conceptions of the national phenomenon' (Stathis 2014, p. 40).

28 Typical of Nikos Svoronos's political career is the following excerpt from an interview: 'The first summary of the *History of Greece* was written when I was asked to write a short

question: Does the identification of Svoronos's views with those of Apostolos Vakalopoulos, Ioannis Philemon, etc., as regards the 'historical continuity' of Hellenism through the 'incessant and unremitting resistance' of the Greek people to the conquerors constitute an isolated circumstance? And further, to what extent do certain leftist approaches to the Revolution constitute ideological uses of history, as compared to those of the official 'national historiography'? These questions shall be addressed in the following sections of this chapter.

5   Historical Approaches in the Context of the Left (1907–1946): From
       Attempts at Scientific Analysis for the Documentation of a
       Socialist Strategy to Ideological Uses of History

5.1   *Georgios Skliros (1907–1919) and Yanis Kordatos (1924)*
The first Marxist treatise that attempted to present a scientific Marxist analysis of modern Greek society on the basis of which the strategy of overthrowing capitalism and replacing it with socialism could be founded was *Our Social Question (To koinonikon mas zitima)* by Georgios Skliros (pseudonym of George Konstantinides, 1878–1919), published in 1907. The work places particular emphasis on the social aspect of the 1821 Revolution as a springboard for the interpretation of Greek society in the early twentieth century. The Revolution is presented as the outcome of class struggle within Ottoman society, specifically as the inevitable consequence of the development of capitalist social relations and the rise of the Greek bourgeoisie.[29]

History for the Greek children in the People's Republics. They accepted what I wrote. They had objections on issues that I did not expect; while they had no objection to my positions on EAM (the National Liberation Front) and the resistance, some objected to my putting England and Russia in the same pot as regards 1821. And they insisted – and some still insist. I had replied to them at the time that if some communists consider themselves to be descendants of the Tsar, of Romanov, I am not ...', *Synchrona Themata*, 35–7 (December 1988), p. 51, quoted in Loukos 2014, p. 84. In addition, according to the testimony of Philippos Iliou: 'When, in 1945, Nikos Svoronos pointed out to Nikos Zachariadis (the General Secretary of the Communist Party of Greece, KKE, 1931–56) that the official theory of KKE on the relations of the new Greece with Byzantium was not in accord with the testimony of historical sources, Zachariadis accepted (in private) the argumentation of Svoronos, with some reservations, but replied: we will discuss (= publish) that later. At the moment I cannot, these theses are not in our interest' (Iliou 2014, p. 26).

29   Chapter 1 of Skliros's book is entitled 'Class struggle as a necessary factor of social progress' (Skliros 1977, p. 85).

The Marxism of Skliros is schematic and simplistic. It is based on the schema of the mechanistic succession of social systems in their historical trajectory towards 'progress': feudalism-capitalism-socialism. In this sense, the reference to the Revolution was an 'introduction' to support the view of the necessity of overthrowing capitalist domination by way of the workers' power. That notwithstanding, Skliros's analysis in this particular work and in his subsequent writings, including his last book *The Modern Problems of Hellenism* (*Ta synchrona problimata tou ellinismou*, 1919), contain interesting positions and remarks, both on the outcome of the Revolution and on the social forces that sustained it.[30]

Skliros's basic position on the nature of '1821' is summarised as follows:

> The Revolution was essentially a bourgeois revolution, brought about by unprecedented economic prosperity of the bourgeois elements within and without the Ottoman Empire, the awakening of national sentiment especially among the developed bourgeois classes and the scholars of the nation.[31]

Based on this position, the following conclusions are drawn:

> With regard to Greece, we said: 1) Greece today ... is an entirely bourgeois state. 2) The Greek revolution ... could only take place when the *bourgeois elements* of the nation had reached great economic prosperity and had awakened the national sentiment and the *idea of the homeland*, which had been introduced by the bourgeois revolutions of western Europe. 3) *Our bourgeoisie* showed all its vitality and vigour while it fought the upper classes: First with the feudal Turks and then with the aristocratic Bavarians. But as soon as it was left alone and in charge, without rivals from above or below, it fell into stagnation and decay. 4) All the remedies that have been proposed to us so far by various '*utopians*' to cure our bourgeois rot have had no effect, because they were *bourgeois remedies against a bourgeois sickness*. Only '*worker, proletarian*' medicines will be able to cure our bourgeois sickness ... If the nationalists wanted to fight us seriously, they had only to undo, to debunk those axioms of ours ... And with regard to Greece they had to prove to us ... That our revolution was not bourgeois at all, but that it was either advanced by the Phanariotes

---

30   For details, see Milios 2017, pp. 45–67.
31   Skliros 1977, p. 114.

and other magistrates or primates, or it happened for simple, ideological, national reasons.[32]

The book provoked intense theoretical controversy for at least two years in the columns of the magazine *Noumas*, which expressed the views of the demoticist movement,[33] amongst whom were socialists (G. Skliros, Alexandros Delmouzos, Costas Hatzopoulos, Nikos Giannios, Markos Zavitzianos and Fotos Politis) and 'nationalists' (Markos Tsirimokos, Ion Dragoumis, Petros Vlastos, Yannis Hatzis and Aristotle Poulimenos); all were also part of the circle of demoticist intellectuals.[34]

Skliros's theoretical intervention took place at a time (1907) when the expansionist-'irredentist' vision of the Greek state, the Grand Idea, was in full swing (see Chapter 8). A strategy for the overthrow of capitalism and the socialist transformation of society either had to be self-contradictory, acknowledging that it remained ill-timed as the task of territorial-political 'integration of Hellenism' into a single state would have to precede it, or would have to oppose the prevailing strategy (and ideological vision) of territorial expansion.

Skliros (and other socialist intellectuals) initially adopted the latter position, and focussed his polemics against the 'nationalists', the intellectuals who prioritised territorial expansion and had adopted the Grand Idea on the 'national question'.

Skliros maintained that the Greek territorial claims were expansionist in nature (that they did not constitute 'demands for national liberation'); with the formation of national consciousness by other Balkan peoples, Greeks did not constitute the majority of the population in the territories they claimed. In 1909, he wrote:

> So while the Greeks were still in their revolutionary frenzy, imagining that in the entire East there were only two nations, the Greeks and the Turks ... the Romanians established their semi-autonomous state ... some 25 years later the Bulgarians would take the first step of their bourgeois national palingenesis.[35]

---

32   Skliros 1977, p. 391.
33   '[A] complex and multifaceted movement that demanded the use of demotic [the demotic language] as the one and only national language' (Patrikiou 2017).
34   See Stavridi-Patrikiou 1976.
35   Skliros 1977, pp. 421–2. Concerning the so-called 'Macedonian struggle', Skliros states: 'It is high time we all understood that it is not worth causing so much trouble for a few

In turn, criticism of Skliros by the 'nationalists' was based, for the most part, on their demand for 'national integration', that is, the demand that all Greek populations of the Ottoman Empire and the territories they inhabited be incorporated into the Greek state, considering (in a way that was more implicit than explicit) that the national claims of other Balkan peoples were of a more 'artificial' or 'fabricated' character. The main exponent of such nationalist views was Ion Dragoumis, who wrote in *Noumas*:

> Because I happened to be born a Greek, and because the Greeks at the present time are not *yet* at the stage of socialism and because they are surrounded by nations with borders that want to devour us ... and because I am not inclined to be devoured by Bulgarians or Russians ... – therefore I want *first to secure my Greek existence ... thereafter to develop my economic powers*, and then let our nation dissolve, let it be cosmopolitanised, let it be socialised, let it do what it wants.[36]

The confrontation between the socialists and 'nationalists' was to be interrupted by the significant historical events of the period 1909–22 (see Chapter 8, note 74). In those few years, the image of the socialist movement in the country also changed (the founding of the Socialist Labour Party of Greece [SEKE] in 1918, which was soon renamed the Communist Party of Greece [KKE], the General Confederation of Greece's Workers – GSEE, 1918, and so on), together with the boundaries and visions of the Greek state.

At a new conjuncture, in 1924, Yanis Kordatos's book *The Social Significance of the Greek Revolution of 1821* was published, which was another attempt to analyse the 1821 Revolution in order to draw conclusions concerning contemporary Greek society and the leftist strategy of the time. The theses contained in the book follow the theoretical thread of the analyses of Skliros (who shortly before his death, in 1919, had published *The Contemporary Problems of Hellenism*, in which he again addressed, amongst other things, the question of the social character of '1821').

---

thousand Slavic-speaking, pseudo-Greek Christian followers of the Patriarchate, because sooner or later we will lose them' (Skliros 1977, pp. 428–9).

36   Cited in Stavridi-Patrikiou 1976, p. 171. Behind the conjunctural-historical demand for 'national integration' there naturally exists the central theoretical position of nationalism that social-class antagonisms are always of secondary importance in relation to 'national interests' and 'national goals'. In the words of Aristoteles Poulimenos, 'social issues cease where the limits of national being begin ... to ... call the struggle of 1821 a "bourgeois revolution" ... is of course inexcusable' (cited in Stavridi-Patrikiou 1976, p. 180).

According to Kordatos in 1924, the 1821 Revolution had the character of a bourgeois revolution, which brought to political power the already economically dominant bourgeoisie. From the second reprint (third edition) of the book, we read:

> The new social class that had been formed, the *bourgeoisie*, in subjugated Greece had achieved *great material growth*. Because of this reason (an objective factor of a Revolution), and the prevailing pan-European upheaval ... (a subjective factor), the *Greek bourgeoisie* was pushed towards the idea of a Revolution against the Turkish yoke. Of course, if the Greek bourgeoisie, then fully fledged, had not enjoyed the material prosperity that it had, with the enormous development of trade and shipping at home and abroad, it would not have been mentally prepared to accept the French revolutionary ideas and embrace such zeal for the doctrines of the French Revolution. Because it was formed as a class and economically was in its greatest prosperity, it therefore wanted to *rise* as a social class seeking first and foremost to expel the Turks, because their domination was the greatest and insurmountable obstacle to its rise to power.[37]

The dominant bourgeoisie was transformed, according to Kordatos, into a modern, industrial bourgeoisie from 1880 onwards, acquiring reactionary characteristics:

> The bourgeoisie throughout the world is now a reactionary class, a class which politically and economically oppresses and exploits the working people. The Greek bourgeoisie, driven by its own interests, follows the same path, the path of reaction. Its progressive role is long gone ... Only the organised working class is a *progressive* class today. Its struggles, inspired by the internationalist ideal of Communism, aim to free humanity from the disasters and horrors of new imperialist wars ... Through its Social Revolution it will not break its own economic and political ties, but will also be the liberator of all oppressed masses.[38]

Kordatos's Marxism is schematic-mechanistic, as is that of Skliros. Methodologically, it is based on 'economism', i.e. the ascription of all social development

---

37   Kordatos 1927, p. 54.
38   Kordatos 1927, pp. 176–7.

to the economy, thus downplaying the importance of class conflict, which it essentially considers to be reflections of economic development.[39]

5.2   The Subsumption of Historical Analysis under Conjunctural Ideological 'Priorities': Y. Zevgos and His Polemic against Kordatos

The general theoretical schema introduced by the interventions of Skliros (1907) and Kordatos (1924) – concerning the character of the 1821 Revolution, the role of the bourgeoisie, the domination of capitalism in Greek society and the socialist-proletarian content of the revolution that would overthrow capitalism – initially expressed the framework of the positions of SEKE-KKE. This framework would radically change in the 1930s following the intervention of the Communist International.

KKE's new conception of the nature of Greek capitalism, and consequently of a new revolutionary strategy, was finally consolidated in January 1934 following the intervention of the Communist International,[40] which led to the decisions taken by the Sixth Plenary Session (1934) of the Central Committee. According to the decisions,

> Greece belongs to the type countries, which in the Communist International programme are characterised as 'countries with an average level of capitalist development, with significant, residual, semi-feudal relations in the agricultural economy …' … The peculiarity of Greece consists in its considerable dependence on foreign capital and its associated unilateral, feeble development of industry … the forthcoming workers' and peasants' revolution in Greece will have a bourgeois-democratic character, with tendencies of rapid transformation into a proletarian socialist revolution.[41]

---

39   'The economic factor is that which creates and regulates social development' (Kordatos 1927, p. 19). This approach was criticised by Seraphim Maximos (1899–1962), an influential Marxist of the time, who wrote in 1928: 'It is true that the Marxism of Skliros is neither free from metaphysical aspects, nor was Skliros himself eventually successful in maintaining his original appearance as a socialist … Regardless of this, his works are of great value and in this respect we consider them incomparably superior to the works of comrade Kordatos, for they were written at a different time and contain more profound work. On the contrary, the works of Kordatos are characterised neither for their methodology nor even for their scientific profundity, *nor, in our opinion, are they a Marxist analysis of Greek history, because they emphasise the "economic factor"'* (Maximos 1982, p. 11; emphasis added).

40   KKE 1968, p. 9.

41   KKE 1968, pp. 19, 23.

This particular theoretical conception of Greek capitalism and communist strategy would from then on form the basis of official Marxist (and broader leftist) thought in Greece.[42] As Philippos Iliou observes, 'an arbitrary historical discourse thus reigned, which not only did not correspond to any historical reality, but did not even seek any connection with them'.[43]

As regards the Revolution of 1821, the followers of the new concepts of a 'backward, semi-feudal and dependent' Greece were faced with the very challenge that had been addressed in 1907 by Skliros to the 'nationalists': '... [W]ith regard to Greece they had to prove to us ... That our revolution was not bourgeois at all, but that it was either advanced by the Phanariotes and other magistrates or primates, or it happened for simple, ideological, national reasons'.[44]

And that is exactly what the proponents of the Greek 'dependency and underdevelopment' narrative have been trying to promote for decades by manipulating historical data. It began with Yannis Zevgos (pseudonym of Yannis Talaganis, 1897–1947), who as early as 1933–34 published a pamphlet entitled 'Why the Revolution in Greece will begin as a bourgeois-democratic one'. His rationale, which he advanced in all the articles and pamphlets he wrote until his assassination,[45] propounds the scheme of 'betrayal' by the bourgeoisie and the primates (*kotsambasides*), the latter being portrayed as 'feudal lords', of the *national struggle* that the *Greek people* waged in 1821. The aims of the Revolution (bourgeois-democratic revolution – national independence) had lain in abeyance since that time, and would be realised by a 'modern revolutionary movement'.

> The Greek merchant-kotsambasides, enjoying the hegemony of the revolution, struggled to detach the nation from the camp of the revolution, to put new shackles on it, thus condemning it to stagnation and decay. They found themselves unable to rely on the volcanic forces hidden

---

42   See Milios 1988, pp. 144–64; see also Elefantis 1976.

43   Iliou 2014, p. 23. Christos Loukos presents the resilience and continuity of these views over time, views that are constantly reproduced not only by left-wing intellectuals, but 'often intersect with opposing political-ideological currents, such as those of nationalism' (Loukos 2014, p. 91). Loukos focusses on typical exponents of these views, such as L. Stringos, K. Moskov, T. Vournas, C. Tsoukalas, V. Filias, P. Rodakis, T. Lignadis, A. Angelopoulos, D. Mantzoulinos, R. Apostolidis, etc. See also Milios 1989. Nevertheless, in recent years KKE has, in a gesture of self-criticism, distanced itself from this tradition. 'The Revolution necessarily expressed the interests of the rising bourgeoisie class and therefore it could not but lead to the formation of a bourgeois state' (KKE 2020, p. 15).

44   Skliros 1977, p. 391.

45   Zevgos 1933a, 1933b, 1935, 1936, 1943, 1945.

in the popular masses ... A cowardly and conservative class, fearful of the Greek people themselves, removed the cause of the revolution from the latter's robust hands and placed it in the hands of the reaction ... *Betrayed, the cause of the fighters of 1821* awaited its fruition. The modern revolutionary movement of the working nation, led by the proletariat, heir of national struggles, will free the country from dependence on foreign capital and on local exploiters, and will pave the way for the Greek people to rise, for its national culture to flourish.[46]

Zevgos sharply criticised Yanis Kordatos concerning the role of the bourgeoisie in the Revolution, which, according to Zevgos, was equal to national betrayal: that 1821 was the work of the 'popular masses' expressed through the 'movement' of *klephts*. He bestowed on Kordatos the appellation 'The "Marxist" Y. Kordatos, historian of the bourgeoisie',[47] arguing that '[T]he movement of the klephts was nothing more than a mass peasant movement directed against the triple form of exploitation: the Turkish bey, the Turkish-like kotsambasides and the clergy'.[48]

Kordatos's rejoinder to Zevgos stressed the following arguments:

All the texts inform us that the struggle for national liberation in its preparatory stage was mainly the work of the merchants and merchant mariners ... Scientific socialism ... teaches us that the problems and anxieties of our time should not be presented as the anxieties and problems of the past ... neither the shopkeepers, nor the poor peasants, nor the serfs took the lead in organising the Friendly Society. The Ph.E. [Philiki Etereia: Friendly Society] was not a 'popular creation' as Lambrinos and Zevgos

---

46   Zevgos 1936, emphasis added. The perception that the tradition of the 1821 Revolution has persisted into the twentieth century, and especially in the resistance against the German occupation, is not a monopoly of the Left. Professor and minister in the anti-leftist government of Panagiotis Kanellopoulos in 1945, Ioannis N. Theodorakopoulos (see the Introduction of the present book) stressed, in a speech addressed 'to the people, at Thiseion square' on 25 March 1945: 'The cycle of the great epic that began in 1821, culminated with the war of 1940–41 and with the unyielding resistance shown by the nation against the occupiers' (Theodorakopoulos 1972, p. 11).

47   Zevgos 1933a.

48   Zevgos 1935, pp. 83–4. In another text, Zevgos argues the same issue: 'Their [the *klephts*'s] struggle is a peasant national class movement, but remains scattered, isolated and at the end of the 18th century begins to take on a clear national character' (cited in Theotokas and Kotarides 2014, p. 51).

would have it. The vast majority of the members of the Friendly Society were bourgeois.[49]

It was Kordatos himself, however, who, having changed his views, projected 'the problems and anxieties' of his time into the past, as I will show in the next part of this section. In other words, from the 1930s onwards, Kordatos essentially followed, like Zevgos, the practice of an *ahistorical* ideological use of history by 'adapting' the 1821 Revolution to the post-1934 official leftist approach of 'incomplete revolution', 'bourgeois-feudal Greece' and the impending 'democratic revolution'.

5.3   *The Fourth Edition (1946) of* The Social Significance of the Greek Revolution of 1821 *as an Ideological Use of History*

The fourth edition of Kordatos's *The Social Significance of the Greek Revolution*, published in 1946, is not a 'completed' edition of the same book (as the author contends), but the publication of a *new book*, with its basic views radically altered from those of the previous editions of the same title.

In this publication, Kordatos initially endeavours to establish the thesis that the bourgeois forces of 1821 were mainly located *outside of Greece* (Western Europe, Russia), and that the Revolution resulted in the class domination of a pre-capitalist 'oligarchy' with which the bourgeoisie were forced to come to terms ('bourgeois-squires'): 'The creation of a Greek State was a necessity for the Greek bourgeois class, which was dispersed outside mainland Greece'.[50]

And yet the bourgeoisie betrayed the Revolution and allied itself with the feudal elements, squires (*kotsambasides*) and *Phanariotes*:

> When one takes into account what happened during the period of the national-liberation struggle by the ruling class and what followed thereafter, one draws the conclusion, which is confirmed by irrefutable facts, that the Revolution of 1821 was betrayed, not only by the kotsambasides and Phanariotes, but also by the bourgeoisie. This is the only historical truth.[51]

---

49   Kordatos 1957, pp. 8–10.
50   Kordatos 1972, p. 133. On the contrary, in the first version of his book, Kordatos stresses that '*within subjugated Greece* a new class, the bourgeoisie, had been born ... which ... had reached great economic prosperity' and therefore 'the Greek people of the Southern Balkans as such are more prepared for the movement' (Kordatos 1927, pp. 68, 70, emphasis added).
51   Kordatos 1972, p. 273.

The power of the 'bourgeois-squire' has since tied the country to foreign powers and forged its dependence on foreign capital:

> From 1823 to the present, foreign capital, having the bourgeois-squires as its agents and mandataries in our country, has sapped the place dry, impoverished the people and left the land in a backward state, so that it can treat us as colonists.[52]

Kordatos then adopts the basic rationale of the official Left of the period, essentially reproducing the core of Yannis Zevgos's approach, shared by other proponents of the 'dependency' schemes of modern Greek society and the strategy of 'democratic revolution'. Moreover, it projects '1821' in the political context of its time (on the eve of the civil war), when EAM and KKE considered 'Anglocracy' as the main pillar of support of the country's 'bourgeois-squire oligarchy': 'Lord Palmerston laid the foundations for the policy of the Foreign Office towards Greece, which for a hundred years or more has been faithfully followed by his successors'.[53]

The new edition of Kordatos's book arbitrarily recasts 'facts' in order to serve the ideological and political purposes of the time of its publication. In other words, relative to the previous version of the book, Kordatos alters his positions and judgments, not only as regards the character of the Revolution, but even concerning specific events and persons. To illustrate this, I will refer to his 'presentation of facts' and his judgments regarding Alexandros Mavrokordatos, perhaps the most controversial personality of the 1821 Revolution, since he had been subject to fierce attacks by all sorts of 'absolutists' (supporters of Kapodistrias and absolute monarchy) since the time of the Revolution.

In the 1924–27 version of *The Social Significance of the Greek Revolution*, we read:

> If there had not been the intervention of the *politically keen* Al. Mavrokordatos, the experienced in warfare and thence valuable elements of Roumeli would not have offered any worthwhile service to the struggles of 1821.[54]

> Professor N.N. Saripolos criticises the democratic character of the constitution, maintaining that a *Dictator* was needed at that time ... From

---

52   Ibid.
53   Ibid.
54   Kordatos 1927, p. 94.

his pro-monarchical and ultra-conservative point of view, the Professor, thus prompted, agrees with the historian Paparrigopoulos, who writes that 'Mavrokordatos contributed to the adoption of a *polyarchic*, not to say *anarchic*, constitution, but achieved nothing but to make it impossible to form a true government'. This is how history is written in Greece. Mavrokordatos is accused of having constructed a polity, not as the historian Paparrigopoulos and Mr. N.N. Saripolos and other captious, reactionary scholars of modern Greece would have wanted, but as the revolutionary *bourgeoisie* would have had it.[55]

Conversely, in the 1946 version of the book, Kordatos states that Mavrokordatos was '*essentially an agent of the British Foreign Office*'.[56] Further, in the second volume of the *History of Modern Greece* (which refers to the period 1821–32), Kordatos goes so far as to identify Mavrokordatos (that is, the political party he represented) with Kapodistrias:

> Kapodistrias ... stressed that the [members of the Society of] Friends must be disavowed and those who are exponents of new [revolutionary] ideas and democrats must be sidelined. Mavrokordatos not only agreed with what Kapodistrias suggested, but also considered his suggestions and opinions as dictates.[57]

With this 'novel' perspective on Mavrokordatos (who headed the so-called 'English' Party, see Chapters 6 and 7), Kordatos essentially places the history of '1821' in the context of EAM's opposition to the British intervention after World War II. While purporting to reinforce the 'struggle for national independence', by misrepresenting history he is in fact aligning himself with the views of those conservative historians whose very theses he criticised in 1924–27.[58]

---

55 Kordatos 1927, pp. 103–4. The position of G. Skliros is similar: 'Hydra was in general hailed as the genuine locus of the bourgeois spirit, of liberal constitutional ideas and the broad views of the genus. That is why it was rightly called "*the little England of the Aegean*". Hydra was also the base for all the educated and liberal elements from outside (Mavrokordatos, Negris, etc.) and it was there that the "*European*" liberal "*political*" party, so appreciated by the public opinion of Europe, was formed. This party, whose soul was the Phanariote Mavrokordatos, represented, so to speak, *the political mind* of the revolution and on the whole it succeeded, fortunately, in imposing its ideas and giving the revolution that noble *bourgeois liberal ideology*, which is so much maligned by our conservative historians' (Skliros 1977, p. 235).

56 Kordatos 1972, p. 133.

57 Kordatos 1957, p. 438.

58 Loukos (1994) presents the opinions of various writers, conservative and left-wing alike,

In the example of Kordatos, we witness how an ideological use of '1821' can transform historical analysis: when the strategy of a proletarian revolution was replaced by a 'democratic revolution', the Revolution of 1821 ceased to 'be' bourgeois. The Revolution did not establish a modern bourgeois state as organiser and bearer of the power of capital; it was considered to have been 'betrayed' by the servile-to-foreigners bourgeoisie, and the regime it established was thereafter described as a 'bourgeois-squire' power, in effect as a compromise between the weak and dependent bourgeoisie and 'feudal remnants'. The 'bourgeois-democratic' revolution was to be carried out in the future by the 'modern revolutionary movement of the working nation, led by the proletariat'!

6   Does History Unite a Nation?

6.1   'Historical Continuity' and 'Popular Resistance'
The theory of the 'popular national revolution' which was 'betrayed, not only by the *kotsambasides* and *Phanariotes*, but also by the bourgeoisie',[59] misleadingly introduces the idea of the 'historical continuity of Hellenism': the 'popular masses' are considered to possess a national consciousness regardless of the prevailing social relations, and even in opposition to the 'servile-to-foreigners bourgeoisie'. Furthermore, aside from the popular masses, not only are the bourgeoisie portrayed as active agents of the Revolution, but the classes and strata considered as belonging to the 'feudal' milieu are as well: *kotsambasides*, *Phanariotes*, primates, etc. Hence, practically all classes of society, even those belonging to the supposedly 'feudal' 'ancien régime', took part in the Greek (i.e. national) Revolution. In accordance with this argumentation, whereby those conveyors of the national idea (and thus, the creation of a

---

on Alexandros Mavrokordatos. It is worth relaying some examples here. Christos Stasinopoulos, a conservative, wrote in 1972 that he considered Mavrokordatos as 'the most blatant saboteur of the unity of the revolutionaries'. Of the intellectuals who shared the views of the traditional Left, Leonidas Stringos wrote in 1966 that Mavrokordatos was 'a representative of the compromising part of the big bourgeoisie and an exponent of Anglophile politics, a great schemer and a man who has no connection with and hates the popular masses, [who] will play the most evil role at the expense of the revolution'; Dimitrios Fotiadis argues that Mavrokordatos was 'the most diabolical of all the Phanariotes who came to Greece ... His spirit has ruled over us until now and does not let us progress', while Tasos Vournas, paraphrasing Stringos, wrote: 'The squire [*kotsambasikan*] front has been urgently strengthened by the arrival of Alexander Mavrokordatos, that evil demon of the Greek revolution, enemy of the popular masses, political schemer and fanatical advocate of British policy in Greece'. All citations from Loukos 1994.

59   Kordatos 1972, p. 273.

Greek state) were both the social classes and groups connected to the capitalist mode of production, as well as those presumed to be *pre-capitalist* classes
and groups, one is forced to logically conclude that the nation bears no correlation to modern (capitalist) social relations, but originates in a primeval
past. In other words, 'Hellenism' should be defined as an everlasting identity, so that 'the kotsambasides, the Phanariotes and some of the warlords
shook hands and formed the "aristocratic" oligarchy of the country', as Kordatos claims.[60]

The myth of the 'national esprit' of the popular masses more often than
not feeds the notion of an interminable confrontation between armed fighters and military leaders on the one hand (whose biographies are in most
cases 'recreated' at will),[61] and politicians on the other (who are usually portrayed as representatives of foreign and/or self-serving interests). This ideological schema is a meeting point for both left-wing and right-wing 'popular-
ised' approaches,[62] and usually culminates in the glorification of the *klephts* as
bearers of an eternal 'Greekness' (latent or manifest national consciousness)
and 'resistance'. It thus again promotes the 'incessant and unremitting resistance' of the Greek people, to which we referred in the previous sections of this
chapter.[63]

It should therefore be of no surprise that in the context of the problematic of
'bourgeois-squire Greece', the 'national continuity of Hellenism' is often projected in a clear and defined way. In *The Social Significance of the Greek Revolution*
of 1946, Kordatos does not hesitate to state:

> In the 14th century things change ... In all the economic centres where
> there is commercial production (Constantinople, Thessalonica, Mystras,
> etc.), a Greek consciousness begins to form, because trade is in the hands
> of the Greeks, who, seeing the Byzantine Empire collapsing, react against
> feudalism and the priesthood.[64]

---

60   Kordatos 1958, p. 11.
61   See Dimitropoulos 2014, Panagiotidis 2014.
62   See Loukos 2014, and note xxx.
63   See also Theotokas and Kotarides 2014. The leftist adherents of the supposed 'national
      movement' of the *klephts* and *armatoloi* (*martolos*) at this point meet Constantinos
      Sathas (1842–1914), who wrote in 1885: 'If ... this nation that rose from the dead occu-
      pied one of the most brilliant pages of this century, if the younger Greeks did not dis-
      grace their ancestors, if the Christian anti-Hellenism that once prevailed in Europe was
      transformed into political philhellenism, we owe all this to the armatoloi' (Sathas 1986,
      p. 9).
64   Kordatos 1972, pp. 35–6.

The last emperor of the Byzantine Empire, Constantinos Palaeologos, possessed a Greek consciousness.[65]

History as a narrative seems at times to unite political factions, even if (or perhaps *when*) *history experienced* as a social process divides the two (even if to the point of civil war, as was the case in 1946).

6.2   From 'Traditional' to 'Modernising' Narratives

In the last decades of the twentieth century, and particularly in the twenty-first century, novel historical methodologies and their corresponding coteries of historians have demonstrated the metaphysical foundation of the discourse of the unbroken continuity of Hellenism[66] and the ahistorical nature of binary divisions that constitute the basic motifs of modern Greek national ideology (in parallel with the 'regime of truth' around which the power relations within the Greek social formation have been arranged): enslaved – free, national yoke – resistance, enlightened West – barbarian East, national – anti-national, etc. Equally, various 'Hellenic-Christian' narratives have been subjected to a catalytic critique (for example, the myth of the supposedly 'secret school' for Greek pupils organised by the Orthodox Church),[67] but also all versions of the approach that counterpose the 'popular' versus 'servile-to-foreigners' aspect of the 1821 Revolution; for example, the narrative of the *klephts* and warlords who through their 'resistance' to the 'Turkish' yoke represented 'the people' as opposed to the 'feudal lords', 'servile-to-foreigners politicians', the *Phanariotes*, foreign powers, etc.

---

65   Kordatos 1972, pp. 51–2.

66   It is worth noting the important publication in 2018 of the collective volume *Hellene, Romios, Graecos: Collective Identifications and Identities* (in Greek), edited by Olga Katsiardi-Hering, Anastasia Papadia-Lala, Katerina Nikolaou and Vangelis Karamanolakis, a publication that includes the contributions presented at a conference in a fully developed form under the same title, organised by the University of Athens in January 2017.

67   Vassilis Kremmydas, in an interview in 2016 posted on 24 March 2018, when asked what he considered to be the biggest myth about the Revolution, replied: 'I would say the one about the alleged raising of the banner by Germanos III of Old Patras at the Monastery of Aghia Lavra on 25 March 1821, where the fighters supposedly took an oath. The Revolution in the Peloponnese did not even begin on that date, but a little earlier. Germanos himself, moreover, mentions in his memoirs that on that day he was in another village. He did indeed raise the banner, but that happened a few days later, in Patras. The legend of Lavra was part of later attempts to link the religious with the newly emerging national identity' (Kremmydas 2018).

In this study, I have attempted to critically evaluate these scientific studies, presenting and commenting on some of their analyses and conclusions which I consider important. This does not mean, of course, that my analysis identifies with most of the theses put forward by these studies. For example, the case of Kapodistrias, who even today remains a widely-respected figure and is considered the founder of the Modern Greek state, proves that some national myths, two hundred years after 1821, have been kept stoked.[68] Another, perhaps even more significant, issue illustrating the differentiation of my reasoning from practically all current books and articles on '1821' is related to the fact that the latter skirt the question of why the Greek Revolution was first proclaimed in the Danubian Principalities – i.e. in present-day Romania – with the leader of the Friendly Society claiming that Bulgaria and Serbia belong to the 'whole of Hellas'! The case presented in the volume edited by Kitromilides and Tsoukalas on the bicentenary of the Revolution (in 2021: see the Introduction of this book) is more than telling.

With regard to the issue that has been extensively discussed in the present chapter, the ideological use of history as a vehicle to defend the everlasting 'revolutionary action' of the *klephts* and *armatoloi* (and therefore the 'incessant and unremitting resistance' of the enslaved Greek people), the intervention of Spyros Asdrachas is of particular significance. Asdrachas uses the concept of 'primitive rebellion' to emphasise precisely both the pre-national character (embedded in the Ottoman social system) of these armed bands, as well as the 'noble' status of their leaders:

> [T]he pressures exerted by the war communities and groups belong more to institutionalised social realities than to exclusively illegal aggregations; they are based on a family and community structure that respects the legal framework of the Ottoman Empire ... the klephts ('thieves') try to substitute themselves for the armatoloi who, in turn, become klephts and resume the same type of pressure, perpetuating thus the mechanism of transference between outlaws and authorities. In this way, both constitute functions that are embedded in the same matrix, that is, the matrix of primitive rebellion, which in addition obeys the mechanism of integration into social structures through the institution of the armatoloi.[69]

---

68   A characteristic case in this respect is the approach of Kitromilides (2021, p. 13), who claims that 'Capodistrias was possibly the most distinguished Greek of his time, with a clear sense of the world and the requirements of modern politics'!

69   Asdrachas 1993, pp. 173–4; see also Asdrachas 2019, pp. 3–16. Besides, the *armatoloi* were not simply 'gendarmes' and collectors of tributes in the area they were guarding. They

The narrative of the 'popular' versus 'servile-to-foreigners' Revolution has at present receded from academic historiography and primarily retains its potency amongst circles concerned with 'national rights' on social media and in the area of journalism.

In whatever void the retreat of this traditional narrative leaves, however, an equally arbitrary problematic creeps in – that of the extreme 'modernisers', who attribute to any manifestation of resistance to (capitalist) power an 'archaic' (and therefore curseworthy) nature. According to this ultra-conservative problematic, the origins of the Greek state were not the Enlightenment and nationalism (the national politicisation of the masses), but the world of Ottoman pashas! 'This was the world of Ali-pashas, whence the Greek state originated'.[70] And there is more. Any claim or protest against capitalist power in Greece is considered to emerge from the *klephtarmatolist* element, the thieving spirit:

> The Greek radical phenomenon today, contrary to the illusions encouraged by its leaders, is perhaps the most conservative and anachronistic in Europe ... Indigenous radicalism does not draw its models from French Jacobinism, but from the indigenous spirit of the klepht and armatoloi element ... The horizontal composition of society is broken in our country by clientelist or armatolik segmentation.[71]

Nevertheless, no matter how much those who advocate the imposition of discipline onto the power structure attempt to eliminate social contradictions, they will continue to be frustrated by social explosions, uprisings and revolutions. After all, the 1821 Revolution was precisely that: the fusion of the social contradictions of the time and their eruption as a struggle to tear down the old world in the name of 'freedom'. It constructed a new, national-capitalist regime, a new form of class and state power, which is today being contested, 200 years later, as its overthrow has become an absolute necessity for the social majority.

---

often assisted the Ottoman army in its military operations, such as with the recapture of the Peloponnese from Venice in 1715. 'The saddest thing is that, along with the Turks, many of the armatoloi of Mainland Greece also joined in the fight against the Peloponnese, who, after having captured the peninsula, returned home loaded with booty' (Paparrigopoulos 1971, Vol. 14, p. 239).

70   Veremis et al. 2018, p. 294.
71   Veremis 2006.

References

About, Edmond 1968, *Ο βασιλεύς των ορέων* [*The King of the Mountains*], Athens: Galaxias.

Agriantoni, Christina 1986, *Οι απαρχές της εκβιομηχάνισης στην Ελλάδα τον 19° αιώνα* [*The Beginnings of Industrialisation in Greece in the Nineteenth Century*], Athens: Historical Archives of the Commercial Bank of Greece.

Agriantoni, Christina 2006, 'Βιομηχανία' ['Industry'], in Kostas Kostis and Socrates Petmezas (eds.), *Η ανάπτυξη της ελληνικής οικονομίας τον 19° αιώνα* [*The Development of the Greek Economy in the Nineteenth Century*], Athens: Alexandria, 219–51.

Althusser, Louis 1977, 'Anmerkung über die ideologischen Staatsapparate (ISA)', in *Ideologie und Ideologische Staatsapparate. Aufsätze zur Marxistischen Theorie*, Hamburg: VSA-Verlag, 154–68.

Anderson, Benedict 2006, *Imagined Communities: Reflections on the Origin and Spread of Nationalism*, London: Verso.

Anderson, Perry 1974, *Lineages of the Absolutist State*, London: New Left Books.

Andreades, Andreas M. 1904, *Ιστορία των εθνικών δανείων* [*History of National Loans*], Athens: Estia.

Andreades, Andreas M. 1925, *Μαθήματα δημοσίας οικονομίας. Εθνικά δάνεια και ελληνική δημόσια οικονομία. Μέρος Α΄. Από της Επαναστάσεως μέχρι της πτωχεύσεως (1821–1893)* [*Lessons in Public Economy. National Loans and Greek Public Economy. Part I. From the Revolution to Bankruptcy (1821–1893)*], Athens: Publishing House of D.N. Tzakas, S. Delagrammatikas & Co.

Andreou, A.I. 1934, 'Εμπόριον' ['Trade'], in *Great Greek Encyclopaedia*, Vol. 10 (Hellas), Athens: Pyrsos, 147–54.

Andreou, Apostolis 1987, 'Ιδιωτική εκπαίδευση. Προσανατολισμός, διάρκειες και τομές. (Ιστορική προσέγγιση)' ['Private Education: Orientation, Durations and Intersections (An Historical Approach)'], *Theseis* 20: 95–134.

Anonymous Hellene, The 1977 [1806], *Ελληνική Νομαρχία, ήτοι Λόγος περί Ελευθερίας* [*Hellenic Nomarchy, or Discourse on Liberty*], Athens: Kalvos.

Anthimos, His Beatitude Patriarch of the Holy City of Jerusalem 1798, *Διδασκαλία Πατρική* [*Paternal Teaching*], http://digital.lib.auth.gr/record/126122?ln=el (retrieved 22 August 2021).

Arendt, Hannah 1993, 'The Nation', in *Essays in Understanding, 1930–1954: Formation, Exile and Totalitarianism*, New York: Schocken Books, 206–11.

Aretov, Nikolay 2014, 'The Starting Point of Bulgaria in National Mythology', *Slavia Meridionalis* 14: 165–88.

Argyroudis, D.I. 1934, 'Καλλιέργεια του καπνού' ['Cultivation of Tobacco'], in *Great Greek Encyclopaedia*, Vol. 10 (Hellas), Athens: Pyrsos, 87–91.

Arsh, Grigori L. 2011, *Η Φιλική Εταιρεία στη Ρωσία. Ο απελευθερωτικός αγώνας του ελληνικού λαού στις αρχές του 19ου αιώνα και οι ελληνορωσικές σχέσεις* [*The Friendly Society in Russia: The Liberation Struggle of the Greek People in the Early Nineteenth Century and Greek-Russian Relations*], Athens: Papasotiriou.

Asdrachas, Spyros 1978, *Μηχανισμοί της αγροτικής οικονομίας στην Τουρκοκρατία. (ιε΄–ιστ΄ αι.)* [*Mechanisms of the Rural Economy in the Ottoman Empire (Fifteenth–Sixteenth Centuries)*], Athens: Themelio.

Asdrachas, Spyros 1982, *Ελληνική οικονομία και κοινωνία ιη΄ και ιθ΄ αιώνες* [*Greek Economy and Society in the Seventeenth and Eighteenth Centuries*], Athens: Hermes.

Asdrachas, Spyros 1993, 'Οι "πρωτόγονοι της εξέγερσης"' ['The "Primitives" of the Rebellion'], in *Σχόλια* [*Commentaries*], Athens: Alexandria, 173–86. Reprinted in Spyros I. Asdrachas 2019, *Πρωτόγονη επανάσταση. Αρματολοί και κλέφτες, 18ος–19ος αι.* [*Primitive Revolution: Armatoloi and Klephts, Eighteenth–Nineteenth Centuries*], Patras: Hellenic Open University Press, 3–16.

Asdrachas, Spyros 2019, *Πρωτόγονη επανάσταση. Αρματολοί και κλέφτες, 18ος–19ος αι.* [*Primitive Revolution: Armatoloi and Klephts, Eighteenth–Nineteenth Centuries*], Patras: Hellenic Open University Press.

Aspreas, Georgios K. 1930, *Πολιτική ιστορία της νεωτέρας Ελλάδος 1821–1928. Τελευταία τριακονταετία* [*Political History of Modern Greece 1821–1928: Last Thirty Years*], Athens.

Axelos, Loukas 2006, *Ρήγας Βελεστινλής. Σταθμοί και όρια στην διαμόρφωση της εθνικής και κοινωνικής συνείδησης στην Ελλάδα* [*Rigas Velestinlis: Milestones and Limits in the Formation of National and Social Consciousness in Greece*], Athens: Stochastis.

Babanasis, Stergios 1985, *Ιδιομορφίες της ανάπτυξης στη Νότια Ευρώπη* [*Peculiarities of Development in Southern Europe*], Athens: Foundation for Mediterranean Studies.

Balibar, Étienne 2005, 'The Construction of Racism', translated from the French by Cadenza Academic Translations, https://www.cairn-int.info/article-E_AMX_038_00 11--the-construction-of-racism.htm (retrieved 22 August 2021).

Balibar, Étienne, and Immanuel Wallerstein 1992, *Race, Nation, Class: Ambiguous Identities*, London: Verso.

Bauer, Otto 1907, *Die Nationalitätenfrage und die Sozialdemokratie*, https://www.marxists.org/deutsch/archiv/bauer/1907/nationalitaet/index.html (retrieved 22 August 2021).

Bauer, Otto 2000, *The Question of Nationalities and Social Democracy*, Minneapolis: University Minnesota Press.

Beaton, Roderick 2013, *Byron's War: Romantic Rebellion, Greek Revolution*, Cambridge: Cambridge University Press.

Beaton, Roderick 2019, *Greece: Biography of a Modern Nation*, Chicago: University of Chicago Press.

Beaton, Roderick, and David Ricks (eds.) 2009, *The Making of Modern Greece: Nationalism, Romanticism, and the Uses of the Past (1797–1896)*, London: Ashgate.

Beaujour, Félix 1800, *A View of the Commerce of Greece: Formed After an Annual Average, from 1787 to 1797*, London: James Wallis.

Benjamin, Walter 1940, *On the Concept of History*, https://www.marxists.org/reference/archive/benjamin/1940/history.htm (retrieved 22 August 2021).

Bouropoulos, A.N. 1931, 'Ληστεία' ['Robbery'], in *Great Greek Encyclopaedia*, Vol. 16, Athens: Pyrsos, 74–6.

Cheston, Charles 1887, *Greece in 1887*, London: Effingham Wilson.

Chiakon Archive [Χιακόν Αρχείον], Vol. 1, 1924, edited by Ioannis Vlachogiannis, Athens: P.D. Sakellariou.

Clair, William St. 2008, *That Greece Might Still Be Free: The Philhellenes in the War of Independence*, Cambridge: Open Book Publishers.

Clogg, Richard 1976, *The Movement for Greek Independence 1770–1821: A Collection of Documents*, London: Macmillan.

Cotovanu, Lidia 2018, 'Οι πολλαπλές αναπαραστάσεις των Ρωμαίων/Γραικών στις Παραδουνάβιες Ηγεμονίες: η μαρτυρία του Ματθαίου Μυραίων (αρχές 17ου αιώνα)' ['The Multiple Representations of *Romans/Graeci* in the Para-Danubian Principalities: The Testimony of Matthaios of Myreon (early seventeenth century)'], in Olga Katsiardi-Hering et al. (eds.), *Έλλην, Ρωμηός, Γραικός. Συλλογικοί προσδιορισμοί και ταυτότητες [Hellene, Romios, Graecos: Collective Identifications and Identities]*, Athens: Eurasia, 431–47.

Dafnis, Grigorios 1961, *Τα ελληνικά πολιτικά κόμματα 1821–1961 [The Greek Political Parties 1821–1961]*, Athens: Galaxias.

Daskalakis, C.E. 1934a, 'Νεώτεροι χρόνοι' ['Modern Times'], in *Great Greek Encyclopaedia*, Vol. 10 (Hellas), Athens: Pyrsos, 575–601.

Daskalakis, C.E. 1934b, 'Αλύτρωτος Ελληνισμός' ['Hellenic Irredentism'], in *Great Greek Encyclopaedia*, Vol. 10 (Hellas), Athens: Pyrsos, 757–8.

Daskalakis, Apostolos V. 1961–62, 'Η έναρξις του αγώνος της ελευθερίας. Θρύλος και πραγματικότης' ['The Beginning of the Struggle for Freedom: Legend and Reality'], *Scientific Yearbook of the School of Philosophy of the University of Athens*, 2nd Period, 12, 9–138.

Daskalakis, Apostolos V. 1979, *Ο Αδαμάντιος Κοραής και η ελευθερία των Ελλήνων [Adamantios Korais and the Freedom of the Greeks]*, Athens: Vayonakis.

Davidson, Neil 2012, *How Revolutionary Were the Bourgeois Revolutions?* Chicago: Haymarket Books.

Detrez, Raymond 1997, *Historical Dictionary of Bulgaria*, Lanham, MD: The Scarecrow Press.

Detrez, Raymond 2014, 'Τι είδους μανία είναι η Γραικομανία' ['What Kind of Mania is Graecomania?'], in Bulgarian Academy of Sciences, *The Balkans: Modernization, Identities, Ideas: A Collection of Papers in Honour of Professor Nadia Danova*, Herakleion: Crete University Press, 399–410.

Dimaras, K.Th. 1989, *Νεοελληνικός Διαφωτισμός* [*Modern Greek Enlightenment*], Athens: Hermes.

Dimaras, K.Th. 1992, *Ιστορικά φροντίσματα, Α΄. Ο Διαφωτισμός και το κορύφωμά του* [*Historical Notes, 1. The Enlightenment and its Peak*], Athens: Poreia.

Dimaras, K.Th. 1994, *Ελληνικός ρωμαντισμός* [*Greek Romanticism*], Athens: Hermes.

Dimitropoulos, Dimitris 2014, 'Παναγιώτης Καρατζάς: Η βιογραφία ενός αγωνιστή του 1821. Από την πρόσληψη στην ανάπλαση' ['Panagiotis Karatzas: The Biography of a Fighter of 1821: From Apperception to Reconstruction'], in Dimitris Dimitropoulos and Vangelis Karamanolakis (eds.), *Οι αναγνώσεις του 1821 και η Αριστερά* [*Readings of 1821 and the Left*], Athens: Contemporary Social History Archives – Avgi, 59–69.

Dimitropoulos, Dimitris, and Vangelis Karamanolakis (eds.) 2014, *Οι αναγνώσεις του 1821 και η Αριστερά* [*Readings of 1821 and the Left*], Athens: Contemporary Social History Archives – Avgi.

Dimoulis, Dimitris 2000, 'Λαός, έθνος και πολίτες στην ελληνική συνταγματική ιστορία του 19ου αιώνα' ['People, Nation and Citizens in Greek Constitutional History of the Nineteenth Century'], *Theseis* 72: 35–89.

Efthymios [Pentagiotis], Hieromonk 1996, *Το Χρονικό του Γαλαξειδίου* [*The Chronicle of Galaxidi*], Athens: Dimiourgia.

Elefantis, Angelos 1976, *Η επαγγελία της αδύνατης επανάστασης* [*The Promise of the Impossible Revolution*], Athens: Olkos.

Engels, Friedrich 1890, 'Foreign Policy of Russian Tsardom', https://www.marxists.org/archive/marx/works/1890/russian-tsardom/index.htm (retrieved 22 August 2021).

Evangelides, Tryphon 1933, 'Σάββας Φωκιανός' ['Savvas Phokianos'], in *Great Greek Encyclopaedia*, Vol. 21, Athens: Pyrsos, 405.

Evangelides, Tryphon 1934, 'Τουρκοκρατία – Ελληνική Επανάστασις' ['Turkish Rule – Greek Revolution'], in *Great Greek Encyclopaedia*, Vol. 10 (Hellas), Athens: Pyrsos, 560–75.

Evelpides, Chrysos 1934, 'Γεωργική οικονομία' ['Agricultural Economy'], in *Great Greek Encyclopaedia*, Vol. 10 (Hellas), Athens: Pyrsos, 73–9.

Evered, Emine Ö. 2012, *Empire and Education under the Ottomans: Politics, Reform, and Resistance from the Tanzimat to the Young Turks*, London: I.B. Tauris.

Filiopoulou, Maria 2019, 'Ο φυλετισμός ως συνεκτικό στοιχείο του ελληνικού εθνικισμού κατά τον 19ο αιώνα. Ο ρόλος του Πανεπιστημίου' ['Racism as a Coherent Element of Greek Nationalism in the Nineteenth Century: The Role of the University'], *Theseis* 148: 101–16.

Finlay, George 1859, *History of the Greek Revolution*, 2 Volumes, Edinburgh: William Blackwood.

Gavriilides, Akis 2005, 'The Differential Racism of Nikos Svoronos', *Theseis* 91: 15–31.

Geib, Gustav 1835, *Darstellung des Rechtszustandes in Griechenland während der türkischen Herrschaft u. bis zur Ankunft des Königs Otto 1*, Heidelberg: C.F. Winter.

Geib, Gustav n.d., *Παρουσίαση της κατάστασης του δικαίου στην Ελλάδα στη διάρκεια της Τουρ-κοκρατίας και ως τον ερχομό του βασιλιά Όθωνα του Α'* [*Presentation of the State of Law in Greece During the Turkish Occupation and until the Arrival of King Otto I*], Athens: Govostis.

Gervinos, Georgios [Georg Gottfried Gervinus] 1865, *Ιστορία της Επαναστάσεως και ανα-γεννήσεως της Ελλάδος* [*History of the Revolution and Rebirth of Greece*], 2 Volumes, Athens.

Giohalas, Titos P. 2006, *Ύδρα – Λησμονημένη γλώσσα* [*Hydra – Forgotten Language*], 2 Volumes, Athens: Pataki.

Giohalas, Titos P. 2011, *Η αρβανιτιά στο Μοριά* [*Albanian Speakers in the Peloponnese*], Athens: Pataki.

Gluzman, Renard, and Gerassimos Pagratis 2019, 'Tracking Venice's Maritime Traffic in the First Age of Globalization: a Geospatial Analysis', in *Maritime Networks as a Factor in European Integration: A Selection of Essays*, Florence: Firenze University Press, 135–53.

Godelier, Maurice 1964, 'La notion de "mode de production asiatique" et le schéma marxiste d'évolution des sociétés', in Centre d'études et de recherches Marxistes (CERM), *Sur le mode de production asiatique*, Paris: Edition Sociales.

Gordon, Thomas, F.R.S. 1872 [1832], *History of the Greek Revolution, and the Wars and Campaigns Arising from the Struggles of the Greek Patriots in Emancipating their Country from the Turkish Yoke*, Edinburgh: William Blackwood.

Gramsci, Antonio 2007, *Prison Notebooks*, Vol. III, New York: Columbia University Press.

Gramsci, Antonio 2011, *Prison Notebooks*, Vol. I, New York: Columbia University Press.

Gregorovius, Ferdinand 1994 [1889], *Μεσαιωνική ιστορία των Αθηνών* [*Mediaeval History of Athens*], Vol. III, Athens: Kritiki.

Grothusen K.-G., J.-G. Da Silva, H. Gross, J. Petrosian, P.F. Sugar, M. Todorova, V. Georgescu, N. Todorov, T. Stoianovitc, N. Vuco, D. Milic, V. Panagiotopoulos, P. Dumont, V. Kazarkova, I.T. Sanders, M. Genc 1980, *Εκσυγχρονισμός και βιομηχανική επανάσταση στα Βαλκάνια τον 19ο αιώνα* [*Modernization and Industrial Revolution in the Balkans in the Nineteenth Century*], Athens: Themelio.

Harlaftis, Gelina 1993, 'Εμπόριο και ναυτιλία τον 19ο αιώνα. Το επιχειρηματικό δίκτυο των Ελλήνων της διασποράς. Η "χιώτικη" περίοδος, 1830–1860' ['Trade and Shipping in the Nineteenth Century. The Business Network of the Greeks of the Diaspora. The "Chi-ote" Period, 1830–1860'], *Mnemon* 15: 69–127.

Harlaftis, Gelina 2006, 'Ναυτιλία' ['Shipping'], in Kostas Kostis and Socrates Petmezas (eds.), *Η ανάπτυξη της ελληνικής οικονομίας τον 19ο αιώνα* [*The Development of the Greek Economy in the Nineteenth Century*], Athens: Alexandria, 421–62.

Harlaftis, Gelina 2013a, 'Η ναυτιλία των Ελλήνων ως μοχλός ενοποίησης των αγορών. Η μεθο-δολογία' ['Greek Shipping as a Lever for Market Integration: The Methodology'], in

Gelina Harlaftis and Katerina Papakonstantinou (eds.), *Η ναυτιλία των Ελλήνων 1700–1821. Ο αιώνας της ακμής πριν την επανάσταση* [*The Shipping of the Greeks 1700–1821: The Century of Prosperity before the Revolution*], Athens: Kedros, 39–90.

Harlaftis, Gelina 2013b, 'Η εισβολή της ναυτιλίας των Γραικών στο μεγάλο εμπόριο της Μεσογείου, 1714–1815' ['The Onrush of Greek Shipping into the Major Commerce of the Mediterranean, 1714–1815', in Gelina Harlaftis and Katerina Papakonstantinou (eds.), *Η ναυτιλία των Ελλήνων 1700–1821. Ο αιώνας της ακμής πριν την επανάσταση* [*The Shipping of the Greeks 1700–1821: The Century of Prosperity before the Revolution*], Athens: Kedros, 224–82.

Harlaftis, Gelina, and Sophia Laiou 2008, 'Ottoman State Policy in Mediterranean Trade and Shipping, c. 1780–1820: The Rise of the Greek-Owned Ottoman Merchant Fleet', in Mark Mazower (ed.), *Networks of Power in Modern Greece: Essays in Honour of John Campbell*, London: Hurst, 1–44.

Heinrich, Michael 2018, *Karl Marx und die Geburt der modernen Gesellschaft. Biographie und Werkentwicklung, Erster Band, 1818–1841*, Berlin: Schmetterling Verlag.

Heinrich, Michael 2019, *Karl Marx and the Birth of Modern Society: The Life of Marx and the Development of His Work*, Vol. 1: 1818–1841, New York: Monthly Review Press.

Hering, Gunnar 2004, *Τα πολιτικά κόμματα στην Ελλάδα 1821–1936* [*The Political Parties in Greece 1821–1936*], Athens: National Bank of Greece Cultural Foundation.

Hobsbawm, Eric J. 1992, *Nations and Nationalism from 1780 to the Present: Programme, Myth, Reality*, Cambridge: Cambridge University Press.

Hobsbawm, Eric J. 1996, *The Age of Revolution 1789–1848*, London: Vintage Books.

Hobsbawm, Eric J. 2006, *The Age of Capital 1848–1875*, London: Abacus.

Hobsbawm, Eric J. 2013, 'Introduction: Inventing Traditions', in Eric J. Hobsbawm and Terrence Ranger (eds.), *The Invention of Tradition*, Cambridge: Cambridge University Press, 1–14.

Hobsbawm, Eric J., and Terrence Ranger (eds.) 2013, *The Invention of Tradition*, Cambridge: Cambridge University Press.

Houmanides, Lazaros T. 1990, *Οικονομική ιστορία της Ελλάδος, τόμ. Β΄: Από της Τουρκοκρατίας μέχρι του έτους 1935* [*Economic History of Greece, Vol. 2, From the Turkish Occupation until 1935*], Athens: Papazisis.

Howe, Samuel G. 1828, *An Historical Sketch of the Greek Revolution*, New York: White, Gallaher & White.

Iliou, Philippos 1974, 'Τύφλωσον Κύριε τον λαόν σου. Οι προεπαναστατικές κρίσεις και ο Ν. Σ. Πίκκολος' ['Render Blind, O Lord, Your People: The Pre-Revolutionary Crises and N. S. Pikkolos'], *Eranistis* 11, 580–626.

Iliou, Philippos 1978, 'Νεοελληνικός Διαφωτισμός. Νεωτεριστικές προκλήσεις και παραδοσιακές αντιστάσεις' ['Modern Greek Enlightenment: Modernist Challenges and Traditional Resistance'], *Bulletin of the Society for the Study of Modern Greek Culture and General Education*, Athens: Moraitis School.

Iliou, Philippos 2014, 'Η ιδεολογική χρήση της ιστορίας' ['The Ideological Use of History'], in Dimitris Dimitropoulos and Vangelis Karamanolakis (eds.), *Οι αναγνώσεις του 1821 και η Αριστερά* [*Readings of 1821 and the Left*], Athens: Contemporary Social History Archives – Avgi, 15–28.

İnalcık, Halil 1967, 'Capital Formation in the Ottoman Empire', *Journal of Economic History* 29: 97–140.

İnalcık, Halil 1978, *The Ottoman Empire: Conquest, Organization and Economy* (*Collected Studies*), London: Variorum Reprints.

İnalcık, Halil 1993, 'State, Sovereignty and Law during the Reign of Süleymân', in Halil Inalcik and Cemal Kafadar (eds.), *Süleymân the Second and his Time*, Istanbul: The Isis Press, 61–92.

İnalcık, Halil 1997, *An Economic and Social History of the Ottoman Empire, Volume 1: 1300–1600*, Cambridge: Cambridge University Press.

İnalcık, Halil, and Cemal Kafadar (eds.) 1993, *Süleymân the Second and His Time*, Istanbul: The Isis Press.

Inglesi, Angeliki 2004, *Βορειοελλαδίτες έμποροι στο τέλος της Τουρκοκρατίας. Ο Σταύρος Ιωάννου* [*Northern Greek Merchants at the End of the Turkish Occupation: Stavros Ioannou*], Athens: Historical Archives of the Commercial Bank of Greece.

Iovva, Ivan 1986, *Οι Δεκεμβριστές του Νότου και το ελληνικό απελευθερωτικό κίνημα* [*The Decembrists of the South and the Greek Liberation Movement*], Athens: Synchroni Epochi.

Kalkandjieva, Daniela 2005, 'The Higher Theological Education of Bulgarian Orthodox Clergy (19th–20th centuries)', in *Studia Universitatis Petru Maior, Historia 5* (Târgu Mureş), 229–42.

Kambouroglou, Pantoleon 1985 [1883], *Ιστορία του Πειραιώς από του 1833–1882 έτους: Γενική κατάστασις, κίνησις εμπορίου, ναυτιλία, βιομηχανία* [*History of Piraeus from 1833–1882: General Condition, Trade, Shipping, Industry*], Athens: Dionysios Notis Karavias Bookstore.

Kamburoglous, Dimitrios G. 1934, 'Δημόσιος και ιδιωτικός βίος επί Τουρκοκρατίας' ['Public and Private Life during the Ottoman Occupation'], in *Great Greek Encyclopaedia*, Vol. 10 (Hellas), Athens: Pyrsos, 801–8.

Kanellopoulos, Panagiotis 1982, ''Ελληνες και Βούλγαροι' ['Greeks and Bulgarians'], in Nikolai Todorov, *Η βαλκανική διάσταση της Επανάστασης του 1821 (η περίπτωση των Βουλγάρων). Ένας κατάλογος των αγωνιστών στη Μολδοβλαχία (Αρχεία Οδησσού)* [*The Balkan Dimension of the Revolution of 1821 (the Case of the Bulgarians): A Catalogue of the Fighters in Moldavia and Wallachia (Odessa Archives)*], Athens: Gutenberg, 9–62.

Karagiannis, Giorgos (24 January 2016), 'Ο αλβανικός μεγαλοϊδεατισμός και το ζήτημα των Τσάμηδων (Ε΄)' ['Albanian Expansionist Aspirations and the Issue of the Cham Albanians'], https://www.imerodromos.gr/tsamiko-5/ (retrieved 22 August 2021).

Karakatsouli, Anna 2016, *'Μαχητές της ελευθερίας' και 1821. Η Ελληνική Επανάσταση στη* διεθνική της διάσταση [*Freedom Fighters' and 1821: The Greek Revolution in its Transnational Dimension*], Athens: Pedio.

Kardasis, Vassilis A. 1987, Σύρος, σταυροδρόμι της Ανατολικής Μεσογείου (1832–1857) [*Syros, Crossroads of the Eastern Mediterranean (1832–1857)*], Athens: National Bank of Greece Cultural Foundation.

Kardasis, Vassilis A. 1993, 'Ελληνική εμπορική ναυτιλία 1858–1914' ['Greek Merchant Shipping 1858–1914'], at the Scientific Symposium in Memory of Nikos Svoronos (30–31 March 1990), Athens: Society for the Study of Modern Greek Culture and General Education, 215–42.

Kardasis, Vassilis A. 1998, Έλληνες ομογενείς στη Νότια Ρωσία, 1775–1861 [*Greek Expatriates in Southern Russia, 1775–1861*], Athens: Alexandria.

Karouzou, Evangelia 2006, 'Θεσμικό πλαίσιο και αγροτική οικονομία' ['Institutional Framework and Rural Economy'], in Kostas Kostis and Socrates Petmezas (eds.), *Η ανάπτυξη της ελληνικής οικονομίας τον 19° αιώνα* [*The Development of the Greek Economy in the Nineteenth Century*], Athens: Alexandria, 175–218.

Katsiardi-Hering, Olga, Anastasia Papadia-Lala, Katerina Nikolaou, and Vangelis Karamanolakis (eds.) 2018, Έλλην, Ρωμηός, Γραικός. Συλλογικοί προσδιορισμοί και ταυτότητες [*Hellene, Romios, Graecos: Collective Identifications and Identities*], Athens: Eurasia.

Katsoulis, Giorgis, Marios Nikolinakos, and Vassilis Filias 1985, Οικονομική ιστορία της νεώτερης Ελλάδας από το 1453 μέχρι το 1830 [*Economic History of Modern Greece from 1453 to 1830*], Vol. I, Athens: Papazisis.

Kautsky, Karl 2009 [1907/08], 'Nationality and Internationality', Part I, ed. by Ben Lewis, *Critique* 37(3): 371–89.

Kautsky, Karl 2010 [1907/08], 'Nationality and Internationality', Part II, ed. by Ben Lewis, *Critique* 38(1): 143–63.

Kitromilides, Paschalis 1990, Η Γαλλική Επανάσταση και η Νοτιοανατολική Ευρώπη [*The French Revolution and Southeastern Europe*], Athens: Diatton.

Kitromilides, Paschalis 1996, Νεοελληνικός Διαφωτισμός [*Modern Greek Enlightenment*], Athens: National Bank of Greece Cultural Foundation.

Kitromilides, Paschalis (ed.) 2013, *Enlightenment and Revolution: The Making of Modern Greece*, Cambridge, MA: Harvard University Press.

Kitromilides, Paschalis 2021, 'Introduction: In an Age of Revolution', in Paschalis M. Kitromilides and Constantinos Tsoukalas (eds.), *The Greek Revolution: A Critical Dictionary*, Cambridge, MA: Harvard University Press.

Kitromilides Paschalis M., and Constantinos Tsoukalas (eds.) 2021, *The Greek Revolution: A Critical Dictionary*, Cambridge, MA: Harvard University Press.

KKE 1968, Επίσημα κείμενα [*Official Texts*], Vol. 4, Political and Literary Publications.

KKE 2020, 1821. Η Επανάσταση και οι απαρχές του ελληνικού αστικού κράτους [*1821: The Revolution and the Beginnings of the Greek Bourgeois State*], Athens: Synchroni Epochi.

Koder, Johannes 2018, 'Ρωμαϊστί. Παρατηρήσεις για τη γλωσσική *romanitas* των Βυζαντινών' ['In Roman: Observations on the Linguistic *Romanitas* of the Byzantines'], in Olga Katsiardi-Hering et al. (eds.), *Έλλην, Ρωμηός, Γραικός. Συλλογικοί προσδιορισμοί και ταυτότητες* [*Hellene, Romios, Graecos: Collective Identifications and Identities*], Athens: Eurasia, 73–85.

Kofinas, G.N. 1934, Ἰστορία των δημοσίων οικονομικών, Α'. Από της επαναστάσεως του 1821 μέχρι της αφίξεως του κυβερνήτου Καποδίστρια' ['History of Public Finances, I: From the Revolution of 1821 to the Arrival of Governor Kapodistrias'], in *Great Greek Encyclopaedia*, Vol. 10 (Hellas), Athens: Pyrsos, 351–4.

Kokkinos, Dionysios A. 1956, *Η Ελληνική Επανάστασις* [*The Greek Revolution*], Volume 1, Athens: Melissa.

Kolias, Aristides 1997, *Οι Αρβανίτες και η καταγωγή των Ελλήνων. Ιστορική, λαογραφική, πολιτιστική, γλωσσολογική επισκόπηση* [*The Arvanites and the Origin of the Greeks: An Historical, Folkloric, Cultural, Linguistic Overview*], Athens: Thamyris.

Koliopoulos, Yannis 1988, *Ληστές. Η κεντρική Ελλάδα στα μέσα του 19ου αιώνα* [*Bandits: Central Greece in the Middle of the Nineteenth Century*], Athens: Hermes.

Kolokotrones, Theodoros 2013, *Memoirs & the History of the Klephts Prior to 1821*, A Bilingual Publication Dedicated to All Greek-Americans, USA: Mitch Fatouros editor/author.

Kolokotrones, Theodoros 1846, *Διήγησις συμβάντων της ελληνικής φυλής από τα 1770 έως τα 1836* [*Narrative of the Events of the Greek Race from 1770 to 1836*], Athens.

Konomos, Dinos 1973, *Μυστικές εταιρείες στα χρόνια της Εθνεγερσίας* [*Secret Societies in the Years of the National Revolution*], Athens.

Korais, Adamantios 1798, Ἀδελφική διδασκαλία προς τους ευρισκόμενους κατά πάσαν την οθωμανικήν επικράτειαν γραικούς' [*Fraternal Teaching to the Greeks throughout the Ottoman Territory*], http://digital.lib.auth.gr/record/56228?ln=el (retrieved 22 August 2021).

Korais, Adamantios 1805, *Τι πρέπει να κάμωσιν οι Γραικοί εις τας παρούσας περιστάσεις: Διάλογος δύο Γραικών κατοίκων της Βενετίας όταν ήκουσον τας λαμπράς νίκας του Αυτοκράτορος Ναπολέοντος* [*What the Greeks Should Do in the Present Circumstances: Dialogue of Two Greek Inhabitants of Venice When They Heard of the Glorious Victories of the Emperor Napoleon*], In Venice: From the Prints of Chrysippos Kritovoulos.

Korais, Adamantios 1819, *Στοχασμοί Κρίτωνος* [*Crito's Reflections*], Paris: from the printing press of Firminos Didotos.

Kordatos, I.K. 1927 [1924], *Η κοινωνική σημασία της Ελληνικής Επαναστάσεως του 1821* [*The Social Significance of the Greek Revolution of 1821*], Athens: G.I. Vassileiou.

Kordatos, Yanis 1957, *Ιστορία της Νεώτερης Ελλάδας* [*History of Modern Greece*], Vol. 2, Athens: Eikostos Aionas.

Kordatos, Yanis 1958, *Ιστορία της Νεώτερης Ελλάδας* [*History of Modern Greece*], Vol. 5, 1900–1924, Athens: Eikostos Aionas.

Kordatos, Yanis 1972 [1946], *Η κοινωνική σημασία της Ελληνικής Επαναστάσεως του 1821* [*The Social Significance of the Greek Revolution of 1821*], Athens: Epikairotita.

Kordatos, Yanis 1983 [1945], *Ο Ρήγας Φεραίος και η Βαλκανική Ομοσπονδία* [*Rigas Pheraios and the Balkan Federation*], Athens: Epikairotita.

Kostis, Kostas 2006, 'Δημόσια οικονομικά' ['Public Finances'], in Kostas Kostis and Socrates Petmezas (eds.), *Η ανάπτυξη της ελληνικής οικονομίας τον 19ο αιώνα* [*The Development of the Greek Economy in the Nineteenth Century*], Athens: Alexandria.

Kostis, Kostas 2013, *'Τα κακομαθημένα παιδιά της Ιστορίας'. Η διαμόρφωση του νεοελληνικού κράτους 18ος–21ος αιώνας* [*'History's Spoiled Children': The Formation of the Modern Greek State Eighteenth–Twenty-First Centuries*], Athens: Polis.

Kostis, Kostas, and Socrates Petmezas (eds.) 2006, *Η ανάπτυξη της ελληνικής οικονομίας τον 19ο αιώνα* [*The Development of the Greek Economy in the Nineteenth Century*], Athens: Alexandria.

Kotarides, Nikos G. 1993, *Παραδοσιακή επανάσταση και Εικοσιένα* [*Traditional Revolution and 1821*], Athens: Plethron.

Kotarides, Nikos G. 2017, *Περί της επαναστάσεως των λεγομένων Ελλήνων. Η μαρτυρία του Ιερομόναχου Γερασίμου (1836)* [*On the Revolution of the So-Called Greeks: The Testimony of Hieromonk Gerasimos (1836)*], Patras: Opportuna.

Koumbourlis, Yannis 2018, 'Εθνική ταυτότητα, εθνικός χαρακτήρας και εθνικό αφήγημα: Ζητήματα ερμηνείας της ιστορίας του ελληνικού έθνους κατά τη μετάβαση από τον Διαφωτισμό στον ιστορισμό' ['National Identity, National Character and National Narrative: Issues of Interpretation of the History of the Greek Nation in the Transition from Enlightenment to Historicism'], in Olga Katsiardi-Hering et al. (eds.), *Έλλην, Ρωμηός, Γραικός. Συλλογικοί προσδιορισμοί και ταυτότητες* [*Hellene, Romios, Graecos: Collective Identifications and Identities*], Athens: Eurasia, 615–31.

Kremmydas, Vassilis 1980, *Συγκυρία και εμπόριο στην προεπαναστατική Πελοπόννησο, 1793–1821* [*Conjuncture and Trade in the Pre-Revolutionary Peloponnese, 1793–1821*], Athens: Themelio.

Kremmydas, Vassilis 1992, 'Υποδοχή των ευρωπαϊκών ιδεών από τον ελληνισμό στο τέλος της τουρκοκρατίας' ['Reception of European Ideas by Hellenism at the End of the Turkish Occupation'], *Theseis* 42: 27–32.

Kremmydas, Vassilis 2016a, *Η ελληνική επανάσταση του 1821 – Τεκμήρια, αναψηλαφήσεις, ερμηνείες* [*The Greek Revolution of 1821 – Documents, Reinvestigations, Interpretations*], Athens: Gutenberg.

Kremmydas, Vassilis 2016b, 'Ελληνική Επανάσταση του 1821: ο πόλεμος και η νίκη της νεωτερικότητας' ['The Greek Revolution of 1821: War and the Victory of Modernity'], interview with Stratis Bournazos, https://enthemata.wordpress.com/2016/03/26/vkrem/ (retrieved 22 August 2021).

Kremmydas, Vassilis 2018, 'Ο Βασίλης Κρεμμυδάς καταρρίπτει έναν έναν τους μύθους του 1821 κι όχι μόνο το κρυφό σχολειό' ['Vassilis Kremmydas Debunks One-by-One the

Myths of 1821, and not only that, of the Hidden School'], interview with Thodoris Antonopoulos, https://www.lifo.gr/articles/book_articles/93091/o-vasilis-kremmyd as-katarriptei-enan-enan-toys-mythoys-toy-1821-ki-oxi-mono-to-kryfo-sxoleio (retrieved 22 August 2021).

Kribas, V.D. 1934, 'Αμπελουργία' ['Viniculture'], in *Great Greek Encyclopaedia*, Vol. 10 (Hellas), Athens: Pyrsos, 93–5.

Kyriakopoulos, Elias G. 1929, 'Βερώνης Συνέδριον' ['The Congress of Verona'], in *Great Greek Encyclopaedia*, Vol. 3, Athens: Pyrsos, 154–5.

Kyrtatas, Dimitris 2011, 'Slavery and Economy in the Greek World', in Bradley Keith and Paul Cartledge (eds.), *The Cambridge World History of Slavery*, Cambridge: Cambridge University Press, 91–111.

Ladogianni, Georgia 1989, *Το περιοδικό «Ιδέα» (1933–1934). Παρέμβαση στην κοινωνική κρίση και την αισθητική αναζήτηση* [*The Periodical 'Idea' (1933–1934). Intervention in the Social Crisis and the Aesthetic Pursuit*], PhD Thesis, University of Ioannina.

Lane, Frederic C. 1973, *Venice, A Maritime Republic*, Baltimore: The Johns Hopkins University Press.

Lenin, Vladimir I. 1972, *Collected Works*, Vol. 3, Moscow: Progress Publishers.

Lenin, Vladimir I. 1974, *Collected Works*, Vol. 2, Moscow: Progress Publishers.

Lenin, Vladimir I. 1977, *Collected Works*, Vol. 29, Moscow: Progress Publishers.

Leontaritis, Georgios 1996, *Ελληνική εμπορική ναυτιλία (1453–1850)* [*Greek Merchant Shipping (1453–1850)*], Athens: Society for the Study of Modern Hellenism – Mnemon.

Liakos, Antonis 1986, *Η ιταλική ενοποίηση και η Μεγάλη Ιδέα* [*Italian Unification and the Grand Idea*], Athens: Themelio.

Liakos, Antonis 2005, *Πώς στοχάστηκαν το έθνος αυτοί που ήθελαν να αλλάξουν τον κόσμο* [*How Did Those Who Wanted to Change the World Reflected upon the Nation?*], Athens: Polis.

Loukas, Ioannis 1998, *Θαλάσσια ισχύς και ελληνικό κράτος (Ο στόλος της Μεγάλης Ιδέας)* [*Sea Power and the Greek State (The Fleet of the Grand Idea)*], Athens: Epikoinonies SA.

Loukos, Christos 1988, *Η αντιπολίτευση κατά του κυβερνήτη Ιω. Καποδίστρια, 1828–1931* [*The Opposition Against Governor I. Kapodistrias, 1828–1931*], Athens: Themelio.

Loukos, Christos 1994, 'Οι "τύχες" του Αλέξανδρου Μαυροκορδάτου στη νεοελληνική συνείδηση' ['The "Fate" of Alexandros Mavrokordatos in Modern Greek Consciousness'], in *Η Επανάσταση του 1821. Μελέτες στη μνήμη της Δέσποινας Θεμελή-Κατηφόρη* [*The Revolution of 1821: Studies in Memory of Despina Themeli-Katifori*], Athens: Society for the Study of Modern Hellenism, 93–106.

Loukos, Christos 2014, 'Ο "κοινωνικός" Καποδίστριας. Η αποκατάστασή του στις αριστερές συνειδήσεις' ['The "Social" Kapodistrias: His Restoration in Leftist Consciousness'], in Dimitris Dimitropoulos and Vangelis Karamanolakis (eds.), *Οι αναγνώσεις του 1821 και η Αριστερά* [*Readings of 1821 and the Left*], Athens: Contemporary Social History Archives – Avgi, 83–95.

Lowry, Heath W. 1993, 'Süleymân's Formative Years', in Halil İnalcık and Cemal Kafadar (eds.), *Süleymân the Second and His Time*, Istanbul: The Isis Press, 21–36.

Lyberatos, Andreas 2018, Ῥωμηοί, Ἕλληνες και Γκαγκαούζοι στη Βουλγαρία του 19ου αιώνα: ανασημασιοδότηση, ταξινόμηση, αυτο-κατανόηση' ['Romioi, Greeks and Gagauzis in Nineteenth-Century Bulgaria: Re-Semanticisation, Classification, Self-Understanding'], in Olga Katsiardi-Hering et al. (eds.), Ἕλλην, Ρωμηός, Γραικός. Συλλογικοί προσδιορισμοί και ταυτότητες [*Hellene, Romios, Graecos: Collective Identifications and Identities*], Athens: Eurasia, 417–29.

Makriyannis, Yannis 2011, Απομνημονεύματα του Μακρυγιάννη. Τo πλήρες κείμενο, μεταγραφή από το πρωτότυπο του Γιάννη Βλαχογιάννη, επεξεργασμένη από τον καθηγητή Γιάννη Καζάζη [*Memoirs of Makriyannis: The Complete Text*, transcribed from the original by Yannis Vlachoyannis, edited by Professor Yannis Kazazis], https://www.imlagada.gr/UsersFiles/admin/documents/Downloads/1_Makrigianni_opt.pdf (retrieved 22 August 2021).

Maleševiç, Siniša 2019, *Grounded Nationalisms: A Sociological Analysis*, Cambridge: Cambridge University Press.

Mamoukas, Andreas Z. 1839, Τα κατά την Αναγέννησιν της Ελλάδος. Ἤτοι συλλογή των κατά την αναγεννωμένην Ελλάδα συνταχθέντων πολιτευμάτων, νόμων και άλλων επισήμων πράξεων, από του 1821 μέχρι τέλους του 1832 [*Testimonies of the Renaissance of Greece: A Compilation of the Constitutions, Laws and Other Official Acts Drawn up During the Rebirth of Greece, from 1821 to the End of 1832*], Piraeus: from the Ilias Christofides Printing House, Volumes I, II, VI.

Mandel, Ernest 1971, *The Formation of the Economic Thought of Karl Marx*, New York: Monthly Review Press.

Marmora, Leopoldo 1983, *Nation and Internationalism: Problems and Perspectives of a Socialist Concept of Nation*, Bremen: Edition CON.

Martone, Eric 2009, 'Pushkin, Alexander (1799–1837)', in Eric Martone (ed.), *Encyclopedia of Blacks in European History and Culture*, Westport, CT: Greenwood, 431–2.

Marx, Karl 1972, 'The Eighteenth Brumaire of Louis Bonaparte', in *Marx-Engels Collected Works* (*MECW*), Vol. 11, 99–197, New York: International Publishers.

Marx, Karl 1973, 'Marx an Engels in Manchester, 14/3/1868', in *Marx-Engels-Werke* (*MEW*), Vol. 32, 42–4, Berlin: Dietz Verlag.

Marx, Karl 1976, 'Ber Bürgerkrieg in Frankreich', in *MEW*, Vol. 17, 313–65, Berlin: Dietz Verlag.

Marx, Karl 1977, 'The Bourgeoisie and the Counter-Revolution', in *MECW*, Vol. 8, 157–78, New York: International Publishers.

Marx, Karl 1978, 'Review: Guizot, Pourquoi la révolution d'Angleterre a-t-elle réussi? Discours sur l'Histoire de la Révolution d'Angleterre, Paris, 1850', *MECW*, Vol. 10, 251–6, New York: International Publishers.

Marx, Karl 1984, 'Mazzinis neues Manifest', in *MEW*, Vol. 12, 579–83, Berlin: Dietz Verlag.

Marx, Karl 1986 [1870–71], 'The Civil War in France', in *MECW*, Vol. 22, 307–59, New York: International Publishers.

Marx, Karl 1990, *Capital*, Vol. 1, London: Penguin.

Marx, Karl 1991, *Capital*, Vol. 3, London: Penguin.

Marx, Karl 1993, *Grundrisse*, London: Penguin.

Marx, Karl, and Friedrich Engels 1998, *The German Ideology including Theses on Feuerbach and Introduction to the Critique of Political Economy*, Amherst, New York: Prometheus Books.

Matalas, Paraskevas 2002, *Έθνος και ορθοδοξία. Οι περιπέτειες μιας σχέσης. Από το 'Ελλαδικό' στο Βουλγαρικό σχίσμα* [*Nation and Orthodoxy. The Adventures of a Relationship. From the 'Greek' to the Bulgarian Schism*], Herakleion: Crete University Press.

Maurer, Georg Ludwig von 1976 [1835], *Ο ελληνικός λαός* [*The Greek People*], Athens: Tolides Bros.

Mavrogiannis, Gerasimos E. 1889, *Ιστορία των Ιονίων Νήσων, αρχομένη τω 1797 και λήγουσα τω 1815* [*History of the Ionian Islands, Beginning in 1797 and Ending in 1815*], 2 Volumes, Athens: 'Palingenesia' Printing House.

Maximos, Seraphim 1973, *Η αυγή του ελληνικού καπιταλισμού. Τουρκοκρατία 1685–1789* [*The Dawn of Greek Capitalism: Ottoman Rule 1685–1789*], Athens: Stochastis.

Maximos, Seraphim 1976, *Το ελληνικό εμπορικό ναυτικό κατά τον XVII αιώνα* [*The Greek Merchant Navy in the Seventeenth Century*], Athens: Stochastis.

Maximos, Seraphim 1982, 'Μερικά προβλήματα από την εξέλιξη του καπιταλισμού στην Ελλάδα' ['Some Problems Regarding the Evolution of Capitalism in Greece'], in *Spartacus, Monthly Journal of Marxist-Leninist Theory and Practice. Left Opposition of the KKE. Essays of 1928*, pp. 10–12 and 89–91.

McGowan, Bruce 1981, *Economic Life in Ottoman Europe: Taxation, Trade and the Struggle for Land, 1600–1800*, Oxford: Oxford University Press.

Meyer, Ioannis [Johann Jakob] 1858, *Ελληνικά Χρονικά 'Μεσολογγίου'* [*Greek Chronicle of 'Missolonghi'*], Volumes I (1824) and II (1825–1826), Athens: X.H. Spanos and N. Nikas.

Milios, Jean [John] 1988, *Kapitalistische Entwicklung, Nationalstaat und Imperialismus. Der Fall Griechenland*. Athens: Kritiki.

Milios, John 1989, 'The Problem of Capitalist Development: Theoretical Considerations in View of the Industrial Countries and the New Industrial Countries', in M. Gottdiener and N. Komninos (eds.), *Capitalist Development and Crisis Theory: Accumulation, Regulation and Spatial Restructuring*, London: Macmillan, 154–73.

Milios, Jannis [John] 1997, 'Der Marxsche Begriff der asiatischen Produktionsweise und die theoretische Unmöglichkeit einer Geschichtsphilosophie', *Beiträge zur Marx-Engels-Forschung. Neue Folge*, 101–13.

Milios, John 1999, 'Asiatic Mode of Production', in *Encyclopaedia of Political Economy*, edited by Phillip Anthony O'Hara, London: Routledge, 18–20.

Milios, Yannis [John] 2017, *Ο 'σοβιετικός μαρξισμός' και οι Έλληνες στοχαστές* [*'Soviet Marxism' and Greek Thinkers*], Athens: Ephemerida ton Syntakton.

Milios, John 2018, *The Origins of Capitalism as a Social System: The Prevalence of an Aleatory Encounter*, London: Routledge.

Milios, John, and Dimitris P. Sotiropoulos 2009, *Rethinking Imperialism: A Study of Capitalist Rule*, London: Palgrave Macmillan.

Milios, Yannis [John], and Thanos Mikroutsikos 2018, *Στην υπηρεσία του έθνους. Ζητήματα ιδεολογίας και αισθητικής στην ελληνική μουσική* [*In the Service of the Nation: Issues of Ideology and Aesthetics in Greek Music*], Athens: Ephemerida ton Syntakton.

Moschovakis, N.G. 1882, *Το εν Ελλάδι Δημόσιον Δίκαιον επί Τουρκοκρατίας* [*Public Law in Greece During the Turkish Occupation*], Dissertation on Readership, Athens: C.N. Philadelpheus.

Moskov, Kostis 1979, *Εισαγωγικά στην ιστορία του κινήματος της εργατικής τάξης. Η διαμόρφωση της εθνικής και κοινωνικής συνείδησης στην Ελλάδα* [*Introduction to the History of the Working-Class Movement: The Formation of National and Social Consciousness in Greece*], Thessaloniki.

Mosse, George L. 1993, *Confronting the Nation: Jewish and Western Nationalism*, Hanover and London: Brandeis University Press.

Mouritsen, Henrik 2009, 'Modern Nations and Ancient Models: Greece and Italy Compared', in Roderick Beaton and David Ricks (eds.), *The Making of Modern Greece: Nationalism, Romanticism, and the Uses of the Past (1797–1896)*, London: Ashgate, 43–9.

Mutafchieva, Vera 1990, *Αγροτικές σχέσεις στην Οθωμανική Αυτοκρατορία (15ᵒˢ–16ᵒˢ αι.)* [*Peasant Relations in the Ottoman Empire (Fifteenth–Sixteenth Centuries)*], Athens: Poreia.

Negris, Theodoros 1824, 'Ανάπτυξις του νόμου της Επιδαύρου' ['Analysis of the Law of Epidaurus'], *Athens Newspaper*, 22 November 1824, quoted in Eleni S. Stoikou, *Όψεις του εθνοφυλετισμού των Ορθοδόξων Αράβων από τα μέσα του 19ᵒᵘ αιώνα έως τον Α΄ Παγκόσμιο Πόλεμο* [*Aspects of the Ethno-Racialism of the Orthodox Arabs from the Mid-Nineteenth Century to the First World War*], Aristotle University of Thessaloniki, Master's Thesis, Department of Modern and Contemporary History, 109–10.

Noutsos, Panagiotis 1982, *Ελληνική Νομαρχία. Συμβολή στην έρευνα των πηγών της* [*Hellenic Nomarchy: Contribution to the Research of its Sources*], Athens: Dodoni.

Noutsos, Panagiotis 1999, 'Νεοελληνικός Διαφωτισμός: Προς τη συγκρότηση μορφών "Γνωσιοανθρωπολογίας"' ['Modern Greek Enlightenment: Towards the Constitution of Forms of "Gnosio-Anthropology"'], in Asterios Argyriou, Konstantinos A. Dimadis, and Anastasia Danae Lazaridou (eds.), *Ο ελληνικός κόσμος ανάμεσα στην Ανατολή και τη Δύση 1453–1981* [*The Greek World Between East and West 1453–1981*], Athens: Ellinika Grammata, 371–80.

O'Meara, Patrick 2003, *The Decembrist Pavel Pestel Russia's First Republican*, Houndmills: Palgrave Macmillan.

Panagiotidis, Stavros 2014, 'Ο στρατηγός Μακρυγιάννης και η ελληνική Αριστερά. Μια περίπτωση συμβολικής αναδρομικής οικειοποίησης' ['General Makriyannis and the Greek Left: A Case of Symbolic Retrospective Appropriation'], in Dimitris Dimitropoulos and Vangelis Karamanolakis (eds.), *Οι αναγνώσεις του 1821 και η Αριστερά* [*Readings of 1821 and the Left*], Athens: Contemporary Social History Archives – Avgi, 71–81.

Panagiotopoulos, Vassilis 1980, 'Η βιομηχανική επανάσταση και η Ελλάδα, 1832–1871' ['The Industrial Revolution and Greece, 1832–1871'], in Grothusen et al., *Εκσυγχρονισμός και βιομηχανική επανάσταση στα Βαλκάνια τον 19° αιώνα* [*Modernization and Industrial Revolution in the Balkans in the Nineteenth Century*], Athens: Themelio, 216–35.

Papadakis, V.P. 1934, 'Πολιτικά κόμματα' ['Political Parties'], in *Great Greek Encyclopaedia*, Vol. 10 (Hellas), Athens: Pyrsos, 850–9.

Papadia-Lala, Anastasia 1984, 'Η Σμύρνη κατά τα ορλωφικά (1770): Εσωτερικές συγκρούσεις και ευρωπαϊκή παρέμβαση' ['Smyrna During the Orlov Revolt (1770): Internal Conflicts and European Intervention'], *Bulletin of the Centre for Asia Minor Studies*, Vol. 5, 133–85.

Papadia-Lala, Anastasia 2018, 'Οι *Greci* στον ελληνοβενετικό κόσμο (13°ς–18°ς αι.). Ο λόγος των πολλαπλών εξουσιών' ['The *Greci* in the Helleno-Venetian World (Thirteenth–Eighteenth Centuries): The Discourse of Multiple Authorities'], in Olga Katsiardi-Hering et al. (eds.), *Έλλην, Ρωμηός, Γραικός. Συλλογικοί προσδιορισμοί και ταυτότητες* [*Hellene, Romios, Graecos: Collective Identifications and Identities*], Athens: Eurasia, 165–80.

Papadopoulou, Theodora 2018, 'Τα ονόματα Ρωμαίος, Έλλην, Γραικός κατά τους μέσους βυζαντινούς χρόνους' ['The Names Roman, Hellene, Graecos in the Middle Byzantine Period'], in Olga Katsiardi-Hering et al. (eds.), *Έλλην, Ρωμηός, Γραικός. Συλλογικοί προσδιορισμοί και ταυτότητες* [*Hellene, Romios, Graecos: Collective Identifications and Identities*], Athens: Eurasia, 87–101.

Papageorgiou, Stefanos P. 2004, *Από το γένος στο έθνος. Η θεμελίωση του ελληνικού κράτους (1821–1862)* [*From Genus to Nation: The Foundation of the Greek State (1821–1862)*], Athens: Papazisis.

Papanastasiou, Alexandros 1992, *Ο εθνικισμός. Κοινωνιολογική μελέτη* [*Nationalism: A Sociological Study*], Athens: Dimiourgia.

Paparrigopoulos, Constantinos 1899, *Τα διδακτικώτερα πορίσματα της Ιστορίας του ελληνικού έθνους* [*The Most Instructive Findings of the History of the Greek Nation*], Athens: Spyridon Kousoulinos.

Paparrigopoulos, Constantinos 1971, *Ιστορία του ελληνικού έθνους* [*History of the Greek Nation*], Volumes 14 and 15, Athens: Galaxy.

Papathanasopoulos, Constantinos 1983, *Ελληνική εμπορική ναυτιλία (1833–1856). Εξέλιξη* και αναπροσαρμογή [*Greek Merchant Shipping (1833–1856): Evolution and Readjustment*], Athens: National Bank of Greece Cultural Foundation.

Papazoglou, K.V. 1933, 'Ναυτικόν' ['Navy'], in *Great Greek Encyclopaedia*, Vol. 21, Athens: Pyrsos, 291–7.

Papoulidis, Constantinos 1989, *Γρηγόριος Γ. Μαρασλής (1831–1907)* [*Gregorios C. Maraslis (1831–1907)*], Athens: Foundation of Balkan Peninsula Studies.

Paraskevopoulos, Georgios P. 1896, *Η Μεγάλη Ελλάς. Ανά την Ρωσσίαν, Ρουμανίαν, Βουλγαρίαν, Σερβίαν, Μαυροβούνιον, Τουρκίαν, Σάμον, Κρήτην, Κύπρον, Αίγυπτον και Παλαιστίνην* [*Great Hellas: Throughout Russia, Romania, Bulgaria, Serbia, Montenegro, Turkey, Samos, Crete, Cyprus, Egypt and Palestine*], Athens.

Paschalis, D.P. 1933, 'Ύδρα – Ιστορία' ['Hydra – History'], in *Great Greek Encyclopaedia*, Vol. 23, Athens: Pyrsos, 589–90.

Patrikiou, Alexandra 2017, 'On the Historiography of the Language Question in Post-1974 Greece', *Historein* 16(1–2), https://ejournals.epublishing.ekt.gr/pfiles/journals/14/editor-uploads/issues/517/main517.html?1=517&2=10249 (retrieved 22 August 2021).

Patronis, Vassilis 2015, *Ελληνική οικονομική ιστορία. Οικονομία, κοινωνία και κράτος στην Ελλάδα (18ος–20ός αιώνας)* [*Greek Economic History: Economy, Society and State in Greece (Eighteenth–Twentieth Centuries)*], Athens: Association of Hellenic Academic Libraries – National Technical University of Athens.

Petmezas, Socrates 2006, 'Αγροτική οικονομία' ['Agrarian economy'], in Kostas Kostis and Socrates Petmezas (eds.), *Η ανάπτυξη της ελληνικής οικονομίας τον 19ο αιώνα* [*The Development of the Greek Economy in the Nineteenth Century*], Athens: Alexandria, 103–52.

Petridis, Pavlos V. 1990, *Πολιτικοί και συνταγματικοί θεσμοί στη νεώτερη Ελλάδα (1821–1843)* [*Political and Constitutional Institutions in Modern Greece (1821–1843)*], Athens: University Studio Press.

Philemon, Ioannis 1834, *Δοκίμιον ιστορικόν περί της Φιλικής Εταιρίας* [*Historical Essay on the Friendly Society*], Nafplion: T.N. Loulakis.

Philemon, Ioannis 1859, *Δοκίμιον ιστορικόν περί της ελληνικής Επαναστάσεως* [*Historical Essay on the Greek Revolution*], Vol. 1, Athens: P. Soutsas and A. Ktenas.

'Philhellenism in England (1821–1827)' 1936, *The Slavonic and East European Review* 14(41): 363–71.

Philippou, Philippos 2015, 'Νικόλαος Γαλάτης, προδότης ή πατριώτης' ['Nikolaos Galatis, Traitor or Patriot?'], seisaxthia.wordpress.com/2015/03/26/nikolaos-galatis-traitor-or-patriot/ (retrieved 22 August 2021).

Photeinos, Elias 1846, *Οι άθλοι της εν Βλαχία Επαναστάσεως το 1821 έτος* [*The Feats of the Revolution in Wallachia in the Year 1821*], Leipzig, Saxony.

Pizanias, Petros (ed.) 2011, *The Greek Revolution of 1821: A European Event*, Istanbul: The Isis Press.

Platis, Vasilis A. 2008, *Ιστορική γεωγραφία και εθνικές διεκδικήσεις των Ελλήνων τον 19° αιώνα* [*Historical Geography and National Claims of the Greeks in the Nineteenth Century*], Thessaloniki, PhD Thesis, School of History and Archaeology, Aristotle University of Thessaloniki, Department of Modern and Contemporary Greek and European History.

Ploumides, Spyridon G. 2018, 'Της μεγάλης ταύτης ιδέας. Οι αφετηρίες της ελληνικής εθνικής ιδεολογίας' ['On this Grand Idea: The Origins of Greek National Ideology'], in Olga Katsiardi-Hering et al. (eds.), *Έλλην, Ρωμηός, Γραικός. Συλλογικοί προσδιορισμοί και ταυτότητες* [*Hellene, Romios, Graecos: Collective Identifications and Identities*], Athens: Eurasia, 555–70.

Polyzoides, Anastasios 1971, *Ανέκδοτα κείμενα από την 'Απόλλωνα', Ύδρα 1831* [*Unpublished Texts from the 'Apollo', Hydra 1831*], Athens: Koultoura.

Poulantzas, Nicos 1973, *Political Power and Social Classes*, London: New Left Books.

Poulantzas, Nicos 1980, *State, Power, Socialism*, London and New York: Verso.

Poulantzas, Nicos 2018, *Fascism and Dictatorship: The Third International and the Problem of Fascism*, London: Verso.

Pouqueville, F.C.H.L. 1824, *Histoire de la Régénération de la Grèce*, Paris: Chez Firmin Didot Père et Fils.

Praktika 1844, *Πρακτικά. Η της Τρίτης Σεπτεμβρίου εν Αθήναις Εθνική Συνέλευσις*, [*Proceedings: The National Assembly of the Third September in Athens*], Athens: Royal Printing Office.

Psalidopoulos, Michalis 2014, *Ιστορία της Τράπεζας της Ελλάδος, 1936–2008* [*History of the Bank of Greece, 1936–2008*], Athens: Bank of Greece.

Psarras, Dimitris 2020, *Πώς συλλογάται ο Ρήγας; Επιστροφή στις πηγές* [*How Does Rigas Reason? Back to the Sources*], Athens: Polis.

Psyllas, Georgios 1974, *Απομνημονεύματα του βίου μου* [*Memoirs of My Life*], Athens: Academy of Athens, Office of Publications.

Reinhold, Karl Dr. 1855, *Πελασγικά.* [*Pelasgics*]. *Noctes Pelasgicae: Dialectos Graeciae Pelasgicas*. Athens: Typis Sophoclis Garbola.
https://books.google.gr/books?id=ugJvYWos14UC&pg=PP8&lpg=PP8&dq=Noctes+Pelasgicae:+Dialectos+Graeciae+Pelasgica (retrieved Nov. 19, 2022).

Rhigas Velestinlis [Pheraios] 2008, *Revolutionary Scripts*, Athens: Scientific Society of Studies Pheres – Velestino – Rhigas.

Rigas [Pheraios] 1996a, *Νέα πολιτική διοίκησις των κατοίκων της Ρούμελης, της μικράς Ασίας, των μεσογείων νήσων, και της Βλαχομπογδανίας* [*New Political Administration of the Inhabitants of Roumeli, Asia Minor, the Mediterranean Islands, and Vlachobogdania*], in Emmanuel S. Stathis, *Το Σύνταγμα και ο Θούριος του Ρήγα. Το αρχικό και το τελικό κείμενο. Κριτική έκδοση* [*The Constitution and the Thourios of Rigas: The Original and the Final Text. Critical Edition*], Athens: Armos, 183–224.

Rigas [Pheraios] 1996b, *Θούριος, ήτοι ορμητικός πατριωτικός ύμνος πρώτος, εις τον ήχον. Μια* προσταγή μεγάλη [*Thourios, or First Stormy Patriotic Hymn, to the Sound. A Great Imperative*], in Emmanuel S. Stathis, *Το Σύνταγμα και ο Θούριος του Ρήγα. Το αρχικό και το τελικό κείμενο. Κριτική έκδοση* [*The Constitution and the Thourios of Rigas: The Original and the Final Text. Critical Edition*], Athens: Armos, 279–98.

Rotzokos, Nikos V. 1997, *Επανάσταση και Εμφύλιος στο Εικοσιένα* [*Revolution and Civil War in 1821*], Athens: Plethron/Dokimes.

Roudometof, Victor 1998, 'From Rum Millet to Greek Nation: Enlightenment, Secularization, and National Identity in Ottoman Balkan Society, 1453–1821', *Journal of Modern Greek Studies* 16: 11–48.

Rubin, Alfred P. 1988, *The Law of Piracy*, Newport, RI: Naval War College Press.

Rubin, Isaac I. 1979, *A History of Economic Thought*, London: Pluto Press.

Sakai, Naoki 2006, '"You Asians": On the Historical Role of the West and Asia Binary', in Tomiko Yoda and Harry Harootunian (eds.), *Japan After Japan*, Durham, NC: Duke University Press, 167–94.

Sakellariou, Michael V. 1978 [1939], *Η Πελοπόννησος κατά την δευτέραν Τουρκοκρατίαν (1715–1821)* [*The Peloponnese During the Second Turkish Occupation (1715–1821)*], Athens: Hermes.

Sakellaropoulos, Theodoros D. 1991, *Θεσμικός μετασχηματισμός και οικονομική ανάπτυξη. Κράτος και οικονομία στην Ελλάδα 1830–1922* [*Institutional Transformation and Economic Development: State and Economy in Greece 1830–1922*], Athens: Exantas.

Sakellaropoulou, Katerina 2017, 'Τα Συντάγματα του Αγώνα: Το δίκαιο της ελευθερίας' ['The Constitutions of the Struggle: The Law of Freedom'], paper presented at the event co-organized on 26 April 2017 by the Institute for Justice and Development and the N. Svoronos Institute, on 'The Constitutions of the Struggle (1821–1832)', 109–17, http://www.publiclawjournal.com/docs/6/2017_2_2_sakellaropoulou.pdf (retrieved 22 August 2021).

Sathas, Constantinos 1869, *Τουρκοκρατούμενη Ελλάς. Ιστορικόν δοκίμιον περί των προς αποτίναξιν του οθωμανικού ζυγού επαναστάσεων του ελληνικού έθνους (1453–1821)* [*Greece under the Turkish Yoke: An Historical Essay on the Revolutions of the Greek Nation Aiming at Throwing off the Turkish Yoke (1453–1821)*], Athens: printed by the children of Andreas Koromilas.

Sathas, Constantinos 1986 [1885], *Έλληνες στρατιώται εν τη Δύσει και αναγέννησις της ελληνικής τακτικής* [*Greek Soldiers in the West and the Rebirth of Greek Tactics*], Athens: Dionysios Notis Karavias Bookshop.

Schwarz-Sochor, Jenny 1958, 'P. I. Pestel: The Beginnings of Jacobin Thought in Russia', *International Review of Social History* 3(1): 71–96.

Shelley, Percy Bysshe 1874, 'Hellas', in *The Poetical Works of Percy Bysshe Shelley*, edited by Mrs. Shelley, London: Edward Moxon & Co, 166–80.

Skarpetis, Vasileios 1934, 'Ναυτιλία' ['Shipping'], in *Great Greek Encyclopaedia*, Vol. 10 (Hellas), Athens: Pyrsos, 200–5.

Skliros, Georgios 1977, Έργα [Works], Athens: Epikairotita.

Skopetea, Eleni 1988, Το πρότυπο βασίλειο και η Μεγάλη Ιδέα [The 'Model Kingdom' and the Grand Idea], Athens: Polytypo.

Σπάρτακος, Μηνιαίο περιοδικό της μαρξιστικής-λενινιστικής θεωρίας και πράξης, τεύχη του 1928 (1982), [Spartakos, Monthly Journal of Marxist-Leninist Theory and Practice, Issues of 1928], Athens: Utopia.

Stalin, Joseph V. 1913, Marxism and the National Question, https://www.marxists.org/reference/archive/stalin/works/1913/03a.htm (retrieved 22 August 2021).

Stasinopoulos, Michael D. 1970, 'Η περί της παιδείας μέριμνα του αγωνιζομένου έθνους και το πρώτον Πανεπιστήμιον' ['The Concern for Education of the Struggling Nation and the First University'], Nea Estia, Tribute to Eikosiena, Christmas.

Stathis, Emmanuel S. 1996, Το Σύνταγμα και ο Θούριος του Ρήγα. Το αρχικό και το τελικό κείμενο. Κριτική έκδοση [The Constitution and the Thourios of Rigas. The Original and the Final Text. Critical Edition], Athens: Armos.

Stathis, Panagiotis 2014, 'Το Εικοσιένα στην αριστερή ιστοριογραφία του 20ού αιώνα' ['1821 in Twentieth-Century Left Historiography'], in Dimitris Dimitropoulos and Vangelis Karamanolakis (eds.), Οι αναγνώσεις του 1821 και η Αριστερά [Readings of 1821 and the Left], Athens: Contemporary Social History Archives – Avgi, 29–43.

Stavrianos, L.S. 1958, The Balkans Since 1453, New York: Rinehart & Company.

Stavridi-Patrikiou, Rena (ed.) 1976, Δημοτικισμός και κοινωνικό πρόβλημα [Demoticism and the Social Problem], Athens: Hermes.

Stavropoulos, Theodoros 1979, Ιστορική ανάλυση του αγροτικού ζητήματος στην Ελλάδα [Historical Analysis of the Agrarian Question in Greece], 2 Volumes, Athens: Nea Synora.

Ste. Croix, G.E.M. de 1984, 'Class in Marx's Conception of History, Ancient and Modern', New Left Review 146: 92–111.

Ste. Croix, G.E.M. de 2004, Athenian Democratic Origins and Other Essays, Oxford: Oxford University Press.

Stoianovich, Traian 1980, 'Αγρότες και γαιοκτήμονες των Βαλκανίων και οθωμανικό κράτος: οικογενειακή οικονομία, οικονομία αγοράς και εκσυγχρονισμός' ['Balkan Peasants and Landowners and the Ottoman State: Family Economy, Market Economy and Modernization'], in Grothusen et al. Εκσυγχρονισμός και βιομηχανική επανάσταση στα Βαλκάνια τον 19ο αιώνα [Modernization and Industrial Revolution in the Balkans in the Nineteenth Century], Athens: Themelio.

Stoianovich, Traian 1992, 'The Conquering Balkan Orthodox Merchant', in Traian Stoianonich, Between East and West: The Balkan and Mediterranean Worlds, Vol. II: Economies and Societies: Traders, Towns, and Households, New York: Aristide D. Caratzas.

Stoianovich, Traian 1994, Balkan Worlds: The First and Last Europe, London: Routledge.

Stoikou, Eleni S. 2008, Όψεις του εθνοφυλετισμού των Ορθοδόξων Αράβων από τα μέσα του 19ου αιώνα έως τον Α΄ Παγκόσμιο Πόλεμο [Aspects of the Ethno-Racialism of the Orthodox

Arabs from the Mid-Nineteenth Century to the First World War], Aristotle University of Thessaloniki, Master's Thesis, Department of Modern and Contemporary History.

Sugar, Peter F. 1983, *Southeastern Europe under Ottoman Rule, 1354–1804*, Washington: University of Washington Press.

Svolos, Alexandros 1972, *Τα ελληνικά Συντάγματα 1822–1952* [*The Greek Constitutions 1822–1952*], Athens: Stochastis.

Svoronos, N.I. 1934, 'Πληθυσμός και κάτοικοι' ['Population and Inhabitants'], in *Great Greek Encyclopaedia*, Vol. 10 (Hellas), Athens: Pyrsos, 223–36.

Svoronos, Nikos 1995, *Η μέθοδος της Ιστορίας* [*The Method of History*], Athens: Agra.

Svoronos, Nikos 2004, *Το ελληνικό έθνος – Γένεση και διαμόρφωση του νέου ελληνισμού* [*The Greek Nation – Genesis and Formation of Modern Hellenism*], Athens: Polis.

Syngros, Andreas 1908, *Απομνημονεύματα* [*Memoirs*], Vol. III, Athens: Hestia.

Σύνταγμα της Επτανήσου Πολιτείας του 1803 [*Constitution of the Ionian State of 1803*], http://www.infokerkyra.gr/protaseis/2-uncategorised/187-syntagma-tis-eptanisou-politeias-tou-1803.html (retrieved 17 August 2021).

Συνταγμάτιον Νομικόν περί ευταξίας και του καθήκοντος εκάστου των κριτηρίων και των οφφικίων του πριντζιπάτου της Βλαχίας (1780) [*Legislative Constitution on the Orderliness and Duty of Each of the Judges and Officers of the Principate of Wallachia*] (1780), https://anemi.lib.uoc.gr/metadata (retrieved 17 August 2021).

Tairako, Tomonaga 2016, 'A Turning Point in Marx's Theory on Pre-Capitalist Societies: Marx's Excerpt Notebooks on Maurer in MEGA IV/18', *Hitotsubashi Journal of Social Studies* 47(1): 1–10.

Theodorakopoulos, Ioannis N. 1972, *Το Εικοσιένα και ο σύγχρονος ελληνισμός* [*1821 and Modern Hellenism*], Athens: Publications of Friends.

Theotokas, Nikos, and Nikos Kotarides 2014, 'Προσλήψεις των κλεφτών από την μαρξιστική ιστοριογραφία' ['Apperceptions of the Klephts by Marxist Historiography'], in Dimitris Dimitropoulos and Vangelis Karamanolakis (eds.), *Οι αναγνώσεις του 1821 και η Αριστερά* [*Readings of 1821 and the Left*], Athens: Contemporary Social History Archives – Avgi, 45–57.

Thiersch, Frédéric 1833, *De l'état actuel de la Grèce et des moyens d'arriver à sa restauration*, Leipzig: F.A. Brockhaus.

Thiersch, Frédéric 1972, *Η Ελλάδα του Καποδίστρια. Η παρούσα κατάσταση της Ελλάδος (1828–1833) και τα μέσα για να επιτευχθεί η ανοικοδόμησή της* [*The Greece of Kapodistrias: The Present State of Greece (1828–1833) and the Means to Achieve its Reconstruction*], 2 Volumes, Athens: Tolides Bros.

Todorov, Nikolai 1982, *Η βαλκανική διάσταση της Επανάστασης του 1821 (η περίπτωση των Βουλγάρων). Ένας κατάλογος των αγωνιστών στη Μολδοβλαχία (Αρχεία Οδησσού)* [*The Balkan Dimension of the 1821 Revolution (the Case of the Bulgarians): A Catalogue of the Fighters in Moldavia and Wallachia (Odessa Archives)*], Athens: Gutenberg.

Todorov, Nikolai 1986, *Η βαλκανική πόλη. 16ος–19ος αιώνας* [*The Balkan City: Sixteenth–Nineteenth Centuries*], 2 Volumes, Athens: Themelio.

Toynbee, Arnold J. 1922, *The Western Question in Greece and Turkey, A Study in the Contact of Civilisations*, London: Constable & Company Ltd.

Toynbee, Arnold J. 1981, *The Greeks and their Heritages*, Oxford: Oxford University Press.

Trikoupis, Spyridon 1993 [1860], *Ιστορία της Ελληνικής Επανάστασης* [*History of the Greek Revolution*], in 4 Volumes, Vol. 1, Athens: Nea Synora.

Trotsky, Leon 1930, *History of the Russian Revolution*, Preface, https://www.marxists.org/archive/trotsky/1930/hrr/ch00.htm (retrieved 14 August 2021).

Tsatsos, Constantinos 1933, 'Η θέση της ιδεοκρατίας στον κοινωνικό αγώνα' ['The Position of Ideocracy in the Social Struggle'], *Idea* 1(6): 360–6.

Tsokopoulos, Vassias 1984, *Πειραιάς, 1835–1870. Εισαγωγή στην ιστορία του ελληνικού Μάντσεστερ* [*Piraeus, 1835–1870. Introduction to the History of the Greek Manchester*], Athens: Kastaniotis.

Tsoukalas, Constantinos 1977, *Εξάρτηση και αναπαραγωγή. Ο κοινωνικός ρόλος των εκπαιδευτικών μηχανισμών στην Ελλάδα* [*Dependency and Reproduction: The Social Role of Educational Apparatuses in Greece*], Athens: Themelio.

Tsoukalas, Constantinos 1981, *Κοινωνική ανάπτυξη και κράτος. Η συγκρότηση του δημόσιου χώρου στην Ελλάδα* [*Social Development and the State: The Constitution of Public Space in Greece*], Athens: Themelio.

Vagenas, Thanos, and Evridiki Dimitrakopoulou 1949, *Αμερικανοί φιλέλληνες εθελοντές στο Εικοσιένα* [*American Philhellene Volunteers in 1821*], Athens.

Vakalopoulos, Apostolos E. 1966, *Η πορεία του γένους* [*The Course of the Genus*], Athens: Publications of Friends.

Vakalopoulos, Apostolos E. 1974, *Ιστορία του νέου ελληνισμού Α´: Αρχές και διαμόρφωσή του* [*History of the New Hellenism A: Its Principles and its Formation*], Athens: Ant. Stamoulis.

Vakalopoulos, Apostolos E. 1980, *Ιστορία του νέου ελληνισμού: Η μεγάλη Ελληνική Επανάσταση (1821–1829) – Οι προϋποθέσεις και οι βάσεις της (1813–1822)* [*History of the New Hellenism: The Great Greek Revolution (1821–1829) – Its Prerequisites and Bases (1813–1822)*], Thessaloniki: Herodotos.

Vakalopoulos, Apostolos E. 1998, *Νέα ελληνική ιστορία 1204–1985* [Modern Greek *History 1204–1985*], 15th edition, Thessaloniki: Vanias.

Vasiliev, Alexander A. 1952, *History of the Byzantine Empire 324–1453*, Madison: The University of Wisconsin Press.

Veremis, Thanos 2006, 'Ριζοσπαστισμός και κλεφταρματολισμός' ['Radicalism and Klepht-Armatolism'], *Kathimerini* 9/4.

Veremis, Thanos, Ioannis S. Koliopoulos, and Iakovos D. Michaelides 2018, *1821, η δημιουργία ενός έθνους-κράτους* [*1821, the Creation of a Nation State*], Athens: Metaichmio.

Vernardakis, Athanasios N. 1990 [1885], *Περί του εν Ελλάδι εμπορίου* [*On Trade in Greece*], Athens: Dionysios Notis Karavias.

Vernardakis, Nikolaos 1962 [1875], *Καποδίστριας και Όθων* [*Kapodistrias and Otto*], Athens: Galaxias.

Vogli, Elpida K. 2007, *'Έλληνες το γένος'. Η ιθαγένεια και η ταυτότητα στο εθνικό κράτος των Ελλήνων (1821–1844)* ['Greeks according to Genus': Citizenship and Identity in the National State of the Greeks (1821–1844)], Herakleion: Crete University Press.

Vournas, Tasos 1956, *Το ελληνικό 1848* [*The Greek 1848*], Political and Literary Publications.

Vournas, Tasos 1989, (Introduction-Selection of Texts-Commentary), *Η Γαλλική Επανάσταση και η Ελλάδα. Ιδεολογικές απηχήσεις του γαλλικού 1789 στον ελληνικό και το βαλκανικό χώρο* [*The French Revolution and Greece: Ideological Echoes of the French 1789 in Greece and the Balkans*], Athens: Tolides Bros.

Xifaras, Dimitris 1992, *Δημοσιονομική πολιτική και οικονομική ανάπτυξη. Κράτος και οικονομία στην Ελλάδα, 1828–1862* [*Fiscal Policy and Economic Development: State and Economy in Greece, 1828–1862*], Diploma Thesis at the Department of History, Faculty of Philosophy, University of Athens, Greece.

Xifaras, Dimitris 1993a, 'Η "ακατάλυτη συνέχεια" του ελληνισμού: Ορισμένες επίκαιρες σκέψεις περί "εθνικής ιστορίας"' ['The "Indissoluble Continuity" of Hellenism: Some Topical Thoughts on "National History"', Part A], *Theseis* 42: 57–79.

Xifaras, Dimitris 1993b, 'Η "ακατάλυτη συνέχεια" του ελληνισμού: Ορισμένες επίκαιρες σκέψεις περί "εθνικής ιστορίας"' ['The "Indissoluble Continuity" of Hellenism: Some Topical Thoughts on "National History"', Part B], *Theseis* 43: 25–46.

Xifaras, Dimitris 1995, 'Η ελληνική εθνικιστική ιδεολογία στο Μεσοπόλεμο: Όψεις διαμόρφωσης της εθνικής ιδέας' ['Greek Nationalist Ideology in the Interwar Period: Aspects of the Formation of a National Theory', Part A], *Theseis* 53: 69–88.

Xifaras, Dimitris 1996, 'Η ελληνική εθνικιστική ιδεολογία στο Μεσοπόλεμο: Όψεις διαμόρφωσης της εθνικής ιδέας' ['Greek Nationalist Ideology in the Interwar Period: Aspects of the Formation of a National Theory', Part B], *Theseis* 54: 61–86.

Ypsilantis, Alexandros 1821a, 'Άνδρες Γραικοί, όσοι ευρίσκεσθε εις Μολδαβίαν και Βλαχίαν!'; 'Αδελφοί της Εταιρείας των Φιλικών' ['Greek Men, those Sojourning in Moldavia and Wallachia!'; 'Brothers of the Society of Friends'], https://karavaki.files.wordpress.com/2012/02/ypsilantis-prok1.pdf (retrieved 14 August 2021).

Ypsilantis, Alexandros 1821b, 'Μάχου υπέρ πίστεως και πατρίδος' ['Fight for Faith and Motherland'], https://www.sansimera.gr/articles/898 (retrieved 14 August 2021).

Zelepos, Ioannis 2018, 'Μετεμορφώθη γαρ και έγινεν ο Ελληνισμός Χριστιανισμός. Έλληνες, ελληνικόν γένος, και Ελληνισμός στον θρησκευτικό λόγο κατά τις παραμονές της Ελληνικής Επανάστασης (τέλη 18ου αι. έως 1821)' ['Hellenism was Transformed and Became Christianity. Hellenes, the Hellenic Genus, and Hellenism in Religious Discourse on the Eve of the Greek Revolution (Late Eighteenth Century to 1821)', in Olga Katsiardi-

Hering et al. (eds.), Ἕλλην, Ῥωμηός, Γραικός. Συλλογικοί προσδιορισμοί και ταυτότητες [Hellene, Romios, Graecos: Collective Identifications and Identities], Athens: Eurasia, 345–59.

Zevgos, Yannis 1933a, 'Ο "μαρξιστής" Γ. Κορδάτος ιστορικός της μπουρζουαζίας' ['The "Marxist" Y. Kordatos, Historian of the Bourgeoisie'], Communist Review 20 (15 October): 19–24.

Zevgos, Yannis 1933b, 'Ο Γ. Κορδάτος σαν ιστορικός της επανάστασης του 1821' ['Y. Kordatos as a Historian of the 1821 Revolution'], Communist Review 21 (1 November): 26–34.

Zevgos, Yannis 1935, 'Η επανάσταση του 1821. Ο χαραχτήρας, οι κινητήριες δυνάμεις και τα προβλήματά της' ['The Revolution of 1821: Its Character, Driving Forces and Problems'], Young Pioneers 3 (March): 82–5.

Zevgos, Yannis 1936, '1821 και ξένες δυνάμεις' ['1821 and Foreign Powers'], Rizospastis (25 March). Reprint: The Rizos of Monday (24 March 1947). http://anasintaxi.blogspot.com/2008/03/1821.html (retrieved 22 August 2021).

Zevgos, Yannis 1943, 'Προς την ολοκλήρωση του Εικοσιένα' ['Towards the Completion of 1821'], Communist Review 12 (April).

Zevgos, Yannis 1945, Σύντομη μελέτη της νεοελληνικής ιστορίας [Short Study of Modern Greek History], Athens: The New Books.

Zioutos, Georgios D. 2009, Το διεθνές εργατικό κίνημα στον 19ο και τις αρχές του 20ού αιώνα [The International Labour Movement in the Nineteenth and Early Twentieth Century], Athens: Stochastis.

Index

www.ingramcontent.com/pod-product-compliance
Lightning Source LLC
Chambersburg PA
CBHW070100030426
42335CB00016B/1957